i

The Tabernacle:

A Journey of Faith

The Tabernacle:

A Journey of Faith

By: Kristen Tschida

Destiny House Publishing, LLC

P.O. Box 19774
Detroit, MI 48219

The Tabernacle: A Journey of Faith
Published by Destiny House Publishing, LLC

Copyright 2011 Kristen Tschida
International Standard Book Number:
ISBN-13: 978-1936867004
ISBN-10: 1936867001
Unless otherwise stated, all scripture quotations are from
the Holy Bible,
New International Version. Scripture references that do not
have the Bible version noted are the author's paraphrase.

Original printing 2011

Cover design, editing and Publication Layout: Destiny
House Publishing

For information:
Destiny House Publishing
www.destinyhousepublishing.com
P.O. Box 19774
Detroit, MI 48219

TABLE OF CONTENTS:

The Tabernacle: A Journey of Faith

Introduction

Welcome to the study of the Old Testament Tabernacle, based on the tabernacle that Moses was instructed to make. Before we get started, I want to explain how this study will work:

We will journey with the Israelites, led by Moses as they travel into the wilderness:
- experiencing freedom from bondage
- trusting in Jehovah to provide for their needs
- entering into a covenant relationship with Him
- engaging in a new way of worship that centers around the presence of the Living Jehovah in the tabernacle.

It is divided into 11 weeks; each week has a "teaching" chapter followed by a study guide. Please read through the teaching, which will add insight to the study itself. With each study guide section, there will be a scripture to memorize and several key questions. If you are leading a group study, use the key questions on the study guide as discussion starters (if time does not lend itself to covering the entire study guide).

I invite you to make this a journey of faith allowing the Holy Spirit to meet you in every chapter. As the Israelites experience freedom from bondage, trust in Jehovah, enter into a covenant with Him, and engage in a new way of worship centering around the tabernacle, let the Holy Spirit lead you and guide you to see the Scripture afresh! Come along with me as we embark on this journey of faith.

For some, this will be the first time that the tabernacle has been studied. For others, this will be very familiar. My prayer for each one who joins us in this adventure is that Jesus would draw you close to His heart, being transformed more into the image of Christ. The tabernacle itself points to Jesus in every way. Get ready for the journey!

I want to pray with you and for you as we begin our journey into the Tabernacle:

Lord, I ask that You would open ears to hear, open eyes to see, open minds to understand and open hearts to receive all that You would have for each one. Oh God, may each one who studies Your Word be *awakened* to a new truth, *invaded* by Your Holy Spirit in their inmost being so that they would be *transformed* from the inside out. AMEN

The Tabernacle

The families of Gershonites (Numbers 3)

The Tribe of Ephraim 40,500	The Tribe of Manasseh 32,200	The Tribe of Benjamin 35,400

The families of Merarites (Num. 3)

The Tribe of Naphtali 53,400	The Tribe of Asher 41,500	The Tribe of Dan 62,700

The families of Kohath (Numbers 3)

The Tribe of Gad 45,650	The Tribe of Simeon 59,300	The Tribe of Reuben 46,500

Moses, Aaron, and Sons (Numbers 3)

The Tribe of Issachar 54,400	The Tribe of Judah 74,600	The Tribe of Zebulun 57,400

CHAPTER 1:
WHO GOD IS IN THE WILDERNESS

In this first lesson, we are going to see the relationship between the Israelites and their God. We will gather glimpses as we travel through Exodus 1—19. We need to understand some background before we dig deep into the Tabernacle itself. What is the relationship the Israelites had with God? How did God choose this people group? Was there something special about them? How does Moses get in the picture? What happens in the wilderness? Who is their God? These are just some of the questions that we will answer as we move through the pages of scripture.

Exodus 1 & 2: Enter Moses

The book of Exodus opens with God's people being oppressed in Egypt. Joseph and all his family have died and a king has come to power who does not know anything about Joseph. This king is afraid of the Israelites and decides that he must *"deal shrewdly with them or they may become even more numerous and, if war breaks out, will join our enemies, fight against us and leave the country"* (Exodus 1:10). Fear is ruling this king.

Fear is such a strong emotion that holds people in bondage. We see a king who is being controlled by fear, which causes him to oppress a people by fear. The king's fear traps not only himself, but he then uses his power to hold others in fear & bondage, too. Have you ever known a person like that (whose power is based on fear), which leads to control?

The king of Egypt places slave masters over the Hebrews in order to oppress them with forced labor (slavery) and tells the Hebrew midwives to kill any boy babies that are born. What fear the king had! He even enlisted the Hebrew women to kill the Hebrew boy babies! But in stark contrast to the king's fear, we see the Hebrew midwives' courage. They would not cower to the fierceness of the king and refused to kill any of the babies. These women feared the Lord and refused to do what the king of Egypt ordered. *"The midwives feared God and did not do what the king of Egypt had told them to do; they let the boys live." (Exodus 1:17)* Even in the midst of oppression, we see the midwives choosing to do the right thing in the eyes of God. What courage they had. They did not fear the human king, they feared the Eternal King. The king then enlists his people, the Egyptians to kill the Hebrew boys and tells them *"Every boy that is born you must throw into the Nile, but let every girl live,"* (Exodus 1:22) The Nile River, which was the source of life, became a place of death for so many.

This brutal scene is what Moses was born into. It was a time of oppression and slavery of the Hebrew people and a time of mass murder of all baby boys born. Moses' father (Amram) was a Levite (the priestly lineage) and his mother (Jochebed) was a Levite woman. When Moses was born, they hid him for three months, to preserve Moses' life. When they could no longer hide him, Jochebed made a basket for Moses, coated it with tar and pitch, placed Moses inside it and sent him *"among the reeds along the bank of the Nile." (*Exodus 2:3) Imagine what that was like for a mother. This River, the Nile, which months before was the sight of bloodshed and terror, Jochebed willingly placed her baby boy in and sent him along, trusting the Lord's plan for her baby's life. This is a well known Bible story, but this week as you study and read the account, ask the Lord to show you something new or give you a fresh insight.

Pharaoh's daughter saw the basket and sent one of her servant girls to retrieve it from the Nile. When she looked inside, she saw the baby and named him Moses which means, "I drew him out of water". Pharaoh's daughter had compassion on him and raised him as her own.

Imagine the life that Moses lived: a much different life than his sister, Miriam or brother, Aaron. While Moses' family was struggling under the heavy hand of the Pharaoh, Moses enjoyed all the affluence and education of the Egyptian culture. We don't know anything of his childhood years and early adult years. The Bible tells us that Moses mother, Jochebed nursed him and when he grew older, the child returned to the palace to be Pharaoh's daughter's son.

What happened in those years of being nursed by his mother? Did Jochebed speak destiny over her son? Did she tell him all about the oppression of his people? Did Moses' father & mother have a prophetic word from the Lord about their child being a deliverer? How often did Jochebed tell Moses how much she loved him? Or did she quietly pray over her little one, knowing that he would be handed over to those who oppressed the Hebrews? We don't know the answers, but I do like to "turn back the pages of scripture" and wonder. For me, it makes the Bible come to life with real people in real situations. How could a mother give her son away? Oh, the pain that she & her husband must have wrestled with, not understanding. Where was God? When would He deliver them? Did he hear their cries for help?

Chapter 2, verse 11 says, *"One day, after Moses had grown up..."* We know at this time that Moses is forty years old. LIFE happened from the time nursing ended until he had "grown up". We have to trust that if God had important details for us to know about his growing up years, that information would have been part of the chapter.

At 40 years old, Moses takes justice into his own hands by killing an Egyptian who was beating a Hebrew (one of his own people). The next day Moses saw two Hebrews fighting and He asked one of them why he was hitting his fellow Hebrew. The Hebrew man responded by asking, *"Who made you ruler and judge over us?",* then asked if Moses was going to kill him like he killed the Egyptian. I do think the Hebrews initial question is interesting to note, for in 40 years time, Moses will be ruler and judge over the Hebrew people.

Did Moses know the call that was on his life? When he killed the Egyptian, did he think he was following God's plan for his life? Did he see himself in that privileged position to be the deliverer or rescuer of the Hebrews? Did Moses have a prophetic word or a vision from the Lord about the call on his life? Acts 7:23-29 says this, *"When Moses was forty years old, he decided to visit his fellow Israelites. He saw one of them being mistreated by an Egyptian, so he went to his defense and avenged him by killing the Egyptian. Moses thought that his own people would realize that God was using him to rescue them, but they did not. The next day Moses came upon two Israelites who were fighting. He tried to reconcile them by saying, 'Men you are brothers; why do you want to hurt each other?' But the man who was mistreating the other pushed Moses aside and said, 'Who made you ruler and judge over us? Do you want to kill me as you killed the Egyptian yesterday? When Moses heard this, he fled to Midian, where he settled as a foreigner and had two sons."* What do you think? This account gives us a little "turning back the pages" to wonder.

After killing the Egyptian, Pharaoh found out. So Moses flees to the wilderness of Midian. Moses enlists in the "School of God in the Desert" and for almost 40 years he spends his time learning at the far side of the desert.

Have you been to this school? I know that I have! I have taken things into my own hands, going before the Lord and it hasn't worked out the way I had planned it! I am sure Moses was thinking that same way. He didn't understand why his fellow Hebrews didn't see him as a hero! Moses did not wait for God's timing and perfect plan. He used his emotional judgment, which always gets us into trouble!

Exodus 3: Moses meets God

Moses meets God here (at the burning bush) after forty long years in the wilderness. Imagine that scene. God uses the ordinary, everyday things to train us in the wilderness. Moses was a shepherd. God used the caring for the flock as training for Moses (another well-known Bible hero, David was trained by the flock as well). Moses is shepherding his father-in-law's flock and at the mountain of God (Mt. Horeb) God meets with him~ in flames of fire. What a sight! This will not be the first time that we see the mountain of God. The Israelites will return to this place. And I am sure that Moses will never forget this encounter with the Living God, the God of Abraham, Isaac, and Jacob.

God tells Moses that He is going to deliver the Israelites from Pharaoh's hand. *"The Lord said, 'I have indeed seen the misery of my people in Egypt. I have heard them crying out because of their slave drivers, and I am concerned about their suffering. So I have come down to rescue them from the hand of the Egyptians and to bring them up out of that land into a good and spacious land, a land flowing*

9

with milk and honey..." (Exodus 3:7-8). I am sure that Moses was thinking "They will be so happy." "Maybe then, I can go back." "Oh, thank you, Lord God." And then the Lord says something that rocked Moses' world, *"So now go. I am sending you to Pharaoh to bring my people the Israelites out of Egypt." (Exodus 3:10).* God will deliver the Israelites, but He will use Moses to do it! At this time in his life, Moses is full of fear and is the reluctant hero of the people. He has tried this before (40 years ago) and it didn't turn out so great for him. In fact, Pharaoh wanted to kill him. He was driven to the wilderness. God assures Moses several times that "he is the man"! Moses has many excuses. Do any of these sound familiar to you?

- Who am I? Who do I say sent me? What if they don't believe me? What if they don't listen to me? I don't speak very well, God. Isn't there someone else you could send?

As I have read this scripture over and over preparing for this study, I have been overwhelmed with a sense of how often I have said those same words to God. Who am I God? Why would you use me? What if they don't believe me? On and on. Personally, when the Lord has asked something of me, I usually give him a list of the more qualified, reminding Him of gifted & talented people. A couple of years ago, I was asked to lead a group to pray for awakening and revival in our city. This has been one of my heart's passions, to see the church wake up and our city to be transformed by the Spirit of the Living God. But, who am I to lead this group? What if they don't listen to me? God, there are many more qualified people in our city to lead this movement. On and on, I had many excuses, just like Moses. And the Lord was saying to my heart, "You are the one. I have chosen you." If God has chosen me, surely he will equip me.

10

Whom God appoints, he anoints. We will see that phrase again! God has dealt with Moses in the wilderness. Moses has learned many lessons that will benefit the Israelites. So, now his schooling is complete and it is time to get that diploma!

Finally, when Moses concedes, he asks God, *"Suppose I go to the Israelites and say to them, 'The God of your fathers has sent me to you,' and they ask me, 'What is his name?' Then what do I say?" (Exodus 3:13)*. God's words to Moses are ***I am who I am***. *This is what you are to say to the Israelites. I AM has sent me to you"*. In Hebrew, the meaning is "I will be that I will be" (meaning who will always be: personal, continuous, absolute existence)!

God's name up to this point was not fully revealed; now His name was revealed in connection with His covenant promise. Jehovah or Yahweh is telling the people that He will be a personal, living, faithful & unchanging God! Yahweh or Jehovah is derived from the Hebrew verb, "havah" meaning "to be" or "being". This word is almost exactly like the Hebrew word, "chavah" meaning "to live" or "life". Jehovah is the LIVING GOD. He ALWAYS exists! The name, Yahweh or Jehovah is used 6,823 times in the Old Testament. God wants His people to know who He is!

Yahweh by the Jewish people is spelled without vowel points, YHWH; there was such a reverence & fear of the Lord that His name would not be said out loud or spelled out. Even today, the name Jehovah (YHWH) is never read in the synagogue nor uttered by the people. Adonai (meaning "the name") is substituted in its place (see Lev. 24:16 for Moses law).

11

Jesus' name means "Yahweh is Salvation"; he is the great I AM. He is with us always. In the Gospel of John, Jesus introduces Himself as "I AM":

I AM the bread of life. (John 6:35)

I AM the light of the world. (John 8:12)

I AM the gate for the sheep. (John 10:7)

I AM the resurrection and the life. (John 11:25)

I AM the way, the truth and the life. (John 14:6)

I AM the true vine, and my Father is the gardener. (John 15:1)

Do you know this Jehovah as a personal, living God, faithful and unchanging? Do you live in reverence before him? He is LIFE and we experience the life in God through Jesus!

Exodus 4—11: LET MY PEOPLE GO!

Moses goes back to Egypt (not without excuses for NOT going, but reluctantly goes back with Aaron). He is sent to tell Pharaoh from the Lord, "LET MY PEOPLE GO!" The tool, that God sends with Moses to perform signs and miracles was a staff, the tool of a shepherd. Moses had been trained in the wilderness caring for the flock of sheep, using a staff. Moses knew this tool. He was used to it. His hand was used to gripping it. God's miraculous power would be shown forth by the same tool that Moses was familiar with using. God is so good to us. He doesn't take us far from what we have been trained with. He uses those things that have been part of our schooling.

Pharaoh's heart was hardened & God sent 10 plagues upon the Egyptians to *"bring judgment on all the gods of Egypt. I am the Lord."* (Ex. 12:12). The ten plagues are: 1) plague of blood, 2) plague of frogs, 3) plague of gnats, 4) plague of flies, 5) plague on livestock, 6) plague of boils, 7) plague of hail, 8) plague of locusts, 9) plague of darkness, 10) plague on the firstborn. You will be studying the various gods that the plagues were sent to judge…to show the power of Jehovah, the ONE who possesses life! What are the "gods of America" that God will bring judgment upon? He is the Lord. He will not share the spotlight with another god. He will not compromise. He alone is Yahweh.

Egypt was a polytheistic society. They worshipped over 80 different gods. So the plagues that God sent upon the land of Egypt was in direct opposition to many of these gods. God was showing that HE ALONE is GOD! *"Even Pharaoh was a god, always the son of Amon-Ra, ruling not merely by divine right but by divine birth, as a deity transiently tolerating the earth as his home. On his head was the falcon, symbol of Hours and totem of the tribe; from his forehead rose the uraeus or serpent, symbol of wisdom and life, communicating magic virtues to the crown. The king was chief-priest of the faith, and led the great processions and ceremonies that celebrated the festivals of the gods. It was through this assumption of divine lineage and powers that he was able to rule so long with so little force."* This is taken from Will Durant's book, The Story of Civilization: Our Oriental Heritage, Vol.1, p. 201).

Exodus 12-15: The Exodus

After the final plague, the plague on the firstborn, Pharaoh released the children of Israel. This was a final statement of God's power. Exodus 12:32 shows that Pharaoh realizes that the God of the Israelites was GOD and that he, Pharaoh and the gods of Egypt were defeated. He even asks Moses to bless him. The Israelites were ready to leave. They had been prepared by Moses and followed all his instructions.

13

The Lord protected all who were under the blood covering. As the Israelites left Egypt, Exodus 12:36 tells us, *"the Lord had made the Egyptians favorably disposed toward the people, and they gave them what they asked for; so they plundered the Egyptians."* Moses reminds them in Exodus 13:3 to *"Commemorate this day, the day you came out of Egypt, out of the land of slavery, because the Lord brought you out of it with a mighty hand."* Already, Moses is reminding the people that it is GOD who has delivered them! God led them with a pillar of cloud during the day & a pillar of fire by night; the pillar spoke of God's guidance for His people & His protection from their enemies—a constant miracle! God leads them to the Red Sea. This was the first "test" for the people. Will they put their trust in God? Will they follow Him? Will they believe? Remember, they have seen God's amazing power displayed in the plagues, the exodus and the pillar of fire and cloud.

The people were frightened because the Egyptians were pursuing them and the Red Sea was before them. They felt they had nowhere to go. Do you ever feel that way; like everything is closing in around you? Enemies on all sides. Nowhere to run. No place for safety. At this point the Israelites had several choices: fight, surrender or trust God and keep moving ahead~ into the Sea. These are the same choices we have in the impossible situations. Learn from the Israelites. Recount God's faithfulness to you in the past. It is good to remember. He was faithful, He is faithful and He will always be faithful.

The people are crying out to God and God tells Moses in Exodus 14:15, *"Why are you crying out to me? Tell the Israelites to move on."* Have you heard the Lord say that to you? Move on. Keep going. I will lead you. I will guide you. I will never let you down. I will never leave you. Move on.

14

The Israelites have seen God's signs and wonders. God has shown His power when He sent the plagues upon the Egyptians, He has led the Israelites by a pillar of cloud and a pillar of fire, He has parted the Red Sea, giving them dry land to go across. He is faithful! God is wooing them into the desert. This is just where He wants them. They have been an oppressed people for 400 years. They have lived in a land surrounded by the pagan gods of Egypt. All this generation has known is of Egypt (bondage & chains). God took the Israelites into the wilderness to show them how much He loved them. He showed them who He was. He met their every need. He chose them as His own.

When we are set free from bondage, we need a respite. The wilderness is God's way of drawing us unto himself, to free us of everything that has been a trap for us. Several years ago our daughter was stuck in "Egypt". As my husband and I watched her, we were noticing that she was withdrawing from us and her countenance was changing. We didn't know any of her friends and she wasn't coming around our home very often. We addressed some issues with Lindsay and her response was that "everything's fine". My husband, being the discerning man that he is, kept observing her and asking the Lord to give Divine wisdom and insight to know what we should do, if anything. After several days of prayer and fasting, the Lord spoke very clearly to Greg's heart to get Lindsay out of her living situation, that she was on a path of destruction if we did not act. So, Greg met with Lindsay and gave her two options: 1) continue to live this life, which is a path leading to destruction or 2) come home to live with us for a time, with some rules in place to help restore order in her life. With tears in her eyes, she agreed to come home. Within a couple weeks, things changed. She was set free from bondage and her respite was our home. The wilderness of the Tschida home is where the Lord met her. He drew her

away to a quiet place to speak tenderly to her.
Hosea 2:14-15 tells us that the Lord allures us into the
desert, so He can speak tenderly to us. Oh Beloved, He
wants us to know Him and to depend upon Him.
Wilderness experiences can be great! There is refreshment
in the desert, for He is the living water. There is sustenance
in the desert, for He is the bread of life! God desires to
show Himself to us in new ways. He loves us.

After the crossing of the Red Sea (into the wilderness),
Miriam and Moses sing a song (Exodus 15) of deliverance.
Freedom. The Israelites can feel the chains fall off. This is
real. They are a people, a nation; free from oppression and
slavery. But, this song doesn't last long.

Chapter 15:22-27 shows the state of the heart of the
Israelites After three days, they were grumbling and
complaining It doesn't take long after the miraculous
crossing of the Red Sea that we see the Israelites showing
their inner selves.

The people are thirsty. It has been three days without
water, in the desert. And the people have not learned to
trust that God will provide for their needs. The Israelites
come to a pool of water and notice that it is bitter. They
grumble against Moses, '*what are we to drink*?' they say.
The Lord shows Moses a tree and tells him to throw the
tree into the waters. The bitter water became sweet. And
the people can drink it. This is foreshadowing the work of
the cross. Jesus bore our bitterness on the cross. He gave
himself willingly so that we can have the sweetness of
eternal life. Oh, how God loves us. He shows His love
over and over. When the Israelites had their thirst
quenched by the sweet water that Yahweh provided, He
gave the Israelites a covenant of healing. If they kept His
commandments and listened to His voice, then God would

keep a covenant of healing. He is **Jehovah-Rapha, the Lord who heals** all our sickness & diseases. The disease we see in the Israelites already is the "disease" of bitterness.

How quickly bitterness can take hold in the heart. Hebrews 12:15 says, *"See to it that no one misses the grace of God and that no bitter root grows up to cause trouble and defile many.* We are to have oversight of our heart. Bitterness has deep roots~ it is an inward feeling of hostility that is exhibited outwardly. If we refuse to listen to the Holy Spirit to forgive, we miss the grace of God and therefore are living in disobedience, the roots begin to grow and will sprout. It will trouble you and defile many. Bitterness is the result of carrying an offense. What is an offense? When somebody fails your expectations or falls below your expectations. We cannot be offended if there are not any expectations. That is the goal! To live in such a way that God is who we go to for all acceptance and provision. For when we keep our eyes on Him, we will not be offended. That is the high calling of knowing God. Too often, believers (the chosen people of God) are so offended by one another, that our witness to the world is ineffective. Hebrews 12:15 becomes a reality too often for too many. Does this cycle resonate with you?

- I am offended by someone I know
- I make a choice to NOT forgive them, because I am hurt so badly (whether it was an intentional wound or not). The bitter root is growing, because of my choices.
- I can't make eye contact with that person when I see him/her, because I am so wounded. I can't seem to forget about what happened. I can't let it go.
- I begin to talk about this person with others. Sometimes in the guise of "prayer", asking someone

to pray for this "offender". Sharing the offense with others can cause them to "carry" my offense.

- The cycle continues with anyone then who has offended me. I need to break the cycle by accepting the Lord's acceptance of me, to trust Him with my needs, my hurts, my pain, my disappointment. I need to make a choice to not hold people to my expectations. When I do hold them to my expectations, I will ALWAYS be disappointed and the opportunity to be offended is a real threat. I want to keep my heart from all bitterness. Proverbs 4:23 says, *"Above all else, guard your heart, for it is the wellspring of life."*

The Israelites had much to be bitter about, by the world's standards. They had spent 400 years (as a people) in oppression & slavery. **BUT,** they had a choice to let the bitterness take hold of their hearts. God not only wanted to free them from the physical oppression, but also from the emotional and spiritual oppression. God is giving the Israelites chances to practice this new found freedom in the wilderness. This takes practice and trust that God is in control and that He doesn't miss anything! Recently I led a group through this study on the Tabernacle. One of the women told me that her grandson thought the Israelites were called the "Miserablites". I have not forgotten that. I do not want to be known as a "Miserablite" (grumbling and complaining). What is inside must come out. I want to have a heart that is guarded and healed. I serve Jehovah-Rapha, the God who heals!

EXODUS 16-18: Daily Provision

God uses this wilderness experience to train His people to totally depend on Him in every area of life. Remember, the only life the Israelites knew was a life of oppression &

slavery. Even though it was a hard life and they had cried out for a deliverer to come, it was "comfortable". They knew what to expect. Each day brought the same misery, pain and hardship, but it was their misery, pain and hardship. When God freed them and led them into the wilderness, they didn't know how to respond. And when times were challenging, the people would grumble and complain against Moses and God. The Israelites needed a renewed mind (to know who they were & what their God was capable of doing). God used the wilderness experience (all 40 years of it) to train them.

The motto of the Israelites could be, "When the going gets tough, the weak think of Egypt". Our Israelite friends did not have a free-man mindset. In chapter 16, we see a need for food. Immediately the Israelites grumble and say to Moses, *"If only we had died by the Lord's hand in Egypt! There we sat around pots of meat and ate all the food we wanted, but you have brought us out into this desert to starve this entire assembly to death." (Exodus 16:3).* What? Have they lost their minds? They barely survived in the brutal environment of abuse under the Egyptians. Pharaoh ruled them with a heavy hand, so they (as a people) would not rise up against him. How the memory of the Israelites has been skewed. Isn't that how it is with us too? When God frees us from oppression from the enemy or where the enemy has held us captive, God miraculously sets us free. Later, when the going gets tough, and grumbling begins to roll off our tongues, we remember our time in captivity with fond memories, almost wishing that we were back there. God, the deliverer has come, but our mind has not been renewed, so we still act as slaves and captives. That is what happened to the Israelites. When God sets us free (parts the Red Sea and leads us into the wilderness to speak tenderly to us, and show Himself to be the Great I AM, desiring to call us His people and to

provide for all our needs) we need to walk out the freedom
He has given us. We need a renewed mind. Soak in
scripture that talks about who we are in Christ, what His
promises are for those who are obedient to Him; trusting
God to provide for all our needs. We see that God
provided miraculously for the Israelites:

1) God provided manna & quail for the Israelites.
   Manna nurtured the people and gave them life for
   40 years, a daily provision for them. Luke 11:3
   "Give us this day our daily bread". The Lord still
   wants to provide for our daily needs. This was the
   bread from heaven. We, the New Covenant
   believers have been given the true bread from
   heaven (John 6), Jesus!

2) God provided water for His people as they
   journeyed through the desert. Water = life!
   Without water we can't survive. God gave water in
   miraculous ways to the Israelites. He made bitter
   water sweet. He brought forth water from a rock
   (Exodus 17 & Numbers 20). The ROCK
   representing Jesus, who is the foundation of our
   faith; the rock in whom we trust and the water
   represents for us, the Living Water, who is Jesus
   (John 4:10-14).

3) God directed them and protected them through a
   pillar of fire by night and a pillar of cloud during
   the day. God wants to be our guide and the leader
   of our life. He desires that we follow him. Jesus
   said in Matthew 4:19, *"Come follow me."*

4) God clothed the Israelites. Deuteronomy 8:4 tells
   us, *"Your clothes did not wear out and your feet did
   not swell during these forty years."* God will meet
   all our physical needs. Matthew 6:25—34 speaks to
   God's physical provision for our needs.

The Lord desires that we would totally rely on Him. He is **Jehovah Jireh ~ The Lord, my provider**. In all areas, He is Jehovah Jireh! What areas are you holding back from Him? How have you seen God as your Jehovah-Jireh (provider)?

While the Israelites were in the wilderness, there were still battles to fight. That is true for us today, as well. In the wilderness, Jesus was tested by the enemy (Luke 4:1-13). Battles come. The enemy doesn't play fair and will come at a weak point. The Amalekites were a brutal tribe of warriors who did not "play fair". They would attack those who were weak and defenseless (sounds like the enemy doesn't it?). This was the first people group that the Israelites had to contend with in the wilderness. The scriptures tell us that they were armed for battle when they left Egypt (Exodus 13:18b). Moses sends Joshua (a warrior) and some men to fight the Amalekites. *"As long as Moses held up his hands, the Israelites were winning, but whenever he lowered his hands, the Amalekites were winning. When Moses' hands grew tired, they took a stone and put it under him and he sat on it. Aaron and Hur held his hands up~ one on one side and one on the other~ so his hands remained steady till sunset." Exodus 17:11-12.* There are battles we fight when we are in the wilderness, that we need the help of others to lift our hands. God calls us to relationship with one another. We are not to battle alone. We are to stand together, side by side, wielding our swords together. At times, we all need an "Aaron or Hur" to hold our hands steady and lifted high unto the Lord, to have the victory.

When the battle was won, Moses built an altar to the Lord & called it: **The Lord is my banner (Yahweh-Nissi).** A banner is the pole-like standard beneath which armies or communities rallied. When lifted up, it called the people

21

together for battle, for meeting or instruction. This phrase
could have been a battle cry! At the altar, Moses was
honoring God as the giver of the victory! What a victory it
was for the Israelites! God is the ultimate Victor. *"But
thanks be to God, who always leads us in triumphal
procession in Christ and through us spreads everywhere
the fragrance of the knowledge of Him"*
(2 Corinthians 2:14).

Exodus 19: The Covenant

In the third month the Israelites arrived at the Mountain of
God (Mt. Horeb), which is where Moses met God in the
burning bush.. Moses went up to the mountain and the
Lord spoke to him. God desired to have a covenant with
the Israelites. He gave these words to Moses to say to the
people: *"Now if you obey me fully and keep my covenant,
then out of all nations you will be my treasured possession.
Although the whole earth is mine, you will be for me a
kingdom of priests and a holy nation."* (Ex. 19:5-6) What a
gift to the Israelites. They were a slave people, an
oppressed people, and a captive people. God changes all
that with His sweet words to the community by calling
them a treasured possession, a kingdom of priests and a
holy nation. Can you imagine what those words sounded
like to the Israelites? Did they think, "who are we that we
would be your treasured possession?". "What have we done
to have you call us kingdom of priests?". "How could we
be a holy nation?" Those beautiful words are who we are,
too. In I Peter 2:9, as the New Covenant people, these
words are given to us, *"But you are a chosen people, a
royal priesthood, a holy nation, a people belonging to God,
that you may declare the praises of him who called you out
of darkness into his marvelous light.".* We are chosen. We
are a royal priesthood, a holy nation, a people belonging to

God. It is not based on how good we are or what we deserve. God has chosen us, just as He chose the Israelites to be His people.

God has shown his protection, provision and is now declaring that this people are His own. He loves them. He desires to dwell among them. He is a covenant God! He is the I AM WHO I AM. God is a personal God.

He is Jehovah or Yahweh: The Covenant God
He is Yahweh-Nissi: The Lord is my banner
He is Jehovah-Jireh: The Lord, my provider
He is Jehovah-Rapha: The Lord who heals

As we embark on the tabernacle, we now have an overview of the relationship the Israelites have with their God. We will dig deeper into these chapters in the study guide on the pages that follow.

STUDY GUIDE
Chapter 1: Who God Is In The Wilderness
(Exodus 1—19)

Scripture to memorize: *"Do not be afraid. Stand firm and you will see the deliverance the Lord will bring you today. The Egyptians you see today you will never see again. The Lord will fight for you; you need only be still."*
Exodus 14:13-14

Key Questions:
- Have you had a wilderness experience; a place of desolation in your spiritual, physical, emotional or financial life?
- How did God show Himself during that time? (Review the names of God that were shared this week)
- During that season (or if you are in it now), take an attitude check: Would it be said of you that you had the "Miserable Attitude" —grumbling & complaining? What words describe your attitude as you have experienced the wilderness?

Day 1: Moses is the Man
(Exodus 1-4)

Moses was born into a time of oppression and slavery for the Hebrew people. *"Now, Joseph and all his brothers and all that generation died, but the Israelites were fruitful and multiplied greatly and became exceedingly numerous, so that the land was filled with them. Then a new king, who did not know about Joseph, came to power in Egypt. 'Look,' he said to his people, 'the Israelites have become much too numerous for us. Come let us deal shrewdly with them or they will become even more numerous and, if war breaks out, will join our enemies, fight against us and leave the country." (Ex. 1:6-10)* The king lived in fear and caused great oppression for the Hebrews. *"He made their lives bitter with hard labor in brick and mortar and with all kinds of work in the fields; in all their hard labor the Egyptians used them ruthlessly." (Ex. 1:14)* The king of Egypt told the midwives to kill all Hebrew male babies when they were born; and this is the time & place where Moses enters the scene. The midwives would not do as they were instructed, because they had a fear of the Lord. Moses was hidden in the house of Amram (dad) & Jochebed (mom) until he was 3 months old. Then he was placed in a basket and sent down the Nile. *"Then Pharaoh's daughter went down to the Nile to bathe...she saw the basket among the reeds and sent her slave girl to get it." (Ex. 2:5)* Pharaoh's daughter takes the baby, calls him Moses & raises him as her own.

Moses was raised in the Egyptian palace & customs, but he remained true to his heritage as a Hebrew. *"One day, after Moses grew up, he went out to where his own people were and watched them at their hard labor. He saw an Egyptian beating a Hebrew, one of his own people. Glancing this way and that and seeing no one, he killed the Egyptian and hid him in the sand." (Ex. 2:11-12)* The next day as Moses was out, he saw two Hebrew men fighting and he asked them why they were hitting one another. One of the men responded, *"'who made you ruler and judge over us? Are you thinking of killing me as you did the Egyptian?' Then Moses was afraid and thought, 'What I did must have become known.'" (Ex. 2:14)* Pharaoh found out what happened & tried to kill Moses, but he fled to Midian. And this begins Moses' wilderness training...

1) What were the conditions of Egypt that Moses was born into? Have you had a time when you were in bondage (personally, financially, physically, spiritually, emotionally) where you cried out to the Lord to free you from the "slavery of Egypt"?

2) Read the account of Moses birth (Ex.1:15—2:10). List all the people who were faithful to God to do what was right in His eyes:

3) In verse 13 of chapter 2, one of the Hebrew men say to Moses, "Who made you ruler and judge over us?" This is an interesting question posed to Moses. Why?

4) We know from Acts 7:23 that Moses was 40 years old when he went to visit his people in their hard labor. His first 40 years were spent in the palace of Pharaoh being trained in wisdom, language, and culture (Acts 7:22). He was being groomed to be a leader of the Egyptians. However, God had more refining to do in Moses, so he took him to the desert to be taught in the school of God! Have you spent time in the desert? Why? What were the circumstances that led you into the wilderness?

Life continues on, even in the wilderness. And Moses marries and has children and lives in the land of the Midianites (the Midianites were descendants of Abraham through his 2nd wife, Keturah, and were therefore a kindred people to Moses. They lived in western Arabia and the eastern part of the Sinai Peninsula. —NKJ footnote on Exodus 2:15). During this time period, God is setting his plan into motion to use Moses to deliver His people from their oppression. *"So God looked on the Israelites and was concerned about them." (Exodus 2:25).* As Moses was tending to his father-in-laws flock, he noticed a bush that was on fire and did not burn up. He walked over to it and God called to him from within the bush. *"Moses! Moses!" And Moses said, "Here I am." (Ex. 3:4)* God speaks with Moses and tells him the plan to rescue His people. *"So I have come down to rescue them from the hand of the Egyptians and to bring them up out of that land into a good and spacious land, a land flowing with milk and honey—the home of the Canaanites, Hittites, Amorites, Perizzites, Hivites and Jebusites. And now the cry of the Israelites has reached me, and I have seen the way the Egyptians are oppressing them.* ***So now go. I am sending you to Pharaoh to bring my people the Israelites out of Egypt."*** *(Exodus 3:8-10).* What? Who? Me? What? God said to Moses, "You are the man!" And Moses responds with, "No I am not!" ☺ Moses gives God all the reasons why he can't be the man! 1) He asks, "Who am I?" 2) Who do I tell them sent me? 3) What if they don't believe me? 4) But, I can't speak well. 5) Please send someone else! For every reason he couldn't do it, God had an answer…Moses is the man!

5) Moses had an unusual kind of calling. Describe that scene. (Exodus 3:1-6)

6) (Exodus 3:14) Who does God say that HE is: _____ This is God's name Jehovah or Yahweh. This is the covenant name of God. It occurs 6823 times in the Old Testament. This name of God was too sacred to be uttered by the Israelites, so it was written "YHWH" without vowel points.

7) Read through Moses' reasons for **not** being the one God should send (Exodus 3: 11—4:17). Can you relate to any of his excuses? Have you ever used a

similar excuse when God has asked you to do
something for His Kingdom?

8) How has the wilderness trained Moses?

*"Moses and Aaron brought together all the elders of the
Israelites, and Aaron told them everything the Lord had
said to Moses. He also performed the signs before the
people, and they believed. And when they heard that the
Lord was concerned about them and had seen their misery,
they bowed down and worshipped." Exodus 4:29-30*

Day 2: Encounter with Pharaoh
(Exodus 5-7:13)

Moses and Aaron approach Pharaoh and tell him to let
God's people go. Pharaoh makes an arrogant, prideful
statement, *"Who is the Lord, that I should obey him and let
Israel go? I do not know the Lord and I will not let Israel
go." (Ex. 5:2)*. Pharaoh was considered to be a "god". He
was the religious and political leader of the day. So he had
a difficult time believing that the God of the Israelites (an
oppressed & slave people) would be a threat to him.

1) How does Pharaoh show his "strength & power" of
the people? (Exodus 5:4-9)

2) What were some of Pharaoh's reasons for this
impossible task: Moses goes to meet with the Lord
after Pharaoh's unreasonable demands upon the
Hebrew slaves. Moses shares his heart of concern
over the Israelites with the Lord. It reveals that
Moses is shortsighted. God has such a bigger plan
that Moses can't keep in focus (Exodus 5:22-23).

3) Have you ever had a "plan" of how God should work things out in your life and when it doesn't happen the way you thought, you question the Lord about it?

The Lord comforts Moses and reminds him of who HE is: *"Then the Lord said to Moses, 'Now you will see what I will do to Pharaoh: Because of my mighty hand he will let them go; because of my mighty hand he will drive them out of his country.' God also said to Moses, 'I am the Lord. I appeared to Abraham, to Isaac and to Jacob as God Almighty, but by my name the Lord I did not make myself known to them.'" (Exodus 6:1-3)*

The Lord tells Moses that the Patriarchs knew Him as El-Shaddai, which is the name of God that means "God Almighty", the one who is enough; the all powerful. Now the Lord is saying that He is going to reveal Himself in a new way. He was the covenant God, Jehovah (Yahweh) and He had made a covenant with Moses and was going to fulfill it by releasing the Israelites from bondage and bringing them into a land of plenty.

4) How have you seen the Lord as "El-Shaddai" (God Almighty) in your own life?

Moses goes to the Israelites to tell them all that the Lord has said, and the oppression and brutality of the bondage has closed their ears to the words of redemption. (Exodus 6:9)

5) Have you known someone who did not listen to words of freedom because of *"their discouragement and cruel bondage."?*

God **commands** Moses and Aaron to bring the Israelites out of Egypt! God means business and he will not have his leaders wavering and discouraged. Moses reminds God of his limitations—AGAIN! Really, like God doesn't know his limits and imperfections. Come on Moses! God is on your side.

Chapter 7 opens with God telling Moses that he would stand before Pharaoh as a representative of God and Aaron would be the prophet (spokesperson—mediator between God and man). Wow. That is some assignment. *"Moses and Aaron did just as the Lord commanded them. Moses was 80 years old and Aaron 83 when they spoke to Pharaoh." (Exodus 7:6-7)* Moses has spent his first 80 years being trained for this day & time. This is God's appointed hour for Moses—and he did just as God commanded him.

Everything we go through is training for us, too. Moses knew the Egyptian customs & culture. He knew what he was up against. He also had the training in the wilderness, so he was given the charge of caring for flocks. He had to be gentle and always on guard for some enemy to attack.

6) What training have you been through? Ask the Lord to bring to your mind situations, schooling or desert training that has helped you in your assignment from the Lord for this appointed time.

Day 3: The Ten Plagues on Egypt
(Exodus 7:14—11:30)

The plagues that God sent upon the land of Egypt was "against all the gods of Egypt" (Ex. 12:12).

1. Plague of blood~Exodus 7:14-24 *Nile turned to blood by the staff striking the water; all fish died; no one could drink the water (which was life to the Egyptians). *Water=Life *God showing He had the power over all	1. Nile was the life of the Egyptian culture. The god Khnum was the guardian of the Nile. Hapi was the "spirit of the Nile". Osiris was the god of the underworld (Egyptians believed the Nile was his bloodstream). Nu was the god of life in the Nile. Egyptians considered the Nile sacred.
2..Plague of frogs~Exodus 8:1-15*Frogs everywhere—in the water, land, in homes, bedrooms, etc. *Frogs died in the houses, in the courtyards and the fields. They were piled in heaps!	2. The frog was considered the goddess Heqt, the wife of the creator of the world. Heqt is always shown with the head & body of a frog. Frogs were so sacred that even killing one by accident was punishable by death!
3..Plague of lice (flees/gnats)~Exodus 8:16-19*"Kinnim" is the Hebrew word; it comes from a root word meaning "to dig". It is probable that this insect would dig under the skin *this plague the demonic magic could not duplicate, because the enemy cannot create life, only destroy it.	3. Geb was the god of the earth (soil); the Egyptians gave offerings to Geb for the bounty of the soil & here was a plague from "the dust of the soil".
4. Plague of flies ~ Exodus 8:20-32 *this is the first plague where God made a distinction between the Israelites and the Egyptians *some scholars believe this was swarms of beetles (the scarab beetle is a dung beetle that feeds on dung in the field & are more destructive than termites); other scholars believe it was the blood-	4. Amon-Ra, the creator and king of the gods had the head of a beetle; the Egyptians pictured this god as a scarab beetle pushing a round ball of dung (representing the sun) in front of it

sucking gadfly (which was responsible for much blindness in the land)	
5. Plague on livestock ~ Exodus 9:1-7 *this plague was against all domesticated animals *horses and cattle were sacred to the Egyptians	5. The god Apis was represented as a bull and had been worshipped in Egypt since 3,000 BC; the Apis bull supposedly had the power of prophecy. Hathor was the cow-headed goddess of the desert (the symbolic mother of Pharaoh)
6. Plague of boils ~ Exodus 9:8-12 *this plague was probably a skin anthrax, a black abscess that develops into a puss; this was always accompanied by painful boils that affected the knees, legs and soles of the feet	6. The god of medicine was Imhotepi; the god in charge of healing was Serapis
7. Plague of hail ~ Exodus 9:13-35 *a very unusual occurrence, for the region around Cairo normally receives only 2 inches of rain/year.*flax & barley crops were destroyed, so this took place around January	7. Nut-- sky goddess (picture is that of a woman resting on hands and feet, her body forming an arch, representing the sky; her limbs are the pillars on which the sky rested). Shu was the wind god, Seth was the protector of the crops
8. Plague of locusts ~Exodus 10:1-20 *In ancient times, locusts could destroy an entire village food supply in a matter of minutes	8. Nepri was the god of grain, Ermutet was the goddess of childbirth and crops, Thermuthis the goddess of fertility and harvest
9. Plague of darkness ~ Exodus 10:21-29 *darkness came with NO light to see at all; for 3 days darkness lay on the land of Egypt	9. Amon-Ra was considered one of the greatest blessings in all the land of Egypt. Ptah, the chief god of Memphis, the one who created the moon, the sun and the earth. Tem was the god of the sun.

10. Plague on the firstborn ~ Exodus 11:1-12:30 *this plague showed the inability of all the gods of Egypt to protect their subjects. *Firstborn was not only an heir of a double-portion of his father's inheritance, but represented special qualities of life; a major portion of a family would be inherited by the firstborn son *Israelites placed the blood of the lamb over the doorposts of their homes, so the angel of death would "Passover"; the redemptive power of the blood saved the firstborn son in each Hebrew household;	10. Meskhened, the goddess who presided at the birth of a child; Isis, the god of fertility; Selket, the guardian of life; Renenutet was the cobra-goddess and guardian of Pharaoh

Where were the gods of Egypt, as the Lord God, Almighty was showing His power with his mighty hand? Where were they? Why did they remain silent? How would the people of Egypt have responded to their gods? What were they thinking as God showed His power over and over?

Exodus 12:12 *"...and I will bring judgment on all the gods of Egypt. I am the Lord."*

Today, take some time to thank the God Almighty for all He has provided for you. HE IS ENOUGH! HE IS LORD! He has rescued you from the oppression of the enemy! *"...commemorate this day, the day you came out of Egypt, out of the land of slavery, because the Lord brought you out of it with a mighty hand." (Ex. 13:3)*

Day 4: Freedom
(Exodus 13:17—15:21)

"By day the Lord went ahead of them in a pillar of cloud to guide them on their way and by night in a pillar of fire to

give them light, so that they could travel by day or night. Neither the pillar of cloud by day nor the pillar of fire by night left its place in front of the people."
Exodus 13:21-22

How much God loved His people. He had driven them out of the land of slavery and He was to lead them to the Promised Land. He personally was doing the leading—by a pillar of cloud or a pillar of fire. He was always with them. Imagine what that would have looked like.

1) Take a few minutes to draw the pillars. Use your imagination—our minds think in color & pictures. It will solidify the image if you can picture it:

The Israelites don't get very far when they begin to grumble & complain. Remember those two words: grumble & complain (it's what they do much of the time in the wilderness). The Lord leads the Israelites around so that Pharaoh would think they were confused (this was part of God's plan). The Egyptians pursue the Israelites and when the Israelites see the army of Pharaoh coming after them, they begin to panic. They don't trust God, and begin their lament before Moses, *"It would have been better for us to serve the Egyptians than to die in the desert."* (Ex. 14:12). Moses encourages the people. *"Do not be afraid. Stand firm and you will see the deliverance the Lord brings today. The Egyptians you see today you will never see again. The Lord will fight for you; you need only be still."* (Ex. 14: 13-14). How many of us need to hear those words? Do NOT be afraid. Stand firm. The Lord will fight for you. He will deliver you. Nothing has changed. Our God is the same God that He was for the Israelites! Trust Him to deliver you.

Let's take a look at this key scripture for the week, Exodus 14:13-14. It is interesting that the Israelites were armed for battle when they left Egypt, and yet Moses is telling them that God will fight for them. They need to be still.

- "Do not be <u>afraid</u>" (Hebrew means "to be frightened"; "to have fear") ~ Moses is giving a command. In the midst of the enemy closing in on them (or so it appears), Moses tells them DO NOT BE AFRAID!
- "<u>Stand firm</u>" (Hebrew means "to stand one's ground; to commit oneself; to stand before; to stay"). The Israelites are not to run or be afraid, but to stay put; not to flee in fear of the enemy. Who were they committed to? The Lord?
- "and you will see the <u>deliverance</u>" (Hebrew means "help; rescue from a dangerous circumstance or harmful state). If they stand firm, they will see (witness) help! It is important that they keep their eyes fixed on their deliverer.
- "the <u>Lord</u> will bring you today. The Egyptians you see today you will never see again." (Hebrew for Lord is "Yahweh"—the One True God; their covenant God). The Israelites had just witnessed the plagues upon Egypt which were against all the gods the Egyptians worshipped. Trust Him! He will bring it to pass all that He says, for He can be trusted. He is "I AM WHO I AM".
- "The Lord will <u>fight</u> for you" (Hebrew means "to fight against; attack"). Yahweh will do it on your behalf!
- "You need only to be <u>still</u>" (Hebrew means "to be silent; to be quiet; make no moves). Interesting that the meaning has to do with being silent. The Israelites have mouths that grumble and complain. When mouths are silenced, stillness will abound.

35

2) Using the definitions of the underlined words, above, write out an expanded version of verses 13 & 14. In order to memorize scripture it can be helpful to make it personal.

Read the account of the parting of the Red Sea in Exodus 14: 15-31. Water lay ahead of the Israelites, the Egyptian army behind them. Here were they choices: fight, surrender to the Egyptians or trust God to fight for them. The Israelites went forward lead by Moses. God had told Moses, *"Tell the Israelites to move on." (Ex. 14:15).* The pillar of cloud that held the Lord's presence protected Israel and God made a way for the Israelites to cross through the Red Sea on dry ground. As the Egyptians made their way into the sea, God confused the army and wheels fell off the chariots, so they had a difficult time moving. Even the Egyptian army realizes the power of Yahweh, *"Let's get away from the Israelites! The Lord is fighting for them against Egypt." (Ex. 14:25).* WOW! None of the Egyptian army survived. The Lord caused the waters of the sea to cover them.

3) What does this mean to you? How can you apply this true account to something in your life?

The song of Moses and Miriam is a beautiful song of God's deliverance for His people. It is divided into sections. Read Exodus 15.

4) Prelude (vs.1): Write vs. 1

5) What He is (vs. 2-3):

6) What He has done (vs. 4-13):

7) What He will do (vs. 14-18):

8) Postlude--contrast of the defeat of Egypt & the deliverance of Israel (vs. 19):

9) Chorus (vs.21): Write vs. 21

Revelation 15:2 & 3 tells us that we (the believers) will again sing the song of Moses when we stand beside the sea of glass, before the throne, worshiping the King of Kings. *"And I saw what looked like a sea of glass mixed with fire: and standing beside the sea, those who had been victorious over the beast and his image and over the number of his name. They held harps given them by God and sang the song of Moses, the servant of God and the song of the Lamb."*

Day 5: Miracles in the Wilderness
(Exodus 15:22—19:6)

This was an amazing start to the miracles that the Israelites experienced in the desert. The Lord protects them & leads them by a pillar of cloud & a pillar of fire. He has provided a dry land rescue (parting the Red Sea) and then closed the sea on the Egyptians. He is faithful to His Word. Certainly the Israelites will trust Him completely from this point on. But remember the favorite words of the Israelites: grumble & complain. This celebrating & singing to the Lord doesn't last too long. In fact, it doesn't even last a week! After crossing the Red Sea, they wander for 3 days without finding any water. *"So the people grumbled against Moses, saying 'What are we to drink'?" (Ex. 15:24).* Moses cried out to the Lord and the Lord showed Moses a tree (or piece of wood) & he threw it in the water and the bitter water became sweet.

1) Marah means bitter. Wells and pools in that region of the world were often bitter. Wells were the provider of water, which brought life. Water = life. What well are you getting water from? Is that well bitter? Could you call that well Marah?

A tree was put into the bitter water. Can you think of a time in history when a tree was used to change bitterness to sweetness? The cross. Isn't it interesting that the first wilderness miracle (to provide WATER, which gives LIFE) is done by using a tree? *"He himself bore our sins in his body on the tree, so that we might die to sins and live for righteousness; by his wounds you have been healed."* 2 Peter 2:24. *"Then Moses cried out to the Lord, and the Lord showed him a tree. When he cast it into the waters, the waters were made sweet." (Exodus 15:25)* God instituted a decree and a law for the Israelites to follow. He promised to deliver the Israelites from the diseases that afflicted the Egyptians. He is showing Himself as: Jehovah-Rapha, the Lord who heals.

2) Bitterness seems to be the "disease" that the Israelites suffer from the most. Their attitudes needed to be healed. Have you ever suffered from bitterness? What effects did you notice in your life?

The Israelites continue to move about in the desert and *"In the desert the whole community grumbled against Moses and Aaron. The Israelites said to them, 'If only we had died by the Lord's hand in Egypt! There we sat around pots of meat and ate all the food we wanted, but you have brought us out into the desert to starve this entire assembly to death."*

(Ex. 16:2-3). What? Their memory is a little skewed! They have fond memories of Egypt! What? Egypt was a place of oppression and cruel bondage.

But in God's love for these people, He provides for them miraculously. *"I have heard the grumbling of the Israelites. Tell them, 'At twilight you will eat meat, and in the morning you will be filled with bread. Then you will know that I am the Lord your God.'" (Ex. 16:12)* This manna nurtured the people and gave life for 40 years. The "bread from heaven" was a white, small, thin flake. It was a daily provision; gathered according to need; people needed to gather it (the Lord provided all that they needed, but they had a responsibility to go get it). He is Jehovah Jireh—the Lord, my Provider. In all areas, He is Jehovah Jireh!

Through the desert experience, the Lord was training His people to depend totally on Him in every area of life. That is the Lord's goal for each one of His children—to depend totally on Him in every area of life.

3) "Give us this day our daily bread" Luke 11:3. How is God, Jehovah Jireh to you today? What ways has He trained you to depend totally on Him? What areas are you holding back?

Another miracle we see in this text is the victory in battle that the Lord provided for His people. Even in the desert we have to fight battles. Remember, *"The Israelites went up out of Egypt armed for battle." (Ex. 13:18)*. When the battle was won, Moses built an altar and called it, "The Lord is my Banner", which is Yahweh-Nissi. (A banner is the pole like standard beneath which armies or communities rallied. When lifted up, it called the people together for battle, for meeting or for instruction. This phrase could have been a battle-cry. At the altar Moses was honoring God as the giver of the victory over the Amalekites. ~ NKJ footnote on Exodus 17:15).

> 4) Yahweh-Nissi ~ Use the space provided to describe how the Lord is your banner!

"In the third month after the Israelites left Egypt—on the very day—they came to the Desert of Sinai. After they set out from Rephidim, they entered the Desert of Sinai, and Israel camped there in the desert in front of the mountain." *Exodus 19:1-2*

"Now if you obey me fully and keep my covenant, then out of all nations you will be my treasured possession. Although the whole earth is mine, you will be for me a kingdom of priests and a holy nation." Exodus 19:5-6

We are ready to embark on the study of the Tabernacle. This history of the Israelites was important to prepare your hearts for what the Lord had done already. He is worthy to be praised. He is trustworthy. He loves His people.

He has shown Himself to be:
- Jehovah-Jireh: the Lord, my provider
- Jehovah-Rapha: the Lord who heals
- El-Shaddai: God Almighty
- Yahweh-Nissi: The Lord is my Banner
- Jehovah or Yahweh: The Covenant God

God's heart is for His people. He desires to dwell among them. We saw that this week with the pillar of cloud and pillar of fire—he led them & provided protection for the Israelites. He gave water and food to the Israelites—provided all their needs. Yet, we saw how they "grumbled and complained". May we not be like the Israelites. Let's begin this study with grateful hearts to our Covenant God. He is doing a new thing. Spend some time thanking Him for all He is!

Chapter 2:
The Tabernacle, A Divine Pattern

When we left the Israelites, they were in the wilderness. They have come to the mountain of God, Mount Sinai. God has led them in this vast wilderness for three months. He has shown Himself in power and fire, first to Moses (in the burning bush) and then to the Israelites. God has been their source of life in the wilderness and He has spoken, calling the Israelites to be His chosen people, a kingdom of priests and a holy nation. He is a personal, loving God who longs to dwell among the people.

In your study guide this week, you will be journeying through Exodus 19—24 in great detail. The focus in this chapter will be an overview of the Tabernacle, which begins in Exodus 25. There are 50 chapters in the Bible that discuss the Tabernacle, which is an indication that we should know something about it! More than 20 times during chapters 25—40 of Exodus, these words are written concerning the Tabernacle: "*as the Lord commanded Moses.*" God gives the exact pattern for the Tabernacle. He doesn't miss a detail. And Moses follows perfectly all the directions God gives.

There are five different names used for the same structure, the place where God dwells among His people:

1) The first name is seen in Exodus 25:8 "*Then have them make a <u>sanctuary</u> for me, and I will dwell among them.*" A sanctuary is a consecrated or holy place devoted to God

2) In Exodus 25:9 "*Make this <u>Tabernacle</u> and all its furnishings exactly like the pattern I will show*

you." Tabernacle is the dwelling place of God among His people.

3) The third name is found in Exodus 26:36 "*For the entrance to the <u>tent</u> make a curtain of blue, purple and scarlet yarn and finely twisted linen…*" The tent indicates a temporary dwelling for the presence of God.

4) In Exodus 29:42 the words are written, "*For the generations to come this burnt offering is to be made regularly at the entrance to the <u>Tent of Meeting</u> before the Lord…*" Tent of Meeting was where God met with the Israelites, His chosen people.

5) Lastly we see in Exodus 38:21 "*These are the amounts of materials used for the tabernacle, the <u>tabernacle of the Testimony</u>, which were recorded at Moses' command by the Levites under the direction of Ithamar son of Aaron the priest.*" The law was given to Moses and was kept in the Ark of the Covenant, the Tabernacle of the Testimony, located in the Holy of Holies.

Hebrews 8:5 gives us a context for the Tabernacle that is constructed in the desert. "*They serve at a sanctuary that is a copy and shadow of what is in heaven. This is why Moses was warned when he was about to build the Tabernacle: 'See to it that you make everything according to the pattern shown you on the mountain.'*" This Tabernacle was a copy and a shadow of what was to come. This pattern was a type of spiritual reality. It represents for us <u>a journey of faith</u>. We will see that as we walk through the Tabernacle how each curtain, veil, post, base, metal, color, fabric, piece of furniture, and each area of the tabernacle all point to our relationship with Christ and the ministry of Jesus.

The Tabernacle is where God would dwell with His people for nearly 400 years (from the Exodus to the time of King Solomon building the Temple). The Tabernacle we will be studying moved with the people. God gave the perfect design for the Tabernacle and gave directives on how it was to be put up and taken down for travel.

The Tabernacle was placed at the center of the Israelites camp. It was the center of their worship life. In the vastness of the desert wilderness, stood the structure of the sanctuary. It was 150 feet long by 75 feet wide (1/2 of a football field). The linen curtain walls were 7 ½ feet high all the way around and the Inner Court (which contained the Holy Place and the Most Holy Place) inside the linen frame had walls standing board to board 15 feet high. It was an obvious sight in the midst of sand and rock.

The twelve tribes were camped around the tent. This too, was God's perfect design. The placement of the people and the construction of the Tabernacle itself were all given to Moses on the mountaintop, by God Himself~ the Divine Designer. Including women and children most scholars believe there were between 2-3 million people. That doesn't include all the animals that were brought out of Egypt. It is estimated that the encampment around the Tabernacle extended about 12 miles! Can you imagine that sight?

Numbers 2 gives the placement of the tribes around the Tabernacle. *"The Lord said to Moses and Aaron: 'The Israelites are to camp around the Tent of Meeting some distance from it, each man under his standard with the banners of his family."* (Numbers 2:1-2) The numbers of men that were counted were twenty years old and older. Children were not counted, neither were women. In the middle of the wilderness, each man camped under his standard with the banner of his family. There is order in the camp.

There is a diagram on page 3 to show the layout of the camp. You will be filling in the diagram as we move along through the studies. What tribe might be your heritage? As I read through the descriptions of each tribe, I wonder from which tribe my lineage traces. I am a worshipper. I connect with the Lord through worship. Because of that, I like to think that I am from the tribe of Judah, which means "praise of Jehovah". As you read through the names of the tribes, what resonates with your heart? Where might your heritage come from?

- On the east side of the Tabernacle there were 186,400 men (20 years +): the tribes of **Judah** (74,600), **Zebulun** (57,400), **Issachar** (54,400). Judah means "praise of Jehovah". The tribe of Judah was the ruling tribe of God. It was out of this tribe that the Kings came. King David is of this tribe and so is Jesus (see Matthew 2:6). Blessing, joy, strength and victory were theirs. Zebulun means "abiding". This tribe lived along the seashore and would be a haven for ships (Genesis 49:13). They were as a light to those in the darkness. The name Issachar means "reward". This tribe willingly accepted what was before them and what they had. The descendants of Issachar were mighty men in David's army because of their ability to understand the times and knew what Israel should do (I Chronicles 12:32).
- On the south side of the Tabernacle were 151,450 men (20 years +): the tribes of **Reuben** (46,500), **Simeon** (59,300), **Gad** (45,650). Reuben was the firstborn of Jacob. His name means "behold a son" . Genesis 49:3 says, *"Reuben, you are my*

firstborn, my might, the first sign of my strength, excelling in honor, excelling in power." The name Simeon means "one who hears" or" obedient one". They settled in the valley, near pastures for the flocks. Gad means "good fortune". The Gad tribe were men who were ready for military service (I Chronicles 5:18). They were trained for battle.

- On the west side of the Tabernacle were 108,100 men (20 years +): the tribes of **Ephraim** (40,500), **Manasseh** (32,200), and **Benjamin** (35,400). Ephraim means "to be doubly fruitful, productive". Ephraim was given the double portion of the blessing by Jacob (Genesis 48:14). Manasseh means "one that makes to forget". He was Joseph's oldest son, however Jacob (his grandfather) gave the younger son the oldest son's blessing. Benjamin was the last born son of Rachel and Jacob. Benjamin means" son of my right hand" (Genesis 35:18). The right hand is symbolic of strength, protection and virtue. So, Benjamin is the son of strength, protection and virtue.

- On the north side were 157,600 men (20 years +): the tribes of **Dan** (62,700), **Asher** (41,500) and **Naphtali** (53,400). Dan means "to judge, to plead a cause". (Samson will come from the tribe of Dan—Judges 14-16). The name Asher means " blessed, happy, to prosper". Genesis 49:20 tells us about the prospering of this tribe and future generations. Naphtali means "to wrestle". *"About Naphtali he said, 'Naphtali is abounding with the favor of the Lord and is full of blessing; he will inherit southward to the lake."* *(Deuteronomy 33:23).*

- The Levites (**Levi** means "joined or attached") were not counted along with the other Israelites. They were placed closest to the Tabernacle. Numbers 2:53 says, *"The Levites, however, are to set up their tents around the Tabernacle of the Testimony so that wrath will not fall on the Israelite community."* Numbers 3 gives us the placement of the Levites:

  ~ The Gershonite clans were to camp around the west side behind the Tabernacle (they were responsible for the care of the Tabernacle and tent, its coverings, the curtain at the entrance to the Tent of Meeting, the curtains of the courtyard, the curtain at the entrance to the courtyard surrounding the Tabernacle and altar, and the ropes.)

  ~ The Kohathite clans were to camp on the south side of the Tabernacle (they were responsible for the care of the ark, the table, the lampstand, the altars, the articles of the Sanctuary used in ministering, and the curtain.)

  ~ The Mararites were to camp on the north side of the Tabernacle (they were responsible for the care of the frames of the Tabernacle, its crossbars, posts, bases, all its equipment, and everything related to their use, as well as the posts of the surrounding courtyard with their bases, tent pegs and ropes.)

  ~ Moses and Aaron and his sons were to camp to the east of the Tabernacle, toward the sunrise, in the front of the Tent of Meeting. (They were responsible for the care of the sanctuary on behalf of the Israelites. They were to minister before the Lord and be the mediators between the people and God.)

There are no surprises. God knew just where each tribe was to be placed and the Israelites trusted God and camped where they were told to camp. This is a sign of obedience from the Israelites. There wasn't any grumbling or complaining, "But my tribe wants to be on the west side, not the north side," or "Why do the Levites get to be on the east side of the tabernacle?" God told them what to do and they obeyed.

God has shown Himself to be merciful, faithful, Jehovah, the Lord who provides, the God who heals, the Victor, and the Living and Covenant God. In Exodus 24, we see Moses ascending the mountain of God where he stayed for 40 days and nights (Exodus 24:15-18). It is here that God gave the pattern for the tabernacle, because His desire was to dwell with His chosen people. During those 40 days and nights, Moses did not eat or drink. He was in the presence of God, who is the Living Water and the Bread of Life. There was no need to meet the physical needs of the body, for Moses' spiritual needs manifested into a physical sustaining power.

God has provided for the Israelites these three months and has endured their "miserablite" attitude. We see in the beginning of Exodus 25 a startling statement. God tells Moses, *"Tell the Israelites to bring me an offering. You are to receive the offering for me from each man whose heart prompts him to give." (Exodus 25:1)* Before God gives any direction for the building of the tabernacle, this was top priority. God was looking for willing hearts. He was taking a 'heart inventory' on the Israelite nation. They have grumbled and complained, showing their heart attitude and now God is asking them to bring Him an offering. He was looking for an offering from anyone whose heart would prompt him to give. This showed the Lord what the Israelites were putting their trust in. How would they respond to God? Did they trust God enough to let go of the gold, silver, bronze, yarn, precious gemstones, spices, and oils? Would they hold back? Would they put their trust in the Living God or in their "stuff" which looks like security (even though we know that at any moment it can all be taken)?

This is the same startling statement that God makes to us today. He is still looking for willing hearts. In fact, it is always about the heart. God sees through the exterior and looks at the heart. He is only concerned about the heart condition. Man is so prone to turn away from God and put trust in his own resources, which become a substitute for God. So before anything else, God establishes with His chosen people that He is interested in their hearts!

In Romans 12:1 Paul urges us to offer our bodies as living sacrifices to God~ to serve Him willingly, in all areas. *"I appeal to you therefore brethren, and beg of you in view of all the mercies of God, to make a decisive dedication of your bodies, presenting all your faculties, as a living sacrifice, holy, devoted and consecrated and well pleasing to God, which is your reasonable, rational, intelligent service and spiritual worship," (Amplified Bible translation).* Will we willingly give of ourselves to the Lord? Each one of us (believers) have been delivered and rescued from "Egypt". God has miraculously set us free from bondage. Where are our hearts? Do we willingly offer our bodies as living sacrifices~ to be holy, devoted and consecrated to God?

2 Corinthians 9:7 Paul again is telling us that God wants a cheerful giver. God wants His people to have hearts willing to give. *"Each man should give what he has decided in his heart to give, not reluctantly or under compulsion, for God loves a cheerful giver."* Do we

cheerfully give to the Lord from finances? What would
God see if the tabernacle (the physical tent) were to be built
today so He could dwell among His people? Is my heart
prompted to give? Is yours? I heard this little quote a long
time ago that has stayed with me. **"If you want to know
what (who) someone loves, look at their checkbook."**
What do we spend our money on? What are checks/debit
cards used for? Too often the answer is "Me" or "My
family" or "My needs". Before you continue reading, I
would like you to take a few minutes to ask these tough
questions:

- Is my heart willing to give to the Kingdom?
- Am I living in such a simplistic lifestyle that there is
  money to give when my heart is prompted by the
  Holy Spirit?
- If I were to look at the check book or debit receipts,
  where is my money going?
- What is my heart devoted to?
- From what bondage did God free me?
- Do I have a "Miserablite" attitude~ grumbling,
  complaining, whining?

If you need an attitude change, tell the Lord. He is faithful.
He loves you & waits to hear from you. His ear is always
inclined to His children. He will change your attitude and
give you a willing heart to give in all areas!

As for the Israelites, you have to give them credit! Check
out Exodus 36:6-7. *"Then Moses gave an order and they
sent the word throughout the camp: 'No man or woman is
to make anything else as an offering for the sanctuary.'
And so the people were restrained from bringing more,
because what they already had was more than enough to do
all the work."* Moses had to say "STOP GIVING! WE
HAVE TOO MUCH!" Can you imagine? We certainly

could learn something from our ancestors in the area of giving! What a dream it would be for a pastor, missionary or ministry leader to have to say to the people of God, "Stop giving. We have too much!" Oh Lord, would it be? The Israelites had hearts that were willing to give to their Jehovah.

What were these offerings the Israelites were instructed to bring? And where did they come from? Exodus 12:35-36 tells us where they got the offerings. *"The Israelites did as Moses instructed and asked the Egyptians for articles of silver and gold and for clothing. The Lord had made the Egyptians favorably disposed toward the people, and they gave them what they asked for; so they plundered the Egyptians."* The Israelites left Egypt wealthy! They had a lot of STUFF! Did they ever wonder, while they were traveling over rock & sand "What are we to do with this gold?" "This yarn is so heavy. Do I really need to continue to take this on the journey?" And how did they know what to ask for? When they were fleeing Egypt, the Bible tells us that the Egyptians were favorably disposed toward the Israelites and gave them what they asked for. God was even in the asking, for they did not know what they would need. I wonder, as I like to do, with "turning the pages of the Bible", did they have a knowing from God as to what they were to ask for? The Bible passage in Exodus 12 tells us that they plundered the Egyptians! Plundered them!

There is a spiritual truth that runs throughout this story of the Israelites. **What God did with the Israelites in the realm of the seen, He does with us in the realm of the unseen.** For us, when we left Egypt, we were given spiritual riches beyond compare. We plundered the enemy. Ephesians 1:3 says to us, *"Praise be to the God and Father of our Lord Jesus Christ, who has blessed us in the*

heavenly realms with every spiritual blessing in Christ."
And 2 Corinthians 2:14 begins, *"But thanks be to God, who always leads us in triumphal procession in Christ..."*
Christ disarmed the enemy. He stripped him of all that he is. His power was taken away. Jesus plundered the enemy, so that in Him, we have His power to plunder the enemy. Colossians 2:15 says, *"And having disarmed the powers and authorities, he made a public spectacle of them, triumphing over them by the cross."* Praise be to our Lord and Savior. Begin reading in Ephesians 1:3-14 and write out the spiritual blessings that you have experienced. You may want to continue this exercise throughout the New Testament, recording the spiritual blessings you have received in Jesus Christ.

Let's take a look at the offerings that the Israelites were to present. Exodus 25:3-7 records them for us. We will take a look at each of these gifts.

The Metals:
- **Gold** signifies holiness, purity and deity. Gold is rare, so it is worth a lot. Matthew 2:11 gives an account of what the magi bring to the newborn King, Jesus. They present him with a gift of gold (representing his kingship). Revelation 21:18 & 21 speak of the heavenly city for those whose names are written in the Lamb's Book of Life. The city is pure gold and the street of the city was of pure gold, as clear as glass, which shows us what God really thinks of gold. It is a common commodity in God's Kingdom. What a sight that will be!
- **Silver**, the next metal the Israelites were to bring signifies redemption. We see this in Matthew 26:14-15. Judas handed Jesus over for thirty silver coins.

- And the last metal given as an offering is **bronze**. Bronze signifies judgment. Numbers 21:4-9 gives a foreshadowing of the cross. The Israelites were grumbling and complaining again and the Lord sent venomous snakes (probably an adder or sand viper) among the people. Snakes bit the people and many Israelites died. The people came to Moses in repentance; asking that God would take the snakes away. God had Moses make a bronze snake, and put it up on a pole. If a snake bit anyone, they were to look at the bronze snake and live. In Revelation 1:15, the feet of the Son of Man are described as being bronze. The feet of judgment. The first judgment of sin was laid upon Jesus. For those of us who recognize that we are sinners and that Jesus bore our sin upon the cross, repent and surrender our lives in full submission to Him, we are like the Israelites who look to the bronze snake to live. Our life is eternal with Christ (in the Holy City made of gold)! For those who refuse to surrender their lives to Christ, they will meet the feet of Jesus in judgment at the Last Day.

We see Jesus in all the metals. He is represented in the gold~ Holy, pure and a King whose reign will never end. And He is represented in the silver~ redemption is found in Him. Lastly, the bronze represents the judgment that He took on Himself for our sin.

Yarn:
Exodus 25:4 tells us the colors of yarn or thread that would be offered to make the designs in the fabric.
- **blue**~ which signifies revelation and communion, and heaven.
- **purple**~ which signifies royalty and authority.
- **scarlet**~ signifying bloodshed and sacrifice.

Jesus is represented in each of these thread colors. The revelation and communion that He brings is seen in the color of the sky (blue) and He is royalty and has all authority (purple) and poured out His blood by His sacrifice on our behalf (scarlet). Following the colors in verse 4 of chapter 25, the Word speaks of the offerings of **fine linen.** Fine linen is worn by royalty and it is also the clothing of the priests. Exodus 39 gives the instruction for making the garments for the priests. Fine linen is what was used. We also see King David in 2 Samuel 6:14 dancing before the Lord in the procession of the Ark wearing the clothing of a priest, the fine linen garments. We, the saints (believers of the Lord) will wear fine linen. Take a look at Revelation 19:7-8, *"Let us rejoice and be glad and give Him glory! For the wedding of the Lamb has come and His bride has made herself ready. Fine linen, bright and clean was given her to wear (Fine linen stands for the righteous acts of the saints)."* The fine linen of the priests foreshadows the spiritual reality that we are His priests of a new covenant. Remember, **everything God did with the Israelites in the realm of the seen, He does with us in the realm of the unseen**.

Coverings:
Goats' hair, rams' skins dyed red, and sea cows' hides (or badger skins or dolphin skins~ depending upon what version of the Bible you are reading. Whatever animal it speaks of, it would have been a water mammal that was prevalent in the Red Sea) were spoken of next in Exodus 25. The **goats' hair** was used as a covering for the Tabernacle. The **rams' skins** were dyed red (the color of sacrifice) were also used in the covering of the Tabernacle and the outer layer of covering was **sea cows' hides** (which were a grayish color, able to withstand the storms of the desert; waterproof). The tabernacle was an ugly site from the outside. There would be nothing that would attract one

to the Tabernacle, just as Jesus had nothing to attract us to Him physically (Isaiah 53:2 *"He had no beauty or majesty to attract us to him, nothing in his appearance that we should desire him."*). How do we get the skins of animals? Bloodshed and death. Even in the coverings of the Tabernacle, we see the cross of Christ foreshadowed. We will look more closely at these curtains and coverings in a few chapters.

Wood:
Acacia wood is the next offering that was to be presented. This was a wood that was very accessible in the desert region of Sinai. Acacia wood is a hard, incorruptible and indestructible wood. Acacia wood is used to construct most of the pieces of furniture that will be used in the Tabernacle itself. Jesus is seen in this wood. As a product of earth (the wood and humanity), Jesus was incorruptible and indestructible. No evil could penetrate who He was. He lived a perfect humanity. He was all God and all man. There was and never will be another like Him.

Oil & Spices:
Verse 6 of Exodus 25 tells us that **olive oil** and **spices** were to be brought as an offering. The olive oil was used for the light in the Tabernacle and the spices were used for the anointing oil and also for the fragrant incense that would be used at the Altar of Incense.

- Olive oil comes from a plant, which is a symbol of salvation. We also see the olive plant used as a covenant with Noah (in Genesis 8). After the rain stopped, Noah sent out a raven and it did not return to the Ark. Noah then sent a dove and he returned with a freshly plucked olive leaf in his beak (Genesis 8:11). This plant can grow in areas where no other plant grows, which explains why it was

56

from this plant that the dove brought a leaf. The olive oil is a symbol of the Holy Spirit. It represents the anointing of the Holy Spirit that God pours into us, inside our spirit when we are born again. This anointing is part of the new covenant in Jesus. The olive oil that the Israelites had was a pattern and a shadow of what was to come.

- The anointing oil (made from spices) is different than the olive oil. The anointing oil symbolizes the anointing that is put upon a person. It is an anointing for what God has called you to do. The olive oil represents an anointing within and the anointing oil represents an anointing upon.

- Spices were used in the mixing of the fragrant incense. The spices brought were ground into powder, and then placed on the altar as an offering. This incense was to be: holy, pure, fragrant, ground/crushed, and continual. Jesus is holy (I Peter 1:15-16), pure (I John 3:3), fragrant (2 Corinthians 2:16), ground/crushed (2 Corinthians 4:8-10), and continual (Hebrews 7:25).

Precious Stones:

Lastly, the Israelites were instructed to present as an offering onyx stones and other gems to be used in the special garments of the priests. Each stone represented the twelve tribes of Israel. The high priest would wear these stones in the breast piece over his special linen garments. As he entered the Holy of Holies, where the presence of the Lord dwelt, the high priest carried the tribes of Israel (the chosen ones) over his heart. Jesus, the Great High Priest carries us, His chosen ones over his heart. These stones are also mentioned in Revelation 21:18-21. We see that they are the twelve foundations of the Heavenly City! Jesus is the cornerstone (the true foundation) and we are building on Him. I Peter 2:5 says, *"As you come to him, the living*

Stone~ rejected by men but chosen by God and precious to him~ you also, like living stones, are being built into a spiritual house to be a holy priesthood, offering spiritual sacrifices acceptable to God through Jesus Christ."

God is the perfect designer. He has taken these Israelites as His very own. He has delivered them, provided for them, protected them and desires to live among them. They will be His people and He will be their God. The perfect plan is in place. Moses will see to the construction of the tabernacle. And the Israelites, with willing hearts, brought the gifts & offerings that will be used in the construction of the tabernacle.

May it be that we are those with willing hearts to bring the offerings that are asked of us by God, our Deliverer.

STUDY GUIDE
Chapter 2: The Tabernacle
(Exodus 19-25)

Scripture to memorize: Exodus 25:8 *"Then have them make a sanctuary for me, and I will dwell among them."* (NIV)

Key Questions:

1) God desires to dwell among us. We make the choice to come close or stay at a distance. What must we do (according to James 4:8) to be closer to the Lord?
2) What commandment stood out to you as you studied them this week? Any new revelation or a conviction?
3) What have you learned (or been reminded) of the fear of the Lord (especially in Day 4 & 5)? Having a reverence for who God is, YHWH

Day 1: At A Distance
(Exodus 19-20)

The children of Israel have now arrived at Mount Sinai. The rest of Exodus, all of Leviticus and Numbers 1-9 record the events that took place here. There is a turning point here in history of how God deals with His chosen nation Israel. Exodus 19:5-6 establishes a new order in which God would deal with His people. If they obey, then He would bless. *"Now therefore, if you will indeed obey My voice and keep My covenant, then you shall be a special treasure to Me above all people; for all the earth is Mine. And you shall surely be to Me a kingdom of priests and a holy nation."* A covenant means "to bond or fit together". It is a binding agreement between two parties. This is one of the most important words in the Bible, appearing more than 250 times in the Old Testament.

The people are quick to respond, *"We will do everything the Lord has said."* We know the rest of the story—their actions did not match up with their words at this time!

1) Has that been a part of your past or your present? How?

The Lord is going to confirm to the people of Israel that Moses is HIS MAN! He wants the nation to put their trust in Moses, because Moses has been to the mountaintop to receive the Words of the Lord. (See Exodus 19:9)

Moses tells the people to consecrate themselves before they meet with God. They have 3 days to get ready (physically & spiritually clean). As they are preparing, God sets boundaries around the mountain to protect the people. When God sets boundaries, it is always for our best & our protection (Psalm 16:6 *"The lines have fallen for me in pleasant places;"*). R. Alan Cole writes, "Since the mountain was holy (not permanently, or in itself, but on this occasion, and rendered so by the descent of God), then anything that touched it would also become 'holy' or devoted to God. For a living creature that meant sacrifice, which, in turn, meant death." (p. 155 Exodus).

Imagine this scene: The nation of Israel is consecrating themselves and thunder & lightning (representing God's power) are descending on the mountaintop. The trumpet blast (Hebrew word: "Shofar"; a trumpet made from a curved animal horn) to announce the descent of the Lord "He is HERE"! The people trembled in the camp and *"Moses brought the people out of the camp to meet with God, and they stood at the foot of the mountain. (Ex. 19:17).* The mountain is covered with smoke, the

60

mountain trembles and the trumpet gets louder & louder. Moses spoke and God answered Him by voice. The Lord called Moses to the top of the mountain, and Moses went up.

2) Describe a time in your life that you have experienced the power and presence of the Lord that caused you to tremble.

What an amazing picture ~ that the God of the universe, the Creator of the world, desires to have a people to call His own.

3) Read Exodus 20:18-21 which tells us the condition of the Israelites' hearts.

4) What was their response?

5) Has this ever been your response? Explain.

6) Read James 4:8. God desires to dwell among us. He wants us to draw near to Him, not stand far off. What does this verse tell us we must do to draw near to Him? Our hands speak to our actions. Our hearts speak to our desires and motives. Double-mindedness speaks to our mixed motives.

7) Write out a prayer of repentance, asking the Lord to cleanse your hands and purify your heart and to give you a single-minded devotion—to draw near to Him.

DAY 2: The Ten Commandments (Part 1)
(Exodus 20)

The Israelites had been brought out of Egypt by God's mighty hand. They had lived in a land where the worship of many gods was practiced. Jehovah (the Covenant God) was establishing the law for His people so they would know how to live in relationship with their God and with others. What an amazing time in history! God's moral law is given and all His people are held to this standard. Let's review those commandments or the "Words". Today, we will look at the first four commandments. These speak of our relationship to God (the vertical) connection. The last six commandments (which will be studied on day 3) speak of our relationship to people (the horizontal connections). Jesus summarized these commandments in Matthew 22:37-39 by saying, "Love God and Love Others"!

Exodus 20:2 *"I am the Lord your God."* This is Jehovah, the always existing, independent, Almighty, personal God. He is calling Himself in relationship to the Israelites by saying "your God". He has always been known as "the God of Abraham, Isaac and Jacob". He is making this distinction—this new relationship that the people will have with Him. He loves them and has delivered them from bondage.

The commandments are explanation of the "how" to keep covenant with God. Remember in Exodus 19:5-6 God tells the Israelites, "If you obey me fully and keep my covenant…"

There is freedom in walking according to the law of the Lord. God establishes laws to protect us, free us, and keep us healthy (physically, emotionally & spiritually). We will take a look at some of the verses from Psalm 119 as we walk through the commandments. Invite the Holy Spirit to open your eyes to see these in a new way; fresh insight as we take a look, as if for the first time!

1st commandment: **"Have no other gods before me"** (vs. 3) The Israelites have been rescued out of a polytheist nation. God is establishing a prohibition of worshipping any other gods except Jehovah. Hosea 2:17 says, *"I will remove the names of the Baals from her lips; no longer will their names be invoked."* We studied the various gods of Egypt that held the Egyptians in bondage last week as we looked at the ten plagues upon that land. God gives the commandment again to His people in Exodus 23:13 when He says, *"Be careful to do everything I have said to you. Do not invoke the names of other gods; do not let them be heard on your lips."* Those gods were "obvious" to us as we read through the list. But what gods have you worshipped? What names of Baal (false god) have been invoked from your lips? We have many gods in the American church. Anything that takes first place in your life is taking the place of Jehovah.

Deuteronomy 30:17 says, *"But if your heart turns away and you are not obedient, and if you are drawn away to bow down to other gods and worship them..."* Has your heart turned away? Ask the Lord to show you if you have been drawn away to bow down (worship) to other gods (idols),

Here are some examples of common "gods" in our American culture, in the church as well as the secular world: a) convenience, b) time, c) money, d) things of the world, e) children, f) spouse, g) work, h) entertainment/media, I) sports, j) religious rituals, k) "doing" for the Lord, l) addictions, m) hobbies, n) intellect, o) selfish pleasures, p) house, q) schedules, r) gifts & talents, s) comfort, t) guilt, u) fear, v) confidence in self,

w) retirement funds/savings/401K, x) exercise, y) materialism, z) sleep

1) Search your heart and ask the Lord, what gods have you worshipped? It's the things that we love that are the hardest to give up. Which of these idols would be hard for you to give up? Confess that to the Lord. He will cleanse your heart. Repent and turn to Jehovah, the ONLY TRUE GOD!

2nd commandment: **"Use no carved image"** (vs. 4-6) God forbids worshipping any images; including any image of Him. Israel was surrounded by nations who worshipped carved images; they just left one three months prior to this time. The Israelites were unique among the neighboring nations. This can be difficult, because there is a "comfort" in blending in or being like everybody else. ☺ God has called us a "peculiar nation"! I am sure the nations surrounding the Israelites called them a peculiar people! God's Words to His people in Exodus 19:5-6 are that they are a treasured possession! They will not look like everyone else! Would we say, as the psalmist, *"The law from your mouth is more precious to me than thousands of pieces of silver and gold." (Psalm 119:72).* If you remember, silver and gold were (and are) used to make an image to worship.

2) Why do you think God set this commandment in place? The Israelites could have made beautiful carvings of the image of the mountain with the smoke & fire or they could have made a pillar of cloud or a pillar of fire. What was God's motive behind this commandment?

*Take a look at Isaiah 44:6-20.

3rd commandment: **"Do not use God's Name in vain"**
(vs. 7) This means to swear by God's name that a false
statement is true. It also means any profanity, or swearing
to fulfill a promise, or any oaths made by using God's
name. It also means taking His Holy name & using it in a
common way. God is HOLY and His name is HOLY!

   3) Are you breaking this commandment in casual
      conversation?

4th commandment: **"Remember the Sabbath"** (vs. 8-11)
The Bible first mentions the Sabbath in Genesis 2:2-3, but
this is the first time that it is given as a formal ordinance to
follow. God is concerned about His people and establishes
a day of rest for us. Adam & Eve were created on day six,
so their first full day of existence began on the Sabbath.
We are designed by God to live & work **from** the Sabbath.
We seem to live **for** the Sabbath. What a difference in how
we live. The Sabbath existed for the fields and slaves and
animals that were owned by the Israelites.   Take a look at
Exodus 23:10-12.

   4) Are you faithful to the Sabbath? Why/why not?

Psalm 119 is a beautiful passage of scripture. The author
writes of the love of God's law! Oh that we would love
HIS law. Psalm 119:20 *says, "My soul is consumed with
longing for your laws at all times."*

   5) Write these four commandments in your own words
      to make them personal for you. You could write
      them as a prayer of covenant between you & your
      God!

DAY 3: The Ten Commandments (Part 2)
(Exodus 20)

We will continue our study of the Ten Commandments; looking today at the last 6 that deal with our relationships with others in our lives. God's ultimate commandment is that we "love one another." Romans 13:9-10 says, *"The commandments, 'Do not commit adultery', 'Do not murder', 'Do not steal', 'Do not covet', and whatever other commandment there may be, are summed up in this one rule: 'Love your neighbor as yourself'. Love does no harm to its neighbor. Therefore love is the fulfillment of the law."*

5th commandment: **"Honor your father and mother."** (vs. 12) This begins the commandment of dealing with others. How interesting that it has to start in the family! The Israelites would find themselves wandering in the desert for 40 years together. WOW! Imagine living that close with your parents! And we have seen how well they keep their emotions in check (they grumble & complain at every chance)! ☺ God is calling them to be a people who are humble, loving & full of forgiveness toward one another. This commandment came with a promise to the Israelites & it is again repeated in the New Testament in Ephesians 6:2~honor your parents, so you will have a long life in the land that the Lord is giving you.

To honor means to prize highly, to show respect, to exalt.

1) Would you say that you honor your parents? What if we asked your parents? What would they say?

2) If you are a parent, do you parent in a way that your children would easily honor you? Ephesians 6:4 is a command to fathers (parents): "Do not exasperate

your children"—which means to not make them angry (doing something that "pushes their buttons").

6th commandment: **"You shall not murder"** (vs.. 13) This commandment is not speaking of accidental killings or suicide, wartime killing or capital punishment. This is the intentional decision to take one's life. John adds to this in the New Testament when he says, *"Anyone who hates his brother is a murderer, and you know that no murderer has eternal life in him."*. He judges our motives and thoughts. Bring your thoughts into captivity to Jesus, so they are not allowed to have full-access in your mind.

3) Is there anyone that you have been so angry at that your thoughts toward him/her were of evil intent? Repent of those thoughts. Ask the Lord to cleanse your mind & to bring blessing on that individual.

7th commandment: **"You shall not commit adultery"** (vs. 14). This commandment covers all forms of sexual unfaithfulness (adultery, pornography, lustful thoughts, sexual relations outside of marriage). God is concerned about purity of heart & mind. Take a look at Matthew 5:27-30. Jesus spoke with words that pierced like arrows into the heart.

4) Read Psalm 119:9-11. How can a young person keep his/her life pure? How can you encourage a young person to keep his/her life pure?

8th commandment: **"You shall not steal"** (vs. 15) This commandment covers all forms of stealing. The Israelites lived so close to one another in the camps that this commandment gave the security to the people that no one would break in and steal. The heart of this command, too, deals with the heart and its motives. Ephesians 4:28 says, *"He who has been stealing must steal no longer, but must work, doing something useful with his own hands, that he may have something to share with those in need."* Jesus' focus is always on others.

5) Can you think of something that people steal that they would say "well that's not stealing"?

9th commandment: **"You shall not bear false testimony."** (vs. 16). This commandment deals with words rather than with deeds. Among the things named in this commandment would be exaggeration in speech, flattering compliments that aren't meant, lies, slanderous remarks, backbiting, gossip, telling half truths (which are lies). Paul gives us this commandment with more detail in the New Testament (Eph. 4:25, 29—32. We are to: put off falsehood & speak truthfully, only say things that are helpful to build others up, get rid of all bitterness, rage, anger, brawling, slander, malice, be kind and compassionate, forgiving one another. Now that's a list!

6) How can your speech improve (with the insight from this commandment)?

10th commandment: **"You shall not covet."** (vs. 17) To covet means to earnestly desire or long after. A wish to have something our neighbor has may be innocent; but to long for it, excessively, is sinful. A wonderful verse to sum up this verse is Hebrews 13:5 which says, *"Keep your lives free from the love of money and be content with what you have, because God has said, 'Neither will I leave you; never will I forsake you.'."*

7) Have you known someone who has struggled in this area; he/she is consumed with a longing for something that is not his/her own?

Psalm 119:14-16 *"I rejoice in following your statutes as one rejoices in great riches. I meditate on your precepts and consider your ways. I delight in your decrees; I will not neglect your word."* Write a prayer to the Lord rejoicing & delighting in His laws!

DAY 4: The Covenant Confirmed
(Exodus 24)

Moses told the people all the words of the Lord, beginning in chapter 20, with the Ten Commandments to the end of chapter 23, with all the laws & ordinances that God established for the Israelites.

The people agree to obey. *"Everything the Lord has said we will do."* (Exodus 24:3) After the Israelites promised obedience and entered into the covenant agreement with God, it was necessary to have these laws written out, in order for them to be remembered and preserved for generations to come. So we see in Exodus 24:4 that Moses writes all the words of the Lord. To confirm the covenant, Moses acts as the mediator between the people and God. This covenant could not be done without sacrifice, shedding & sprinkling of blood. He builds an altar (of earth) as commanded in Exodus 20:24 and sets up twelve stone pillars. The altar represented the throne of God and the twelve stones represented the twelve tribes of Israel. These were the two parties who were entering into contract or covenant.

The *Book of the Covenant* was not a covenant to be binding until a sacrifice had been offered, so we see in Exodus 24:5-6 the offerings made.

1) Burnt offerings were completely consumed by fire. Read Leviticus 1:10. What animal(s) were used in the burnt offering?

The peace offering (fellowship offering) was an offering of celebration. The animals used in this offering were the bull, sheep or a goat. Only certain parts of the animal were burned. The blood of these animals was poured out before the Lord (see Leviticus 3:1-17).

2) Read Hebrews 9:18-20. What are the words recorded in vs. 20?

Exodus 24:6—8. Half of the blood was sprinkled on the altar & the other half was sprinkled on the people showing that both God and the Israelites were bonded by this covenant. God was bound to His people to support, defend and save them. The people were bound to God to fear, love and serve Him. The Israelites have been "covered in the blood". WOW!

3) Describe that scene. What would the "mood" have been? What do you feel as you read this account?

Moses, Aaron, Nadab & Abihu and the 70 elders of Israel went up the mountain.

4) Read Exodus 24:10. God was showing Himself to the leaders of Israel to give them a worship experience they would never forget. He revealed a part of Himself. What is under His feet?

This is a sapphire stone (deep blue stone) known in Mesopotamia. Take a look at Ezekiel 1:26 (God is seated on a sapphire throne) and Revelation 4:6 (a sea of glass). WOW! For women, the beauty of a crystal sea or a throne made of this stone. Imagine!

These leaders spent time in the presence of Jehovah/YHWH. They ate & drank on the mountain. What an experience!

Moses is called up further on the mountain (Ex. 24:15--18) and the cloud covered the mountain & the glory of the Lord settled on Mt. Sinai. Moses sat in silence for 6 days and on the 7th day; the Lord spoke to Moses in the cloud. Moses continues his climb up the mountain and he stayed on the mountain for 40 days & nights. Seeing the glory of God upon the mountain like a consuming fire (see Hebrews 12:28-29).

   5) The glory of YHWH was evident by what? (Exodus 24:15—18)

God "settled" or dwelt (vs. 16) on the top of the mountain. This speaks of the 'Shekinah' glory of the Lord—the outward manifestation of His presence to men.

   6) Have you experienced this 'Shekinah' glory of the Lord in your life?

Here, on the top of the mountain, Moses meets with God. He does not eat or drink for the whole 40 days & 40 nights. The "bread of life" and the "living water" sustained him. God gives the directions for the tabernacle, the place where His presence may dwell with His people. A place to hold his 'Shekinah' glory!

Moses was gone so long, the Israelites may have thought that Moses was consumed by it, and therefore they more easily fell into idolatry. They used the gold that was given to them by the Egyptians (the gold that was to be used in the construction of the tabernacle) for Aaron (the high priest) to make the golden calf. How could there be such a shift in their hearts so quickly? *"Then the Lord said to Moses, 'Go down, because your people whom you have brought up out of Egypt, have become corrupt. They have been quick to turn away from what I commanded them and have made themselves an idol cast in the shape of a calf. They have bowed down and sacrificed to it and have said, 'These are your gods, O Israel, who brought you out of Egypt.'"* (Exodus 32:7-8). These are the same people who 40 days earlier had said, in Exodus 24:7, *"We will do everything the Lord has said; we will obey."* How could they do this, with the glorious and terrifying sight of God's glory before their very eyes? How could they break covenant so quickly? God calls the time on the mountain "quick" and the Israelites thought the time was "so long". Something to note: **Time to us and time to God are usually two different periods.** We are such a busy people. God is calling us to Himself. One of the first heart conditions that need to be corrected for the Israelites, and for us as well, is the issue of time. TIME = LIFE. We will see this concept again as we study the tabernacle. God wants our time. And to Him, since He is on the outside of time, He has no parameters.

DAY 5: The Pattern of the Tabernacle
(Exodus 25)

"The next seven chapters deal with the instructions for building the tabernacle, setting up the priesthood, and related legislation. Fully 50 chapters in the Bible are devoted to the tabernacle, showing its importance in God's sight. The tabernacle was a tent-like structure, which was to be God's dwelling place among His people. Each part of the tabernacle teaches us spiritual lessons concerning the Person and work of Christ and the way of approach to God. The priesthood reminded the people that sin had created distance between God and themselves, and that they could draw near to Him only through these representatives appointed and made fit by Him." Believer's Bible Commentary (p. 115)

Exodus 25 begins the account of the tabernacle. This is a dramatic turn, for the Lord is asking the Israelites to give to Him with willing hearts; those whose heart prompts him to give. The Israelites have been a people who are known for their grumbling & complaining and asking God to meet all their needs. Now God is giving them an opportunity to give back to Him! The Lord provides the directions for the tabernacle & the people provide the resources and materials. For almost 400 years, the Tabernacle was the place for God to dwell among His people and a place where His people could commune with Him. The Tabernacle was a visual reminder to the Israelites of Jehovah or YHWH whom they served. Every aspect of the Tabernacle points to God's redemptive plan of Salvation through Jesus Christ.

Read Exodus 25:1-9 and answer these questions:

1) What three metals are to be offered?

2) What three colors?

3) What textile?

4) The hair from what animal?

5) What two kinds of skins

6) What specific kind of wood?

7) What will make the oil for the light & anointing oil & incense?

8) What stones?

9) What name is given to the building and what is its purpose?

10) Who is giving the pattern for the tabernacle?

God gives specific direction for the pattern of the tabernacle. Not a detail is missing. More than 20 times in Exodus we read, *"As the Lord commanded Moses"*. There are 5 names given to the tabernacle:

- "A sanctuary" (Exodus 25:8) – a consecrated or holy thing or place; devoted to God
- "Tabernacle" (Exodus 25:9) – a dwelling place of God among His people
- "Tent" (Exodus 26:36) – indicates it is a temporary dwelling
- "Tent of meeting" (Exodus 29:42) – this is where God met with His people
- "The Tabernacle of the Testimony" (Exodus 38:21) – the law given to Moses was kept in the ark of the covenant, located in the Holy of Holies

As we move through the tabernacle, in the pages ahead, ask the Holy Spirit to meet with you on this journey of faith. Invite Him to lead you and guide you into all truth as we study the structure and furnishings of the tabernacle~ giving insight as to how it applies to your life! Let the Lord have a sanctuary in your heart.

CHAPTER 3:
The Outer Court: The Bronze Altar

Entering the Tabernacle requires that you to step through the curtain at the East entrance, the only way into the outer courtyard. Exodus 27:9--19 gives the dimensions and details of the outer court of the tabernacle. The Tabernacle was set up with posts (7 ½ feet high) placed around the 150 foot x 75 foot perimeter. There were 20 posts on the north and south sides and 10 posts on the west and east sides. White fine linen curtains were attached to the posts on the north, south and west sides. The entrance into the outer courtyard was a curtain made of fine linen woven with blue, scarlet and purple which extended thirty feet on the east side of the tabernacle. There were 22 ½ feet on each side of this colorful curtain of fine white linen curtains. The entrance gate was centered & beautiful; a contrast from the rest of the linen curtains. It beckoned one to enter. It was an inviting sight, bringing color and beauty in the midst of the wilderness.

The wilderness of our culture moves people near the curtain, for it beckons, still today. The gate, the entrance, the only way is Jesus. We see Him in the woven blue, scarlet and purple curtain. The blue represents communion, heaven and revelation. Jesus came from heaven to make His dwelling among us (John 1:14) to give forth revelation and new insight, with being the fulfillment of the law. And His desire was to commune with the people of God, the chosen ones. This is the same desire that God has in making a dwelling for His Glory that we see in the construction of the tabernacle. The purple yarn woven in the fabric describes the royalty and authority that Jesus has over all creation. And the scarlet speaks to the cross; the bloodshed for the atonement of the sins of the world. As one entered the gate or entrance into the outer court of the tabernacle, the ministry of Jesus was being displayed. He beckons one to come into the courtyard. Step through the gate to experience a life of freedom and growth; a stark contrast to the vast wilderness in which we live.

When speaking to the Pharisees, Jesus says of the Kingdom of God, *"God's law and prophets climaxed in John; now it's all kingdom of God—the glad news and compelling invitation to every man and woman" (Luke 16:16 Message Translation)*. The curtain speaks of the invitation to enter into a life with Christ Jesus. It is a compelling invitation to every man and woman. My life changed completely when I stepped through the curtain. In John 10:9 Jesus tells us, *"I am the gate; whoever enters through me will be saved. He will come in and go out and find pasture."* What a promise. After stepping through the curtain, provision, healing, freedom, growth, peace and intimacy with Jesus has been my treasure. Once I went through the gate, there was no turning around. Nothing this world could offer me compares to what knowing Christ has provided. In Philippians 3:8-9 Paul says it this way, *"What is more, I consider everything a loss compared to the surpassing greatness of knowing Christ Jesus my Lord, for whose sake I have lost all things. I consider them rubbish, that I may gain Christ and be found in him, not having a righteousness of my own that comes from the law, but that which is through faith in Christ~ the righteousness that comes from God and is by faith."* This is good news!

Each one of us is on a journey of faith. And each person has to make a choice, whether to pass through the gate or not. No one can make the decision for you and you cannot "get in" because your parents walked through the gate or because you were raised in a church, were baptized, did good things, helped the poor, or gave money to various ministries. The Bible is very clear. There is only one way into the Kingdom of God and that way is JESUS. Only Jesus. John 14:6 Jesus says, *"I am the way, the truth and the life. No one comes to the Father except through me."*

His grace leads us into the outer court. Noah Webster's dictionary defines grace as " The divine favor toward man; the mercy of God, as distinguished from His justice; also, any benefits His mercy imparts; divine love or pardon; a state of acceptance with God; enjoyment of the divine favor". Each one must wrestle with the truth that our sin nature must be dealt with. Death is the punishment for sin. And not one of us is excluded from the truth of sin. For all have sinned. It is our nature. *"For all have sinned and fall short of the glory of God" Romans 3;23.* There is no good in us apart from Christ. For us today, this is a spiritual reality with no physical reminder of our need. But for the Israelites, the set up of the tabernacle structure was a visual reminder of their spiritual condition.

A physical border was created by posts, frames and curtains which was a daily reminder of the separation between the people and God. The boundary was established. Levite tribes were placed around the tabernacle structure to protect the tribes of Israel from accidentally coming upon the presence or Holiness of the Lord. We don't see a physical representation in this time of history. Would it help to have a physical structure reminding us of our separateness?

Spiritually we are separated from God until a decision is made to enter the tabernacle through the gate. The journey of faith begins here outside the gate at the east entrance. There are those who have not yet chosen to move past the curtain~ to take the first step of faith. As we discover the Tabernacle and its significance for our lives today, my prayer is that all who read and participate in the study will be moved by the love of God to take the first step or the next step in your individual journey towards deeper intimacy with the Lord, as depicted in a physical structure, the Tabernacle.

Stepping through the East entrance, the curtain, the first object in the outer court is seen~ the bronze altar. It was the largest piece of furniture in the Tabernacle and it was set up to face the Holy Place (inner court). Along the dust, sand and rock was the bronze altar. There was only one other piece of furniture in the outer court and that was the bronze basin. But, no one could go any further into the outer court without making atonement (which means "at-one-ment" or the state of being one or being reconciled).

Sacrificial animals were offered on this altar and their blood was shed for the sins of the people. Blood was shed from morning until evening for the atonement of sins. For the Israelites, the altar provided a temporary atoning of sins. *"In fact, the law requires that nearly everything be cleansed with blood, and without the shedding of blood there is no forgiveness,"* (Hebrews 9:22).

There are several references to the bronze altar in the Old Testament. It is called:
　　1) Altar of acacia wood (Exodus 27:1)
　　2) Altar of burnt offering (Exodus 30:28)
　　3) Bronze altar (Exodus 38:30)
　　4) The altar (Leviticus 1:5, 8:11)
　　5) My altar—the Lord's table (Malachi 1:7)

The word "altar" has two meanings: 1) "Lifted high" or "ascending" and 2) "the slaughter place". In reference to the bronze altar, the animals were sacrificed (the slaughter place) and the burning of the sacrifice was a sweet aroma to the Lord as it was "lifted high" before Him. The cross was the slaughter place (altar) for our Savior, the willing sacrifice to take on Himself the sins of the whole world (Isaiah 53). Imagine, every sin of every generation, every person who has ever lived, is living now or will live in the future was placed on Christ. The atoning sacrifice for sin was fulfilled in Jesus' sacrifice. Hebrews 7:27 tells us, *"Unlike the other high priests, he does not need to offer sacrifices day after day, first for his own sins, and then for the sins of the people. He sacrificed for their sins once for all when he offered himself."*

There is power in the blood of Jesus, once it is applied. Until it is applied, the blood only has potential power. Remember the story of the Israelites at Passover (the final plague). God instructed the Israelite families to shed the blood of a lamb and place the blood over the doorposts so that the angel of death would Passover. What if the lamb had been sacrificed, and the blood collected, put in a bowl and placed on the table? That would not have saved them from the angel of death. There would be no power in that blood; just potential. So it is for us. When Jesus died on the cross, everyone has the opportunity to apply the blood (for salvation). There is potential, but no power until it is applied. Have you accepted Christ's blood sacrifice for the forgiveness of your sins?

Here are some of the effects of Christ's blood:
1) sanctification
2) overcoming power
3) gives life
4) propitiation
5) justification
6) communion with God the Father, God the Son and God the Holy Spirit
7) redemption
8) forgiveness

9) brought near to God
10) peace with God
11) conscience is cleansed
12) name is written in the Book of Life
13) delivered from God's judgment and wrath
14) entrance into the Holy of Holies
15) continually cleansed by the blood

The bronze altar speaks of Christ's atoning work on the cross, which was a once and for all sacrifice, so that all who put their faith in His blood will have their sins atoned for. There is no more need for a continuous blood sacrifice. After pressing through the curtain, the stark reality is that we are sinners who need a Savior. We are redeemed by His blood, once and for all.

Exodus 27 gives us the directions for constructing the bronze altar. The materials used were acacia wood and bronze. Acacia wood was found in the Sinai Desert. It was a hard, indestructible, incorruptible wood. It could survive the harsh environment because its roots grew very deep. The tree itself didn't grow very tall. Most Acacia trees only grow to a height of 15-30 feet. The strong odor in the wood of this tree would keep it from disease and animal invasions. Insects would not borough into it either.

The wood itself was a product of the "earth" which speaks to Jesus' humanity. Isaiah 53:2 says, *"He grew up before him like a tender shoot, and like a root out of dry ground."* The acacia wood signifies the perfect humanity displayed by Jesus Christ. He was without sin, without blemish, without "spot", without "wrinkle", and without any negative thing. His human life withstood all the evil around him. Hebrews 7:16 tells us that Jesus became a *"priest not on the basis of a regulation as to his ancestry but on the basis of the power of an indestructible life."*

Wood is a central theme for Jesus' life: a food trough at his birth became his bed. His life work was as a carpenter and His life's physical end would be on a wooden cross (the altar).

This altar made of acacia wood was about 4 ½ feet high and 7½ feet square. There were horns at all four corners pointing outward at each corner, with a bronze network and a bronze ring at each of the four corners of the network. The four corners represented going into all the world (east, west, north and south) to bring the good news of the gospel to all creation (see Matthew 28:18-20). Poles were used to carry the bronze altar when traveling.

The horns speak of salvation, strength and power. Luke 1:68-69 tells us how Jesus is foreshadowed in the horns, *"Praise be to the Lord, the God of Israel, because he has come and has redeemed his people. He has raised up a horn of salvation for us in the house of his servant, David."* Jesus was a willing sacrifice on the altar (the cross). When we imagine the animal sacrifices offered, the animal itself would not have been a willing sacrifice. Horns can be used to tie down an unwilling sacrifice. What about you? Are you a willing sacrifice or an unwilling sacrifice? I would have to say that I can be both! There are times when it would be better for me to be tied down, so I cannot move off the altar. I am learning to be a willing sacrifice. In Romans 12:1, Paul says, *"Therefore, I urge you, brothers, in view of God's mercy, to offer your bodies as living sacrifices, holy and pleasing to God~ this is your spiritual act of worship."* Paul calls us to offer our lives as a willing sacrifice.

The Random House Dictionary defines willing as "1) disposed or consenting; inclined, 2) cheerfully consenting or ready". It is an adjective, which is a describing word (for all of the grammar teachers). An adjective describes a noun (person, place or thing). So, ask yourself again: Am I a willing (disposed or consenting; inclined, cheerfully consenting or ready) sacrifice? As a living sacrifice, we can "crawl" off the altar. Paul is encouraging us to stay on the altar and willingly give our lives to the Lord as a spiritual act of worship. This takes practice. It doesn't happen overnight. In order to be a living sacrifice, I need to tell my body and my mind daily what I will think and what I will do; not to let emotions or feelings or flesh lead me along. Romans 12:2 gives us a little more insight so we can be a living sacrifice. How do we offer our lives to the Lord as a spiritual offering? *"Do not conform any longer to the pattern of this world, but be transformed by the renewing of your mind. Then you will know what God's will is~ His good, pleasing and perfect will."*

To be a living sacrifice we need to:
1) not conform any longer to the pattern of this world
2) be transformed by the renewing of the mind with God's Word.

In what ways are you conformed (similar to; complying with; in harmony) to this world? As we get God's Word into our minds (meditating on the Word, memorizing it, studying it), we will be transformed (changed). That is a promise. God's Word is alive and active and it will change you and me. We need to be diligent in "feeding" on the Word. Get a new diet! A diet of God's Word! Then you (and I) won't need the horns to tie us down on the altar, instead we will be willing sacrifices to God.

Another interesting event took place at the altar. The horns were a place of refuge. We see in I Kings 1:49-53 that Adonijah found mercy at the horns of the altar. Everything that touches the altar becomes holy, because the altar itself is holy. Solomon, the new king-to-be replied that if Adonijah is found worthy, he will be spared. Adonijah was taken off the altar and sent home. In the next chapter of I Kings, we see another example of Joab seeking refuge at the horns of the altar (I Kings 2:28-34). However, the altar of God gave no protection to anyone who broke the law. Joab's fate was different than Adonijah's. Solomon's men killed Joab on the altar because he refused to come down. They buried him on his property in the wilderness. Joab had shed innocent blood and the altar could not be a place of protection for this man. The altar is holy, and communicates holiness to anyone who touches it (if they aren't holy already). When these men (Adonijah and Joab) grabbed the horns of the altar, each became sanctified. If found guilty, like Joab, he would be killed; because of a sacrilege, but if he is innocent, like Adonijah, he protects himself because of the holiness.

The horns are a place of refuge for those of us who believe. As we cling to the cross, the altar provides rescue, salvation, strength, and power.

The two poles used to carry the bronze altar were made of acacia wood. They were overlaid with bronze and the poles were inserted into the rings so they would be on two sides of the altar when it was carried. The poles were a reminder to the Israelites that they were on a journey; that this wilderness was not their home. For us, the poles represent the same thing! We are not to get too comfortable here on this earth. We, too, are on a journey, like our Israelite ancestors. They traveled in the desert for forty years~ to never settle down for any length of time. We too, should not "settle down" here. This world is not our home. Peter reminds us in I Peter 2:11 *"Dear friends, I urge you, as aliens and strangers in the world, to abstain*

from sinful desires, which war against your soul." We long
for another country~ a heavenly country; our true home.

After the completion of the Tabernacle, the Glory of the
Lord filled the Holy of Holies. *"On the day the Tabernacle,
the Tent of the Testimony, was set up, the cloud covered it.
From evening till morning the cloud above the Tabernacle
looked like fire. That is how it continued to be; the cloud
covered it, and at night it looked like fire. Whenever the
cloud lifted from above the Tent, the Israelites set out;
wherever the cloud settled, the Israelties encamped. At the
Lord's command the Israelites set out, and at his command
they encamped. As long as the cloud stayed over the
Tabernacle, they remained in camp" (Numbers 9:15-18).*
The Lord provided direction and guidance for His people.
They remained in the camp until the cloud lifted from the
Tabernacle, then they would set out. There was an order to
how they marched which is seen in Numbers 10:11—28.
The marching order was: Judah, Issachar, Zebulun,
Gershonites and Merarites, Reuben, Simeon, Gad,
Kohahites, Ephraim, Manasseh, Benjamin, Dan, Asher and
lastly Naphtali.

The materials to construct the poles point to the ministry of
Jesus. The acacia wood (representing Jesus' perfect
humanity) and the bronze overlay (the judgment laid on
Jesus because of our sin). Bronze is used in the outer court
of the Tabernacle. The outer court was a place of judgment
on sin. The bronze altar and the bronze basin (which we
will study in detail next chapter) were the two vessels in the
Tabernacle courtyard. We see that the metal used in the
outer court is bronze which symbolizes judgment.
Scripture has many references to bronze being used in
terms of judgment:

- Judges 16:21 (Samson) *"Then the Philistines seized him (Samson), gouged out his eyes and took him down to Gaza. Binding him with **bronze shackles**, they set him to grinding in the prison."*
- I Samuel 17:5-6 (Goliath of Gath) *"He (Goliath) had a **bronze helmet** on his head and wore a coat of scale armor of **bronze** weighing five thousand shekels, on his legs he wore **bronze greaves**, and a **bronze javelin** was slung on his back."*
- Psalm 107:15-16 (God's unfailing love) *"Let them give thanks to the Lord for his unfailing love and his wonderful deeds for men, for he breaks down **gates of bronze** and cuts through bars of iron."*
- Jeremiah 1:18 (God's judgment) *"Today I have made you a fortified city, an iron pillar and a **bronze wall** to stand against the whole land~ against the kings of Judah, its officials, its priests and the people of the land."*
- Isaiah 48:4 (Stubbornness of Israel) *"For I knew how stubborn you were; the sinews of your neck were iron, your forehead was **bronze.**"*
- Revelation 1:15 (Feet of Jesus to judge the earth) *"His feet were like **bronze** glowing in a furnace, and his voice was like the sound of rushing waters."*

The judgment of our sin was placed on Jesus. He bore the weight himself. God's Word tells us that death is the penalty for sin. Sin must be judged and Jesus willingly laid down his life for us. 2 Corinthians 5:21 says, *"God made him who had no sin to be ***sin** for us, so that in him we might become the righteousness of God."* *Sin = sin offering (which was one of the gifts offered on the bronze altar).

There are pans, shovels, a sprinkling bowl, meat forks, fire pans (or censors) used at the bronze altar (Exodus 27:3).

These are the five utensils; five representing the number of grace. God's grace toward us is seen in this altar and the utensils. His grace abounds unto us.

1) Pans~ were used to remove the ashes of the sacrifices from the altar. The ashes point to the finished work of Jesus on the cross (altar). John 19:30 says, *"When he had received the drink, Jesus said, 'It is finished'. With that, he bowed his head and gave up his spirit."*

2) Shovels~ were used to move the ashes to a clean place outside of camp. John 19:41 tells us of the clean place that Jesus was place into. *"At the place where Jesus was crucified, there was a garden, and in the garden a new (fresh, clean, unused) tomb, in which no one had ever been laid."*

3) Sprinkling bowl~ the blood from the sacrifice on the altar was drained into a basin and poured at the base of the altar. The sprinkling bowl represents Jesus and His blood poured out on our behalf. Hebrews 9:12-13 says, *"He did not enter by means of the blood of goats and calves; but he entered the Most Holy Place once for all by his own blood, having obtained eternal redemption. The blood of goats and bulls and the ashes of a heifer sprinkled on those who are ceremonially unclean sanctify them so they are outwardly clean."*

4) Meat forks~ were used to move the sacrifice on the altar. They represent the hands of those who nailed Jesus on the cross (altar). Luke 23:33 *"When they came to the place called the Skull, there they crucified him (Jesus), along with the criminals~ one on his right, the other on his left."*

5) Fire pans (censors)~ carried the fire from the bronze altar to the altar of incense. This represents the fragrant offering (incense) of intercession that Jesus

makes on our behalf before the Father. Hebrews 7:25 *"Therefore he is able to save completely those who come to God through him, because he always lives to intercede for them."* John also tells us in I John 2:1 *"My dear children, I write this to you so that you will not sin. But if anybody does sin, we have one who speaks to the Father in our defense~ Jesus Christ, the Righteous One."*

Every detail in perfect design, all points to the work of Jesus Christ. The bronze altar was designed and constructed according to the pattern that Moses was given on the mountain. At the dedication of the temple, we see fire fall from heaven. Leviticus 9:23-24 gives the miraculous sight. The Tabernacle has been constructed and the people along with the priests and Moses have gathered in God's presence to offer sacrifices upon the altar. *"Moses and Aaron then went into the Tent of Meeting. When they came out, they blessed the people; and the glory of the Lord appeared to all the people. Fire came out from the presence of the Lord and consumed the burnt offering and the fat portions on the altar. And when all the people saw it, they shouted for joy and fell facedown."* Imagine that sight! Our God is a consuming fire! All the Israelites are on their faces in worship to their covenant God. He has lit the fire on the altar with fire from His presence~ heavenly fire! However, the priests had a part to play; keeping the fire burning. Leviticus 6:12-13 give instructions for the priests. *"The fire on the altar must be kept burning; it must not go out. Every morning the priest is to add firewood and arrange the burnt offering on the fire and burn the fat of the fellowship offerings on it. The fire must be kept burning on the altar continuously; it must not go out."* So, we too, who belong to Him must keep the fire burning on the altar, continuously. God ignited the fire in our hearts, but we must keep the fire burning. Let that be our anthem!

The fire must be kept burning on the altar continuously, it must not go out.

We also see that each vessel was anointed at the dedication of the Tabernacle, so it would be holy to the Lord; consecrated for His service. Leviticus 8:10-11 speaks to the anointing. *"Then Moses took the anointing oil and anointed the Tabernacle and everything in it, and so consecrated them. He sprinkled some of the oil on the altar seven times, anointing the altar and all its utensils and the basin with its stand, to consecrate them."* Exodus 29:37 tells us that the anointing lasted for seven days. After that time, the *"altar will be most holy and whatever touches it will be holy."* As we present ourselves as living sacrifices, Jesus himself sanctifies us and makes us holy. He anoints us for service unto him. We are holy, because He is holy. *"Both the one who makes men holy and those who are made holy are of the same family. So Jesus is not ashamed to call them brothers,"* Hebrews 2:11.

As I close this chapter, I want to finish with a prayer of dedication that we see in 2 Chronicles 6:12-13. Solomon (David's son) has completed the Tabernacle and gathers the whole assembly of Israel. Solomon is overcome by the goodness and love of the Lord and we see Solomon climb up on the altar~ a living sacrifice and he pours his heart out to the Lord in prayer and dedication. *"Then Solomon stood before the altar of the Lord in front of the whole assembly of Israel and spread out his hands. Now he had made a bronze platform, five cubits long, five cubits wide and 3 cubits high, and had placed it in the center of the outer court. He stood on the platform and then knelt down before the whole assembly of Israel and spread out his hands toward heaven."* What humility! Solomon is overcome by the goodness and love of the Lord. He climbs up on the altar~ a living sacrifice and he pours his heart out to the Lord in prayer and dedication.

His prayer begins…"*O Lord, God of Israel, there is no God like you in heaven or on earth~ you who keep your covenant of love with your servants who continue wholeheartedly in your way…*" *(vs.14)*.

Spend some time before the Lord praising Him for who He is and what He has done to present you holy in His sight.

STUDY GUIDE
Chapter 3: The Outer Court
The bronze altar
(Exodus 27:1-7; 38:1-7; 40:6)

Scripture to memorize: Romans 12:1 *"Therefore I urge you, brothers, in view of God's mercy, to offer your bodies as living sacrifices, holy and pleasing to God—this is your spiritual act of worship." (NIV)*

Key Questions:
1) What does Romans 12:1 mean for you, after our discussion & study of the brazen altar?
2) Are you a willing sacrifice? Do you ever "crawl" off the altar?
3) How can you keep the "fire" burning in your heart? (*"The fire must be kept burning on the altar continuously; it must not go out." Leviticus 6:13)*

We are studying the tabernacle as if we are walking through it, our "journey of faith". The first thing we see when we move past the curtains at the East entrance is the brazen altar (bronze altar). This week we are going to study this altar to see the significance it has in our lives today.

DAY 1: Bezalel and Oholiab

Before we observe the details of the bronze altar, let's take a look at the skilled workers who would construct the furniture for the Tabernacle. Moses addressed the Israelites telling them, *"All who are skilled among you are to come and make everything the Lord has commanded." (Exodus 35:10).* Moses gives the specifics concerning all the materials needed.

1) Read Exodus 35:20-29. How did the community of the Israelites respond?

God has raised up two leaders for the construction of the Tabernacle. This is God's design, too—just like the pattern of the Tabernacle. No one applied for the job of "foreman". God **chose** them and He anointed them for His service.

2) Read Exodus 31:1-6. What are the names of the two men chosen?

God filled Bezalel (name means "in the shadow of God") with the Holy Spirit. This is the first time that the Holy Spirit has been poured out. God is equipping him to do the overwhelming task of designing the Tabernacle. He will need the Spirit of God's anointing to complete the Tabernacle to God's standard. Oholiab (name means "tabernacle or tent of my father") was appointed by God to help Bezalel in the designing of the Tabernacle.

3) Read Exodus 35:31 & 34. What did the filling of the Holy Spirit give them?

God chose Bezalel and Oholiab. We don't know why, but we can conclude that they were men whose hearts were willing to serve. They were available to be used by God. Bezalel and Oholiab were given a special assignment.

When God chooses us to a task or assignment, He will do the empowering. *Who He appoints, He anoints.* God's assignments are always to prove who HE IS, not who we are.

4) What has God called you to do? If you are feeling overwhelmed by the impossibility of the task, you

are in good company and that is just where God wants you to be. He will fill you & equip you to do what He has called you to do. (I Corinthians 12:7). Write out a prayer asking God to fill you up to overflowing.

DAY 2: The Curtains

The outer courtyard had no covering. It was in the open. There were curtains of finely twisted linen made for the walls. Today, you will be using your Tabernacle outline on page 3.

1) Read Exodus 27:9—11. The south & north side are to have how many posts (or pillars) each? _____ Draw the pillars on your diagram (you can make black dots or short lines to represent them). These pillars will hold the linen curtains that are to be woven.

2) How many posts (or pillars) that will hold the curtains are to be on the west end? (See Exodus 27:12) _____ Draw the pillars on your diagram.

Exodus 27:13-16 describes the entrance to the Tabernacle. All came into the courtyard through this gate. This was the only way into the Tabernacle. Read Exodus 27:13-16. The gate (entrance) to the outer court in the Tabernacle faced east.

3) Read Genesis 3:23-24. What happens at the east in this passage.

4) Read Matthew 2:2. What do you see about the east?

What does the east represent? I have a couple of thoughts. With the rising of the sun in the east, we 1) hope in a new day (Lamentations 3:22-23 says *"Because of the Lord's great love we are not consumed, for his compassions never fail. They are new every morning.")* and 2) light illuminates the tabernacle entrance~ this is a reminder daily of God's desire to dwell among His people (John 1:4 says, *"In him was life, and that life was the light of men.").*

The entrance (gate) was 30 feet long and the sides of linen curtains were 22 ½ feet on either side of the entrance—with 3 posts (pillars) to support the linen curtains on each side. Draw this on your diagram. Use black dots or short lines to represent the pillars or posts. Draw a thin white curtain over the dots. The height of the wall of curtains around the courtyard was 7 ½ feet high.

The gate was woven of beautiful blue (signifying revelation, communion, and visitation), purple (signifying royalty & authority) and scarlet (signifying bloodshed & sacrifice). Imagine the contrast between the rest of the curtains of white linen. What beauty invited them into the Tabernacle. On your diagram, draw a combination of blue/purple & scarlet in the gate to represent the beautiful entrance to the Tabernacle.

   5) Read John 10:9. What does Jesus say He is?

This gate (entrance) on the outer court is a representation of Jesus who was revelation, communion, visitation, royalty, authority, & the ultimate bloodshed sacrifice. Before we even enter the Tabernacle we see a foreshadowing of Jesus.

DAY 3: The Bronze Altar (brazen altar)

The bronze altar is the first piece of furniture that you see when you enter the Tabernacle. It was the largest piece of furniture and it was set up to face the Holy Place (inner court)—Exodus 40:6. No one could go any further into the outer court without making atonement for one's sins. The sacrificial animals were offered on this altar and their blood was shed for the sins of the people. This symbolizes Christ's work on the cross on our behalf; so that all who put their faith in HIS blood will have their sins atoned for, once and for all.

1) Read Exodus 27:1-8. The altar was made out of what kind of wood?
What type of metal was used?

Acacia wood was found in the Sinai Desert. It was a hard, indestructible, incorruptible wood. It could survive the harsh environment because its roots grew very deep. The tree itself never grew tall. In fact, most acacia trees only grow to a height of 15-30 feet. This tree was not affected by disease nor animal infestations because of the strong odor in the fiber of its wood. Insects would not borough into it. The wood was a product of the "earth" which speaks to Jesus' humanity. The acacia wood signifies the perfect humanity displayed by Jesus Christ. He was without sin, without blemish, without "spot," without "wrinkle," and without any negative thing. His human living withstood all the evil, negative environments around Him and nothing could successfully attack Him.

The altar was about 4 ½ feet high and 7 ½ feet square. There were horns at all 4 corners pointing outward at each corner, with a bronze network and a bronze ring at each of the 4 corners of the network (4 corners represented going into all the world—East, West, North & South to bring the good news to all creation (see Matthew 28:18-20). The horns speak of salvation, strength & power (Luke 1:68-69). Poles of acacia wood were overlaid with bronze and the poles were inserted into the rings so they will be on 2 sides of the altar when it is carried.

2) Read the following scriptures and note the significance of the horn:
   • Genesis 22:13 ~
   • Joshua 6:1-5 ~
   • I Samuel 16:13 ~
   • Revelation 5:6 ~

The horns were used (at this altar) to tie down the sacrifice. The animal would be an unwilling offering. Jesus laid down His life; He offered it as a ransom for all who would come. He was a willing sacrifice. In our scripture memory verse this week (Romans 12:1), Paul calls us to offer our lives as a willing sacrifice. As a living sacrifice, we can "crawl off the altar"! Paul is encouraging us to stay on the altar & willingly give our lives to the Lord as a spiritual act of worship.

3) Are you a willing sacrifice? Why/why not?

4) What are the utensils or tools used at the altar? (See Exodus 27:3)

Each of these utensils points to Jesus as well. The **pans** were used to remove the ashes of the sacrifices. The ashes point to the finished work of Jesus on the cross (see John 19:30). The **shovels** were used to move the ashes to a clean place outside of camp.

5) Read John 19:41. What clean place was Jesus' body put into?

The blood from the sacrifices on the altar were drained into a basin & poured out at the base of the altar. This **sprinkling bowl** represents Jesus and His blood poured out on our behalf (see Hebrews 9:12-13). The **meat forks** represented the hands of those who nailed Jesus to the cross (Luke 23:33). The **fire pans** (censors) carried the fire from the bronze altar to the altar of incense. This represents the fragrant incense that the intercession that Jesus makes on our behalf before the Father. (I John 2:1 & Hebrews 7:25).

The brazen altar was overlaid with bronze (brass). Bronze (brass) symbolizes judgment of sin. The items in the outer court are overlaid with bronze (brass). Bronze (brass) is the symbol for strength & judgment against sin. In Deut. 28:15-23 we see some of the curses that will come upon the Israelite community for disobedience. One of those curses (in vs. 23) says, *"the sky over your head will be bronze, the ground beneath you iron"*. Obedience brings God's mercy, but disobedience brings God's judgment (see Leviticus 26:19). We also see the judgment on Israel's sin when they were grumbling and complaining to the Lord about the food they were given to eat. God sent venomous snakes to bite them & destroy them (see Numbers 21:4-9). Moses prayed for the people & God told Moses to raise up a bronze serpent upon a pole. When the people looked upon the serpent they would be healed from the judgment of sin.

Jesus became sin for us (2 Corinthians 5:21). The judgment of sin was laid upon Him (Galatians 3:13). When we look upon the cross, we are set free from the curse of death. Jesus paid the price. He was the willing sacrifice, once and for all.

Draw the bronze altar on the diagram.

DAY 4: Sacrifices on the Altar

The Hebrew word for altar is "mizbech" which means "the slaughter place". The brazen altar was the means by which animals were offered as a sacrifice. Their blood was shed for the sins of the people. Sacrifices were made from sunrise to sunset everyday. Thousands of animals were sacrificed and their blood sprinkled on the altar ~ not a pretty sight!   There are 5 different types of offerings that are described in Leviticus 1-7.

- ***The Burnt Offering*** (Lev. 1:1-17 and Lev.6;8-13) comes from the Hebrew word "Olah" which means to "ascend upwards". It refers to the entire offering being consumed by fire and the aroma ascending, which is pleasing to the Lord (Lev. 1:9). The burnt offering was total consumption of the animals. God made provision for all people, in regard to what they could afford to offer. The male of the species was chosen (bull, goat, sheep) because its strength & horns were a symbol of power. The male had to be without any blemish or defect. The brazen altar would have been blood-stained after all the sacrifices presented on it. The word "offering" in Hebrew, "qorban" means "something that is brought to the altar, a voluntary offering.
  1) Read Lev. 1:3-5.   What male animal did the wealthy bring to sacrifice?
  2) Read Lev.1:10.   What male animal did the "middle class" bring to offer?
  3) Read Lev.1:14. What did the poor bring as an offering?

The procedure to follow for the person
offering the sacrifice:

1) Choose a male animal without defect (Lev. 1:3)
2) Present the animal at the gate of the Tabernacle (Lev. 1:3)
3) Lay his hands on the head of the animal (Lev.1:4)
4) Slaughter the animal (Lev. 1:5)
5) Skin the animal (Lev. 1:6)
6) Cut the animal into pieces (Lev.1:6)

The procedure for the priests to follow:
1) Sprinkle the blood of the sacrifice against the altar and all sides (Lev. 1:5)
2) Arrange the wood on the fire (Lev.1:7)
3) Arrange the pieces of the animal on the fire (Lev. 1:8)
4) Burn the entire offering (Lev. 1:8-9)

- **The Grain Offering** (Lev. 2:1-16 and Lev. 6:14-23) ~ This was the only offering that did not involve bloodshed. This was a voluntary offering to the Lord. It was offered from the harvest of the land and was composed of fine flour combined with oil, frankincense & salt. Leaven could not be used. It could be baked into cakes. They were an offering to the Lord of the first fruits. Part of this offering was burned on the altar & part was given to the priests.

The Fellowship Offering (Lev. 3:1-17 and Lev. 7:11-38) ~ These instructions for the fellowship (peace) offering were similar to the burnt offerings. However, the Israelites could choose the type of animal they would bring (bull, cow, lamb, or goat). There was no sex distinction in this offering. In this offering, only portions of the sacrifice were burned (internal organs & fat) and the priests were given the breast & right thigh.

- ***The Sin Offering*** (Lev. 4:1-35 and 6:24-30) ~ This offering was designed for atonement for sin that was unintentional; many of the same instructions for the other animal sacrifices apply here as well. There is a major difference in the sacrifice offered depending on who the offender was: a priest, an elder, a leader, or a member of the community.

- ***The Guilt Offering*** (Lev. 5, Lev. 6:1-7, Lev.7:1-7) ~ This offering was similar to the sin offering. The Israelites were to present their offerings for sins committed in 3 areas.
  1) Sins committed against self (Lev.5:1-13) such as contamination by touching (Lev.5:2-3) –by touching dead people, dead animals, unclean lepers, or people with a discharge from their bodies. Or a sin was committed by thoughtless talk (Lev. 5:4)
  2) Sins committed against God (Lev. 5:14-19) such as personally using things dedicated to God, such as tithes, first fruits or the firstborn of cattle or sheep. Also, they could be unaware of breaking a commandment
  3) Sins against mankind (Lev.6:1-7) such as deceiving his neighbor (Lev. 6:2), dishonesty in social or business dealings (Lev.6:2), acquiring by stealing (Lev. 6:2), or being distrustful (Lev. 6:2), lastly by finding lost property & saying it is his (Lev. 6:3).

Restitution needed to be made before forgiveness happened. He had to confess before a priest in what way he had sinned and then bring a sacrifice of a female lamb or goat from the flock as a sin offering.

Assignment for Day 4: Draw a picture of the brazen altar

Day 5: Fire & Anointing

In the dedication of all the furniture in the Tabernacle, each piece needed to be anointed; consecrated so it will be holy.

1) Read Exodus 40:9-10. What was anointed with regards to the bronze altar?

2) Read Leviticus 8:10-11. How many times was the altar & utensils sprinkled with oil?

Seven is the number of completeness, fullness, perfection. The altar was to be anointed because it was to be holy and sanctified. After this anointing took place, whatever touched the altar after that became holy unto the Lord.

3) Read Exodus 29:37. For how many days did the anointing take place?

4) Read Hebrews 2:11. Who has made you holy?

Let's take a look at our memory verse for this week.
Romans 12:1. *"Therefore, I urge you brothers, in view of God's mercy, to offer your bodies as living sacrifices, holy and pleasing, to God—this is your spiritual act of worship."*
- Urge ~ Greek word "paraklaleo" (verb) meaning to ask, beg, plead, encourage, exhort, call, invite

- Mercy ~ Greek word "oiktirmos" (noun) meaning compassion or mercy
- Offer ~ Greek word "paristemi" (verb) meaning to put at your disposal, to present
- Bodies ~ Greek word "soma" (noun) meaning your body, your mass, human, person
- Sacrifice ~ Greek word "thyisa" (noun) meaning an offering
- Holy ~ Greek word "hagios" (adj) meaning consecrated, acceptable to God, devoted
- Pleasing ~ Greek word "euarestos" (adj.) meaning acceptable
- Worship ~ Greed word "latreia" (noun) meaning in service to God; ministry

  5) Write out this verse with the additional information provided by the Greek definitions. What does this verse mean for you? Make it personal.

In the dedication of the brazen altar (and the whole Tabernacle), the Glory of God came. God Himself lit the fire from His own holiness. The fire consumed the offering from the people. All the people saw the Glory of the Lord (see Leviticus 9:23-24). God initiated the fire, but human hands must continue to keep the fire burning (see Leviticus 6:12-13). The fire was to burn continually! The fire was to NEVER GO OUT!

  6) What can you do to keep the fire burning continually in your life?

Read Lev. 9:23-24. What words come to mind to describe our Great & Glorious God?
What a week! What is the most amazing thing you have learned this week?

What does the bronze altar mean for you?

I stand amazed at all the details our Great God put together. And we are just in the beginning of our walk through the Tabernacle. Tell someone this week about the God whom you serve.

CHAPTER 4:
The Outer Court: The Bronze Basin

Standing between the bronze altar and the Holy Place (the inner court structure) was the only other piece of furniture in the outer court, the bronze basin. All other vessels in the tabernacle were used in reference to God, but the bronze basin was used specifically for the consecration and purification of the priests. It was here that the priests washed their hands and feet in preparation for service before the Lord. No ministry happened until the priest had washed himself in the basin. This was a daily practice.

A priest would enter the outer court through the East gate entrance, sacrifice a burnt offering unto the Lord at the Bronze Altar to atone for his sins, then make his way to the Bronze Basin, where he would wash his right hand, then his right foot, then his left hand and left foot.   The hands speak to the service of the priest and the feet speak to the walk of the priest. The priests lived a life dedicated to the service of God. All defilement had to be washed from his body~ the dust from the courtyard and the blood from the sacrifice. He had to be holy before he could move into his position of service before the Lord on behalf of the community.

Exodus 30:17-21 is the reference for the Bronze Basin. The priests were commanded to wash their hands and feet whenever they presented a sacrifice on behalf of an individual or the community at the bronze altar or whenever they entered the inner court structure (the Holy Place). They also washed after the sacrifice or after coming out of the Holy Place. Moses gave a serious warning to the priests in this passage that if the washing was not done before ministering before the Lord, the priest would die. God's holiness requires holy servants. The priests needed to be clean before God and before man.

Bronze. The metal that is symbolic for judgment. Both vessels in the outer court were constructed of bronze. Judgment of sin is seen in the outer court. The bronze altar was the judgment for sin (our sin nature). The sin nature or the flesh is what we are born into. We are controlled by the sin nature until we are born again, of the Spirit. Galatians 6: 17 says this, *"For the sinful nature desires what is contrary to the Spirit..."* and Romans 8:8 *"Those controlled by the sinful nature cannot please God."* When we are born again, we have been set free from the power of the sinful nature to control our lives. Romans 8:9 is such great assurance, *"You, however, are controlled not by the sinful nature but by the Spirit, if the Spirit of God lives in you."* The bronze basin is a judgment of our sins. The sins that are cleansed at the basin are the thoughts, attitudes, motives and behaviors that need to be put off. This is what is in the mind or heart that needs to be transformed. When a person meets Jesus at the cross, he is given a new nature, *"Therefore if anyone is in Christ, he is a new creation; the old has gone, the new has come!"* (2 Corinthians 5:17). After that time, the transformation comes! There are new habits, new attitudes, new behaviors, and new motives of the heart that will come. The "old" needs to be washed away, so the "new" can be formed in us.

Cleansing, refreshment, purification~ these are all words that have to do with the water of the basin. I am a runner and I especially love running outside in the hot sun, on a summer day. After finishing a long run, with the hot sun beating down on me, I have two thoughts on my mind: 1) a shower~ to cleanse the dirt & sweat off my body and 2) a large glass of water. Water. Cool water. Take a minute to think about water.

What are the thoughts that immediately come to your mind?

- Rushing water
- power of water
- water baptism
- water is the life sustainer
- Jesus is the living water
- the ocean
- the refreshing taste of water on a hot summer day
- the joy of cleansing after working out or being in the garden for an afternoon
- the beauty of a pool that seems to beckon one from the chores of the day
- the sound of waves upon a beach

Oh, the many images and memories that water brings to the mind. Water = Life. Without water, life cannot survive. In Exodus 7 the first plague sent upon the land of the Egyptians was the plague of blood, where the water from the Nile and all water everywhere in Egypt turned to blood. God went right to the source of life~ water. And we see the first miracle that Jesus performs has to do with water. While at a wedding, Jesus has the servants take jars (that were used for ceremonial washing) and fill them with water and when the father of the bride went to taste it, the water had turned to wine (see John 2). In John 4, Jesus has a conversation with the woman at the well. The well was a popular place for women to gather (it was like their "Starbucks"). Jesus speaks to her of living water that he has to offer. Jesus offers living water to all who come thirsty~ to drink deep of the water that refreshes and purifies. *"The water I give him will become in him a spring of water welling up to eternal life."* Water, pure and fresh is a desperate source for life. Recently, my daughter was in Malawi, picking her up from the airport, our first question was: "What did you miss the most?" My husband and I were thinking the answers would have to do with friends, her cell phone☺, movies, her soft bed, or any luxury that brings us comfort in the United States. But, her response was "Water." She missed water. She missed the ability to grab a drink at any time. It was not accessible at all times and she craved it! The availability of a shower after a long day in the dust of the environment was missed. Water, the sustainer of life.

As we dive deep into this bronze basin we will see these two aspects of water:
1) cleansing that the water provides, and
2) refreshment and sustenance that it provides.

The priests of the Old Covenant took the time of cleansing in the Bronze Basin seriously. Let us, the priests of the New Covenant, take the cleansing in the basin seriously.

We are the priests of the Living God, all who have committed our lives to Jesus. We see, in the outer court, the gate that we have entered through, which is Jesus himself. And at the altar came our justification, for His sacrifice atoned for our sin. Jesus became the sin offering on our behalf. The altar (the place of sacrifice) comes before cleansing (the place of purification). There can be no consecration (set apart-ness) without the atonement for sin. Salvation, then consecration. The blood at the bronze altar and the water at the bronze basin come together in the outer court and again at the cross of Christ. John 19:34 tells us, *"one of the soldiers pierced Jesus' side with a spear, bringing a sudden flow of blood and water."* Cleansing for us came in His blood, because we have been washed in His blood, once and for all sins I have ever committed, am committing now or ever will commit. And the daily cleansing comes from the water of His Word.

106

God's Word is our basin; the reflective cleansing. As we spend time in His Word; studying, meditating, memorizing scripture, we are washed in the water of the Word and as we are cleansed, our thoughts, attitudes, motives and behaviors are transformed. Ephesians 5:26-27 speaks of the washing that the Word of God brings, *"...to make her holy, cleansing her by the washing with water through the Word, and to present her to himself (Jesus) as a radiant church without stain, or wrinkle or any other blemish, but holy and blameless."* It is an inside-out transformation.

The cleansing of the Word comes from:

1) **Studying God's Word**~ digging for the treasures that are in the Word of God. God's Word is Truth from cover to cover. In Isaiah 55:11 God states that His Word will accomplish all that He desires it to accomplish. *"so is my word that goes out from my mouth; it will not return to me empty, but will accomplish what I desire and achieve the purpose for which I sent it."* There are many different ways to study God's Word. This is very close to my heart, for I love the Word of God and I am a student of the Word. Deuteronomy 32:47 says, *"They are not just idle words for you~ they are your life."* I am going to give several different ways that I study:

   - **character study:** I find a person in the Bible who I want to know more about: David, Peter, Paul, Mary, Gideon, Elijah, Elizabeth, Hannah, Samuel, John, etc. I use a concordance to find all the Biblical references to that person and begin searching. I take a notebook and draw columns to study their 1) physical characteristics~ what does this person look like, where did he/she live, what time did he/she live in, what country, 2) personality, 3) career, 4) strengths, 5) weaknesses, 6) how they respond to God and does that change over time?, 7) any other outstanding fact. Then after examining the person, I ask some questions: 1) How am I like this person? 2) How am I different? 3) Anything I could learn from them? 4) Anything else?

- **Book study:** Want to study a whole book of the Bible? If this is your first time, I would suggest taking the smaller books in the New Testament. I use an outline form for this study. In my journal I begin reading chapter by chapter, studying one chapter at a time. What is the chapter title? What is the chapter summary? How does it divide? Can I summarize the chapter in one sentence? What application can I take away from this chapter?

- **Word study**: Any words that you want to study? Love, covenant, blood, sacrifice, tabernacle, etc. In this type of study, you will need to use a concordance to see all the times the word is used in the Bible. Do you want to study just the use in Old Testament or just the New Testament? Take each reference; write it in your notebook with the meaning or significance. Keep doing this to see the connection; the many different meanings of the same word; the consistency between Old and New Testaments.

2) **Meditating on God's Word~** Meditating on the Word is different than studying. Meditating is a discipline of going over & over & over the same passage. It might be 1 or 2 verses that God has placed on your heart. When I read the Word daily, there are times that the Holy Spirit will "highlight" something in my heart; it is as if the words/verses jump off the page. So, I will

write it out or just place a book mark in my Bible to go back to it. Then I ask the Holy Spirit to show me what He wants me to understand about that passage. For example, this scripture above, is one that I have meditated on, "They are not just idle words for you, they are your life," Deuteronomy 32:47. This scripture has come to life, because I have meditated on it for so long. It has become part of me! It nourishes my heart & mind.

This is not to be confused with a mantra, which is a part of the meditation of false religions. In that, your mind is to go blank. We want to focus on Jesus. We engage our mind with God's Word, asking the Holy Spirit to give insight to what is read. This is a great discipline. The goal is to "chew on" God's Word. Ezekiel 3:3 puts it this way: Eat the Scroll!

3) **Memorizing Scripture~** Memorizing scripture is taking a verse or a chunk of scripture and locking it in your heart! The goal is to get the Word in your heart, so in those times when a Bible is not available, scripture is in your mind. Psalm 119:11 says, "*I have hidden your word in my heart that I might not sin against you.*" I keep notecards available, so if there is a verse that I need to memorize, I write it down and put it in my car, or on my mirror, or above the sink in the kitchen or laundry room. The goal is to have it in a place that is a common place, so I can meditate on it, to get it deep in my heart. For out of the heart, the mouth speaks.

God's Word is our cleansing basin. The washing of the Word shows us what to put off and what to put on. It transforms us. God's Word is also The Living Water that satisfies. For Jesus is alive in the Word. John 1:14 tells us that *"The Word became flesh and made his dwelling among us. We have seen his glory, the glory of the One and Only, who came from the Father, full of grace of truth."* He is the Water that sustains. He is the drink that satisfies our thirst. As Jesus was talking with the woman at the well, He says to her, *"whoever drinks the water I give him will never thirst. Indeed, the water I give him will become in him a spring of water welling up to eternal life."*

There is some interesting, additional information given about the bronze basin in Exodus 38:8. *"They made a bronze basin and its bronze stand from the mirrors of the women who served at the entrance to the Tent of Meeting."* Mirrors that were used in the construction of the bronze basin were made from polished bronze (or brass). Where did the Israelites get the mirrors? From the Egyptians~ remember when they left Egypt, the Egyptians willingly gave them gold, silver, bronze, jewelry, linens, yarn, and all the other materials that would be used in the construction of the Tabernacle.

* A little background: The Egyptian women always carried a mirror in one hand when they went to the pagan temples to worship. The Israelites were surrounded by the Egyptian culture and customs while living in Egypt, that the Israelite women probably adopted this custom. God was asking the women to give up their old customs and behaviors of worship and surrender all to Yahweh.

What customs or behaviors of worship are you still holding onto?

Mirrors are a source of vanity and pride. Who can walk past a mirror without checking to make sure that make-up is still on and hair is in place? A mirror helps us to know physically if we are put together! The basin was constructed with the mirrors of polished bronze. For the priests, they would have used this reflective bronze to make sure that all dust and blood was removed from hands and feet. The mirror reflected back the cleansed image of the priest. The priest spent time at the basin washing until the reflection showed him that he was clean and ready to minister before the Lord. This was not to be a burden for the priests, but a time of reflection (physically and spiritually) to get ready for service. This cleansing was a time to be consecrated unto the Lord, not to be rushed, but to be savored.

The mirror of God's Word helps us to know if we are put together spiritually! We should savor this cleansing time. James 1:22-25 says, *"Do not merely listen to the Word, and so deceive yourselves. Do what it says. Anyone who listens to the Word but does not do what it says is like a man who looks at his face in a mirror and, after looking at himself, goes away and immediately forgets what he looks like. But the man who looks intently into the perfect law that gives freedom, and continues to do this, not forgetting what he has heard, but doing it~ he will be blessed in what he does."* The Greek word for "looks" in this passage means "to peer within; stay near". So, what does that look like? We need to stay near the Word and do what it says. That is how we are changed and cleansed and transformed. As we behold God's glory by spending time in His Word, we will be transformed more and more into His likeness. 2 Corinthians 3:18 says, *"And we, who with unveiled faces all reflect the Lord's glory, are being transformed into his likeness with ever-increasing glory, which comes from the Lord who is the Spirit."*

Another principle to remember: **We become what we behold.** Proverbs 27:19 tells us, *"As water reflects a face, so a man's heart reflects the man."* What does your heart say of you? What are you beholding? I am not the same person I was 10 years ago. I am not the same person I was 5 years ago. I am not the same person I was 1 year ago, or 6 months ago, or 4 weeks ago. God's Word cleanses me and changes me. What about you? The Old Covenant priests needed to be cleansed from the defilement of the world, in a physical sense, we who are the New Covenant priests need to be cleansed from the defilement of the world, in a spiritual sense.

God is seeking counter-cultural people, who will be consecrated to Him, to be holy as He is holy. I Peter 3:3-4 illustrates for us a picture of living opposite from the world. Peter is speaking to the women in his day, who were surrounded by a pagan culture, not unlike the culture we are submersed into. Let's examine his challenge to the women and see how it relates to us today. I will pull out the sections of this verse and give some clarification as to the meaning. Where do you see yourself in this passage? Are you caught up in the culture we live in; concerned more about the physical than the spiritual?

I Peter 3:3-4, *"Your beauty should not come from outward adornment, such as braided hair and the wearing of gold jewelry, and fine clothes. Instead, it should be that of your inner self, the unfading beauty of a gentle and quiet spirit, which is of great worth in God's sight."*

We will begin with a physical mirror (reflecting what is on the outside):
"Your beauty should not come from outward adornment..."
Adornment has the connotation of something ordered; something set in a certain arrangement (cosmetics comes from this Greek word~ "kosmos"). How much time and money do you spend on outward adornment?

- *"such as braided hair…"* This braiding was an intricate, complex system of braiding that would take much time and money. Many times gold threads would be woven into the braids, so that the hair shimmered. It was a common practice of the Roman women, to be sexually attractive, in connection with the goddess Artemis. Are there certain items of clothing you wear or ways of dressing that could be considered "sexy"?

- *"and the wearing of gold jewelry…"* Jewelry was layered and was worn to impress people; to show off one's wealth. Do you try to impress people with jewelry?

- *"and fine clothes…"* Women would change clothes several times a day depending on the events of the day. Much time, energy and money was devoted to clothes. Are you concerned with brand names of clothing? Will you only shop in certain stores?

Using a spiritual mirror (reflecting what is on the inside):
- *"Instead, it should be that of your inner self…"* The beauty we are to spend time on is happening on the inside; that which is hidden from the physical eyes, which is central to life even though you don't see it. Key principle to remember: **Whatever is on the inside will be produced outside.** What are you producing on the inside? Are you spending time developing that which is hidden from the physical eyes?

- *"the unfading…"* Unfading is something that will not decay; it will not show the effects of age; in fact, the unfading grows more beautiful when one is spending time in the right mirror. 2 Corinthians

4:16 tells us *"Therefore we do not lose heart. Though outwardly we are wasting away, yet inwardly we are being renewed day by day."* Can you see this scripture being manifest in your life? Is your inner life being renewed day by day?

- *"beauty of a gentle and quiet spirit..."* A gentle spirit is meek, friendly, warm, kind, strength under control and a quiet spirit is one who knows how to calm herself; maintaining a state of peace no matter what is going on around her. Does this describe you? Is this your aim?

- *"which is of great worth is God's sight."* One who is working on the inner self is of great worth in God's sight. What a reward! To be of great worth in God's sight!

What do you spend more time and money investing in; the physical appearance or the spiritual heart? Those who are cleansing in the basin, being washed by His Word, having the Word reflect back Christ's image, pursuing Him~ that is of great worth in God's sight. Don't spend your time, energy and money pursuing those things which don't last!

The Bible does not give any dimensions for the Bronze Basin. We don't know what size Moses made the basin. There are several ideas that scholars have concluded, based on the information gathered in the text. I think it is very interesting that dimensions weren't recorded, because for us, the New Covenant priests the basin is God's Word. And His Word is dimensionless! There are no parameters that you can put around the Word of God. He is limitless and His power to change our lives is limitless! God thought of every detail in the construction of the Bronze Basin~ for the Israelites and for us today!

114

Fruit is seen when one spends time at the bronze basin of God's Word.

1. There is a hunger and a thirst for righteousness and the things of God; a desire to please God.
2. There is a hunger for God's Word; a desire to get into His Word; to "eat the scroll".
3. There is a sensitivity towards sin; a desire to live obediently to what God asks.
4. There is a desire to share your faith with others.

Exodus 40:11 tells us of the consecration of the Bronze Basin. *"Anoint the basin and its stand and consecrate them."* The Bronze Basin was sprinkled with **blood**, anointed with **oil**, and it contained **water** for washing. The water of the Word (for cleansing) comes to us through the blood of Jesus and by the Holy Spirit (represented in the oil). As priests of the New Covenant we need to experience all three of these in order to be complete and fulfill the tasks of the Priesthood. I Peter 2:5 tells us that we are called to be a Priesthood, *"you also, like living stones, are being built into a spiritual house to be a holy priesthood, offering spiritual sacrifices acceptable to God through Jesus Christ."* We need to be sprinkled with the blood. We need to have the continual washing of the Word and we need the anointing of the Holy Spirit to be poured over us, so we are consecrated, empowered and complete in Him to do the work of the priest.

STUDY GUIDE
Chapter 4: The Outer Court
The Bronze Basin
(Exodus 30:17-21 & 38:8)

Scripture to memorize: Titus 3:5 *"He saved us, not because of righteous things that we have done, but because of His mercy. He saved us through the washing of rebirth and renewal by the Holy Spirit."*

Key Questions:
1) The message of the outer court: **Salvation before consecration.** What does this statement mean for you & your walk with the Lord?
2) Read 2 Timothy 3:16-17. How have you seen the Word used as a tool for correction in your life?
3) Draw what the Bronze Basin looks like in your life today. Use your imagination. Will you share that with us in our discussion time?

As we move through the outer court of the Tabernacle, the next piece of furniture we see is the bronze (or brass) laver. It was here that the priests washed their hands & feet in preparation for service before the Lord. This laver was only for the priests. Ask the Lord to prepare your heart as you begin this week's study, that you may have understanding and insight, as we step beside the bronze laver.

DAY 1: Materials Used

Read Exodus 30:17—21.

1) What is the basin to be made from?

2) Where is it to be placed?

3) Are there dimensions for the size & shape?

4) Who is commanded to use this basin? When?

5) What would happen to the priest if he didn't wash first?

The Basin was to be placed between the Bronze Altar & the Holy Place (inner court). It came after the altar (as the priest entered the outer court, he made a sacrifice for himself). Once beyond the Altar, he was ready to be in service as a Priest, so he would wash at the Laver to be consecrated for service unto the Living God. The other articles of furniture were used in reference to God, but the Basin was used especially for the Priests. What a privilege for the Priests. No one else would ever wash in the Basin.

For the Basin, there are no measurements given as to its size & shape. We are told that it has a stand (Exodus 31:9). However we have no measurement for that either. The Basin was made of solid bronze and mirrors. Bronze speaks to the judgment of God toward sin. For additional study, here are some references that show the correlation between God's judgment & bronze:
- Judges 16:21
- I Samuel 17:5-6
- Psalm 107:15-16

117

- Jeremiah 1:18
- Numbers 21:5-9
- Isaiah 48:4
- Rev.1:15

Water was put into the Bronze Basin. The word "laver" means a bath or wash basin containing water for the purpose of washing. The Priests were commanded to wash their hands and feet 1) whenever they enter the Tent of Meeting (Holy Place) and 2) before they offer a sacrifice on behalf of an individual or the community at the Bronze Altar. The purpose of the Basin was for the washing & cleansing of the priest from all defilement.

The message of the outer court: **Salvation before consecration.** The altar always comes first, before cleansing: Salvation, then consecration, which prepares you for service. Inside the Holy Place were vessels (furniture) that represented God Himself. No priest dared to enter with any defilement. Before any service could be done for the Lord, there had to be cleansing.

DAY 2: Washing

At the bronze basin, the priests washed their hands and their feet (Exodus 30:19, 21).
- **Hands** speak of what they did; their service, work, what they put their hands to was important so they needed to be cleansed.
- **Feet** speaks to where they went; their lives and ways; their walk had to be a holy walk, so their feet were washed everyday.

Before the Priest could begin his service, he had to have his whole body washed. In Exodus 29:4 & Exodus 40:12 God has told Moses, *"Bring Aaron and his sons to the entrance to the Tent of Meeting and wash them with water."* This "washing" means to wash all over; Moses did the washing and it was done once where the bodies & clothing were washed. This initial cleansing was done once; the daily cleansing was done continuously.

First comes the blood (Bronze Altar), then comes the water (Bronze Basin). At the Bronze Altar we receive justification from our sins, and at the Bronze Basin we are sanctified from flesh. The Bronze Basin represents the ministry of sanctification.

How was blood seen in relation to cleansing in the following passages?
1) Exodus 12?
2) Leviticus 16?
3) The 5 offerings made at the Bronze Altar (Leviticus 1-7)?
4) Luke 22:20?
5) Ephesians 1:7?
6) Hebrews 9:7?

How was water seen in connection with cleansing in the following?
1) Numbers 19?
2) Leviticus 8:6?
3) Leviticus 14:1-8?
4) Zechariah 13:1?
5) Matthew 3:11?
6) Acts 22:16?
7) Hebrews 9:10?
8) Ephesians 5:26-27?

The blood & water (Bronze Altar & Basin) meet at the cross of Jesus. On the cross when Jesus died, the soldiers pierced His side & blood and water came forth (John 19:34). In Christ's once-and-for–all, perfect sacrifice He abolished the Old (Mosaic) Covenant. It is the blood that cleanses us from sin. We are washed in the blood of the Lamb and our garments are made white as snow (Psalm 51:7 & Revelation 7:9—14) and He purifies us from all sin (I John 1:7). The water cleanses us from the flesh. *"He saved us through the washing of rebirth and renewal of the Holy Spirit." Titus 3:5.* Washing, in this verse, means "basin" or "laver". We are to be continually cleansed by the water of the Word (Eph. 5:26)... *"To make her holy, cleansing her by the washing with water through the Word..."* The water is to cleanse, remove defilement, and sanctify us to be presented to Jesus as a radiant church, without stain or blemish, but holy and blameless.

DAY 3: Mirrors

Today we are going to take a look at the mirrors that were used in the construction of the Bronze Laver (Basin).

Exodus 38:8 says, *"They made the Bronze Basin and its bronze stand from the mirrors of the women who served at the entrance to the Tent of Meeting."* An interesting piece of information is given to us here in this chapter. We know that the materials used for the Tabernacle vessels were given by the Egyptians (see Exodus 35). They willingly brought gold, silver, bronze, jewelry, linens, colored yarn, etc. Here we see that the women presented their mirrors to Moses for the task of completing the Tabernacle furniture. Mirrors were always made of burnished metal in early days. The verb "served" or "ministered" is rare & interesting as well. It is used only one other place in regard to women in the service of the Tabernacle (I Samuel 2:22). It is the Hebrew word which means "to fight" or "to do battle", but it is also used of the Levitical service in the

Tabernacle. So, what did these women do? Possibly cleaning or sweeping? Or singing & dancing at festivals (like Miriam in Exodus 15)? Or they could have been the doorkeepers on the Tabernacle, which was a very lowly task (see Psalm 84:10).

These women gave of their mirrors (which is a symbol of vanity & pride). Who can pass by a mirror without checking to make sure make-up is still looking OK, lipstick is on, hair is in place, etc., etc. God took this instrument of vanity and transformed it into an instrument of cleansing. The whole design of a mirror is to reflect back an image—what is in the mirror. We use a mirror to take a physical inventory of what we look like. God took this reflective tool and had the Bronze Basin constructed with it. The Priest looked into the water to cleanse his hands and his feet, and his image was reflected back to him through the mirrors & the water.

1) Read James 1:22-25. What does the Word act as?

God's Word is not a tool of condemnation. There is not condemnation for those who are in Christ Jesus (Romans 8:1). But it is a corrective tool. God's Word reveals who we really are—the inside image, not the outer image.

2) Read 2 Timothy 3:16-17. List all the uses for the Word of God.

3) Read Proverbs 27:19. What is this verse saying?

God uses His Word to transform us. He wants us to reflect the Lord's glory as we are being transformed. *"And we, who with unveiled faces all reflect the Lord's glory, are being transformed into His likeness with ever-increasing glory, which comes from the Lord, who is the Spirit." (2*

Corinthians 3:18) As we behold God's glory by spending time in His Word (our mirror), we will be transformed more and more into His likeness.

Thank you, Lord for the mirrors in the Bronze Basin.

DAY 4: Priests

As Aaron & his sons were born into the priesthood (Exodus 28:1), so each of us are born into the priesthood by means of a new birth (Titus 3:5)—*"he saved us, not because of righteous things we had done, but because of his mercy. He saved us through the washing of rebirth and renewal by the Holy Spirit."*

God has called us, the New Covenant believers *"a chosen people, a royal priesthood, a holy nation, a people belonging to God..." (I Peter 2:9).* We are Priests and called to be Holy, just as God is Holy (I Peter 1:15). God has cleansed us by the blood of Jesus (only He could do that washing). Moses washed the Priests whole bodies before they could minister before the Lord. They had to be cleansed. Jesus washed us (our whole bodies) with His blood sacrifice. We needed to be cleansed. Just as the responsibility was given to the Priests to wash at the Bronze Basin to rid themselves daily of the defilement of the world, the responsibility has been given to us (the priests of the New Covenant) to be washed and sanctified, so there is not defilement from the world on us.

As His Priests, we need to embrace the "Bronze Laver" (the washing basin). We need to be willing to cleanse our hands (**Hands** speak of what we do; our service, work, what we put our hands to) and our feet

(**Feet** speaks to where they went; our lives and ways; our walk has to be a holy walk, so our feet need to be washed everyday).

1) Read 2 Corinthians 7:1. How do you cleanse your body & soul out of reverence for God?

Jesus washed the disciples feet (John 13:5—10). As Jesus grabbed a towel & wash basin (Greek describes a basin for washing—which is the way the Hebrew describes the Bronze Basin), and began to wash the disciples' feet, Peter did not want him to wash his feet. Jesus answered him by saying, "*Unless I wash you, you have no part with me.*" Jesus goes on to tell them that "*a person who has had a bath needs only to wash his feet; his whole body is clean.*" *(*John 13:8, 10). Jesus was the WORD MADE FLESH (John 1:14). The Blood of the Lamb & His sacrifice has cleansed us on our behalf. Now, we need to continually be cleansed (symbolized by hands & feet) to remove the defilement from the world.

2) Read 1 Peter 2:2-5. What are we to do? Who are we?

3) Read Malachi 2:7. What is the Priests responsibility?

The true washing basin is the Word of God. The power of the WORD OF GOD is beyond human comprehension. There were no dimensions given in the Old Testament Bronze Basin that was in the Tabernacle. That is relevant because as we see that Basin as a foreshadowing of the Word & its power to wash us & transform us & convict us & cleanse us & move us from glory to glory & into the likeness of Christ, there is no dimension that could capture

that! Thank you Lord for your Word, which is alive &
active (Hebrews 4:12)! You are the WORD OF GOD!

4) Read Revelation 19:13. What is the name of Jesus?

DAY 5: Consecration of the Bronze Basin

"Anoint the basin and its stand and consecrate them."
Exodus 40:11

The Bronze Basin was sprinkled with ***blood***, anointed
with ***oil***, and it contained ***water*** for washing. The water
of the Word (for washing) comes to us through the
blood of Jesus and by the Holy Spirit (represented in
the oil). These are the three witnesses that John speaks
of in I John 5:7-8 *"For there are three that bear witness*
in heaven: the Father, the Word, and the Holy Spirit;
and these three agree as one. And there are three that
bear witness on earth: the Spirit, the water and the
blood; and these three agree as one." (NKJ)

As Priests of the New Covenant we need to experience
all three of these witnesses in order to be complete and
fulfill the tasks of the Priesthood. We need to be
sprinkled with the blood. We need to have the
continual washing of the Word and we need the
anointing oil of the Holy Spirit to be poured over us, so
we are consecrated, empowered and complete in Him to
do the work of the Priest.

1) On your diagram of the Tabernacle, draw the
    placement of the Bronze Laver (Basin). Use a
    circle to show its placement.

2) Use paper & draw what you think the Bronze Basin may have looked like (based on the information in Exodus 30:17-21 & Exodus 38:8)?

3) Draw what the Bronze Basin looks like in your life today. Use your imagination.

CHAPTER 5:
The Holy Place: The Golden Lampstand

As we step inside the holy place, passing through the veil, it is illuminated by the Golden Lampstand. The Tabernacle is broken into several sections.

The first section was the outer court, which was 150 feet long (on the north & south sides) x 75 feet (on the west and east sides) x 7.5 feet high. 60 posts sat in bases around the perimeter by which white fine linens curtains were hung in order to create a boundary. These curtains created a barrier between God and man. The 30 foot entrance (consisting of a curtain with blue, scarlet and purple fabric) to the outer court was on the east side of the tabernacle structure. Inside the curtain of blue, scarlet and purple was the outer court. The outer court held the Bronze Altar, which met each one who entered the outer court. The next vessel that stood between the Altar and the inner court was the Bronze Basin, which the priests used to cleanse themselves, so they would be free from defilement before they went to minister before the Lord. The outer court deals with salvation and sanctification. These two need to be in order before we can move into the next section of the Tabernacle.

The second curtain or veil leads into the next section of the Tabernacle, the Holy Place. This was the place where the priests would minister before the Lord. The Golden Lampstand, the Table of Showbread and the Altar of Incense were contained in the Holy Place. Beyond the third veil was The Holy of Holies (this perfectly squared room). The only furniture in the Holy of Holies was the Ark of the Covenant. The High Priest would only enter this room once a year on the Day of Atonement. Moses was the only one who had unlimited access to the Holy of Holies.

He would meet with God to receive instruction for leading the Israelites.

The building that held the Holy Place and the Holy of Holies measured 45 feet in length x 15 feet in width. 20 upright frames of 15 feet high stood next to one another along the north side and the south side of the inner court. Eight frames stood next to each other at the west side. Along each of these sides crossbars were added to the structure; four along each side (possibly made in the shape of an x) with a center crossbar extending the whole distance of the building. I refer to this complete inner structure as the Inner Court. This inner court was twice as high (15 feet) as the white linen curtains (7 ½ feet) around the perimeter of the outer court. The inner court was highest structure in camp, signifying its central role in Israel's worship. All worship was centered on the inner court.

On the East entrance into the Holy Place was a veil or curtain made of blue, purple and scarlet yarn with cherubim woven into the fabric. This veil hung on five posts that were overlaid in gold. Gold hooks connected the veil from post to post. Four large curtains or canopies acted as a heavy protective ceiling over the inner court structure. The priest would carefully enter through the second veil (or curtain) made of blue, scarlet and purple woven together by an embroiderer. The only light that shone in this "secret place" was the light of the Golden Lampstand. It illuminated the Holy Place and the priest would minister in the light of this Lampstand. Exodus 25:31-40 gives us the specific details of this Lampstand. It was made of one piece of pure gold, weighing between 75-90 pounds. Crafted from that one piece of gold was a center shaft with six branches connected to it (three on each side); with detailed almond flower cups, buds and blossoms hammered out of the gold. Exodus 25:38 tells us that all of the accessories (wick trimmers and trays) were to be made of solid gold also. The metal gold symbolizes holiness and deity. Scripture tells us that the gold was hammered, so in order to make it pliable, the gold would have to be put into the gold refiner's fire and when the impurities were removed, it would then be shaped by the refiner's hands. The gold then went through a hammering process to be completed. We see Jesus represented in the gold itself through the refining and hammering that he allowed himself to go through on our behalf by the Refiner's hands.

We need to know that as one who follows after Jesus, the Refiner will put us through the fire, skim off the impurities and shape us as He sees fit. Refining is a part of the life of every believer. This refining comes when the Lord "turns up the heat" to see what dross (waste, garbage or impurities) rise to the top, so He can skim them off. In order for us to be pure in heart and mind, we need to submit our whole lives to God's refining. We have a choice. We either say "yes" to the process or "no". In John 15, Jesus uses another example which has the same effect as the refining process. *"I am the true vine, and my Father is the gardener. He cuts off every branch in me that does not bear fruit, while every branch that bears fruit he prunes so that it will be even more fruitful," (verses 1-2).* I want to be more fruitful. I want my life to count for His Kingdom. I want God to prune away or remove the dross, so that I can be more like Jesus. Refine me Lord. Get out the hammer and start pounding away, so I can be shaped by Your hand.

How well do you handle the refining process of your walk with the Lord?

Malachi 3:3 says, *"He will sit as a refiner and purifier of silver; he will purify the Levites and refine them like gold and silver. Then the Lord will have men who will bring*

129

offerings of righteousness." Let the Holy Spirit speak to your heart about what needs to be hammered or refined in your life.

The lampstand had a center shaft with six branches connected to the center shaft (three branches on each side). Symbolically, we can see Jesus as the center shaft of the lampstand and the branches on one side represent the Old Testament with the Old Covenant and the branches on the other side represent the New Testament with the New Covenant. They meet at Jesus. He is the fulfillment and completion of the two.

We can also symbolically see Jesus at the center, with the Jewish nation (Old covenant people) extending from one side of the center shaft and the believers or followers of Christ (New Covenant people) extending from the other side. Romans 11 describes the ingrafted branches that we are, as Gentile Christians. Romans 11:17-18, " *If some of the branches have been broken off, and you, though a wild olive shoot, have been grafted in among the others and now share in the nourishing sap from the olive root, do not boast over those branches. If you do, consider this: You do not support the root, but the root supports you."* What a gift to be grafted into the promised people.

On each of the six branches were three cups shaped like almond flowers with buds and blossoms. Three represents the Trinity (Father, Son and Holy Spirit), who is our foundation. On the center shaft there were four cups shaped like almond flowers with buds and blossoms. Four is the number for the earth. We are to take the Gospel of Jesus Christ to the four corners of the earth; the north, south, east and west.

What is the significance of almond flowers, buds and blossoms? Numbers 17 tells of a time when God gave a sign for the stubborn and rebellious nation of Israel. The nation was grumbling and complaining about leadership in the priesthood. God instructed Moses to gather a staff from the leader of each tribe and to write the name of the head of that tribe each staff. God then gave this promise to the people, *"The staff belonging to the man I choose will sprout, and I will rid myself of this constant grumbling against you by the Israelites," (Numbers 17:5).* The staffs were collected from the twelve tribes and placed before God in the Holy of Holies. The next day when Moses entered the place, he saw that Aaron's staff had not only sprouted, but had budded, blossomed and produced almonds. Aaron's staff was then placed before the Ark of the Testimony to be kept as a sign to those who were rebelling. The almond flowers, buds & blossoms on the shafts of the golden lampstand were a reminder to the priests of God's commitment to His choice of the Levitical priesthood.

In the book of Jeremiah, Jeremiah had a vision which the Lord asks him what he sees. Jeremiah's answer is recorded in Jeremiah 1:11-12 (which gives some insight to the almond tree also). *"I see the branch of an almond tree,"* I replied. *The Lord said to me, 'You have seen correctly, for I am watching to see that my Word is fulfilled."* The almond tree is one of the first to bud in this area of the world. It speaks out the message of life from death, watching as others blossom and bloom and bear fruit.

At the top of this Lampstand were seven lamps. These were filled with olive oil. It was part of the priest's ministry to keep the lamps burning continually by filling them. The oil is representative of the Holy Spirit. We need to be continually filled with the Holy Spirit in order to burn continually. Ephesians 5:18 says to us, *"Be filled with the Holy Spirit."* This verb form for "filled" is a continually filling. You could say the passage like this: *Be being filled with the Holy Spirit.* Every morning, before you get out of bed, ask the Lord to fill you fresh with the power of His Holy Spirit. We cry out, "More Lord, more. We want more of You."

The parable of the ten virgins speaks to the lamps and the oil. *"At that time the kingdom of heaven will be like ten virgins who took their lamps and went out to meet the bridegroom. Five of them were foolish and five were wise. The foolish ones took their lamps but did not take any oil with them. The wise, however, took oil in jars along with their lamps. The bridegroom was a long time in coming and they all became drowsy and fell asleep..."* (Matthew 25:1-5). This passage is a continuation of chapter 24, which gives the signs of the end of the age.   The lamps represent the ministry and the oil speaks to the time spent in the secret place with Jesus; the place of intimacy; the place where we are filled with His Holy Spirit. We must cultivate that time, so that the lamp is filled with oil. The wise are those who seek Jesus before ministry. They are those who desire Him above all else. Their main objective is to experience His presence. The foolish are those who put their ministry before their time with the Lord. They are consumed with the "doing" of ministry and will forfeit His presence. In these days, as we approach the coming of the King of Kings, let's be wise. Our obsession should be Jesus, not what we can do for Him.

This Lampstand was different than a candle. A candle has its own source of light and eventually burns itself out because it runs out of energy. We see too many Christians living their life like a candle, using their own source of power. Eventually they burn out. Have you experienced this? I know that I have. I am a "doer", so I can very quickly fall into the trap of being a candle (using my own energy), instead of being tapped into the Holy Spirit to be a Lampstand.

How can you tell when you are using your own power? Here are several signs:
- Frustration
- weariness
- anxiety
- ministry is obligation
- worry
- fear
- unproductive in busyness
- concerned about what people might think (people-pleasing)
- when the ministry you are involved in has become more important than spending time with the one who you are in ministry for

This is seen in the church at Ephesus. Jesus comes to this church and says, *"You have forsaken your first love. Remember the height from which you have fallen. Repent and do the things you did at first. If you do not repent, I will come to you and remove your Lampstand from its place"* (Revelation 2:4-5).

A couple of questions to ask to keep your heart in check:
- Do I love Jesus more than my ministry?
- Would I be willing to give it up to pursue more of Him?

We need to keep a check on the activities we are involved in and the motives behind those ministries. The Christian life was never meant to live out of our own strength;

instead we are to tap into the source of life, the Holy Spirit ~ to be filled to overflowing so our lamp is continually burning. Oh Holy Spirit, burn in us! Let's be like the Lampstand, which was kept burning by the continual source of oil being poured into them. Keep the main thing, the main thing! John 15:5 reminds us, *"I am the vine; you are the branches. If a man remains in me and I in him, he will bear much fruit; apart from me you can do nothing.* We need to take heed of the warning given to the church in Ephesus: Remember. Repent. Return. Or He will remove the Lampstand.

Exodus 27:21 tells us, *"In the Tent of Meeting, outside the curtain that is in front of the Testimony, Aaron and his sons are to keep the lamp burning before the Lord."* The priests trimmed the wicks of each lamp every morning and every evening with the pure gold wick trimmers and the old wicks were disposed of with the pure gold trays. Any dead material that was not removed from the wick would prevent the light from shining brightly. For us, if our "wick" has collected dead material which is not trimmed off, the oil of the Holy Spirit will not be able to flow through us, causing the light to be dim and eventually die out if not tended.

Are you trimming your wick?
- How sensitive am I to sin in my life?
- Have I invited the Holy Spirit to reveal the dead material?
- Am I willing to trim off the dead material and dispose of it?
- Is the light of Jesus shining brightly to others?

The snuff dish (tray) was the container for the used portion of the wicks. These dead pieces were carried away and disposed of properly. Our sin (the dead material) is carried away and disposed of properly.

Psalm 103:12 says, *"As far as the east is from the west, so far has he removed our transgressions from us."*

The Lampstand has seven lamps, yet is one Lampstand. One speaks to unity and oneness. We are His body, one body, one bride shining the light of Christ into the world. *"There is one body and one Spirit—just as you were called to one hope when you were called—one Lord, one faith, one baptism, one God and Father of all, who is over all and through all and in all." (Ephesians 4:4-6).* I am a part of His body, connected to every other believer and then collectively all the believers make up the church. How are we doing in unity and oneness? It doesn't take a genius to see that there is more division than unity in the church. God's heart would be that His body would be built into the Living structure of His Church, *"you also, like living stones, are being built into a spiritual house to be a holy priesthood, offering spiritual sacrifices acceptable to God through Jesus Christ." (I Peter 2:5).* My heart cries out that we, Christ's body or His bride, would concentrate on loving one another~ seeing our similarities, without compromising the Gospel of Jesus Christ. Jesus prayed for the Church's unity (this is one of the messages in the Golden Lampstand) before going to the cross. It is because of His love for us that we are able to live a life of love and oneness with Him and others. John 17:20-21 says, *"My prayer is not for them alone. I pray also for those who will believe in me through my message, that all of them may be one, Father, just as you are in me and I am in you. May they also be in us so that the world may believe that you have sent me."* To be a light-bearer of the Way, the Truth and the Life, we need to be one in mind and spirit. Who will believe the message of the Cross when those who carry the message cannot even get along?

This Lampstand is significant in the book of Revelation. John has the vision of heaven and in the first chapter of Revelation, the Golden Lampstand is mentioned. This time there are seven Golden Lampstands, not just seven lamps. The Lampstands represent seven kinds of churches that are prevalent on the earth. Jesus himself walks among the Golden Lampstands. *"I turned around to see the voice that was speaking to me. And when I turned I saw seven golden lampstands, and among the lampstands was someone like a son of man, dressed in a robe reaching down to his feet and with a golden sash around his chest."* (Revelation 1:12-13). Jesus is dressed as the high priest walking among the churches to strengthen, encourage and bring warning. Jesus wants his bride prepared for His return. As we take a brief look at each of the seven churches admonished in Revelation, ask yourself this question: Which church do I "attend"?

1) The Loveless Church~ Revelation 2:1-7
   - The church in Ephesus began strong, but at this point in history they have grown weary. Because of this, ministry has become an obligation, not a desire out of love. They have forsaken their first love. Jesus tells them to repent and remember. Repent, which means to turn or to change your way of thinking. Turn away from _____ and turn to Jesus. What is it that needs to be repented? What keeps us from loving Jesus single-hearted? Remember what we do when we are in love! Can't eat or sleep…we just want to be with the one we love! How can that be rekindled in our hearts? What changes need to take place?

2) The Persecuted Church~ Revelation 2:8-11
    • Suffering is the theme of the church in
      Smyrna. Jesus affirms them and encourages
      them to remain faithful in persecution. He
      knows what they are going through. He is
      enough for them. As they draw near to Him,
      they will be strengthened by His mighty
      right hand. Persecution drives the
      persecuted to live very close to their
      message~ they simply cling to the gospel of
      Jesus. How well do we handle suffering for
      the cause of Christ? Are we faithful
      witnesses through persecution? Do we offer
      strength and encouragement to those who
      are suffering?

3) The Compromising Church~ Revelation 2:12-17
    • The problem in Pergamum was that there
      were those who were compromising their
      faith with idol worship and sexual
      immorality of pagan worship. This was one
      of the most wicked cities in the ancient
      world. Jesus knows where they live. He
      understands what they are coming against,
      but He will not tolerate compromise. He
      calls them to repent! How has the church
      today been infiltrated by idolatry and
      immorality? Jesus knows where we live.
      He understands the times and this church
      age, however He will not tolerate
      compromise. His message doesn't change.
      How have we compromised? What idols
      have we allowed in our lives?

4) The Worldly Church~ Revelation 2:18-28

- Compromise is the theme in the church at Thyatira. Jesus sees their compromise and He is calling them to overcome. He commends this church, for they are doing more than they did at first. He recognizes their improved spiritual condition. His concern is with those who would lead His followers into moral and spiritual decline. No matter what is going on around us, we need to hold to the true teachings of the Word. We need to be on guard so that we are not misled by false teachings that creep into the church. How often do we spend time in God's Word? Do we know the voice of the Shepherd, so we follow only Him? Are we easily led astray?

5) The Dead Church~ Revelation 3:1-6

- The message to the church at Sardis is "Wake Up"! This church had a reputation of being alive, but they were dead! Jesus doesn't care about reputation. He doesn't look at the outward, He looks at the heart. Jesus has placed this church on the scales and as in Daniel 5:27, He would say to this church, *"You have been weighed on the scales and found wanting"*. The words "wake up" is from two Greek words meaning "to chase sleep"; a call to be stirred out of their slumber. This is the church in America! We have a reputation of being alive, but in reality we are dead! Oh would we stir out of our slumber. Let's pray Ephesians 5:14 for the church in America,

"Wake up, O sleeper, rise from the dead and Christ will shine on you."

6) The Faithful Church~ Revelation 3:7-13

- God is attracted to weakness. For in our weakness, He is strong. The message Jesus has to the church in Philadelphia is this: Continue to be faithful. Jesus speaks to them, *"I know that you have little strength, yet you have kept my word and have not denied my name."* Are we those who have little strength? Jesus knows. Paul knew this kind of weakness. I Corinthians 12:9 says, *'But he said to me, 'My grace is sufficient for you, for my power is made perfect in weakness.' Therefore I will boast all the more gladly about my weaknesses, so that Christ's power may rest on me."* Christ has the sustaining power. Jesus says, "Hold on".

7) The Lukewarm Church~ Revelation 3:14-21

- Jesus had no compliment or encouragement for the church in Laodecia. They were a lukewarm church, in a city of affluence. It was at the end of several aquaducts which made it a boom town. However, Jesus compares them to the tepid temperature of the water that flowed in the aquaducts; he called them lukewarm. Textiles and wool clothes was a prosperous business in Laodecia. There was a banking industry and a medical school where eye-salves were developed and produced. Yet Jesus says that they are "wretched, pitiful, poor, blind and naked. I counsel you to buy from me gold refined in the fire, so you can become rich; and white clothes to wear, so you can cover your shameful nakedness, and salve to put on your eyes, so you can see." (Revelation 3:17-18). Jesus hates pride. In this church were people who were puffed up because of their wealth. The call here is to: Repent! Turn around; change direction; change your way of thinking; that is the only hope for this church. His refining fire transforms us so we are conformed into His image. Where do we see pride in the church? Do we have it all together on the outside, but on the inside are all messed up? Any lukewarmness?

These churches were the seven lampstands spoken of in Revelation. They were to be the shining the light of Christ. Only two of the churches in Revelation are not admonished. What is Jesus thinking as He walks among the churches in America today? What kind of lampstand are we? We are to shine the light of Christ brightly. Matthew 5:14-16 says to us, *"You are the light of the world. A city on a hill cannot be hidden. Neither do people light a lamp and put it under a bowl. Instead they put it on its stand, and it gives light to everyone in the house. In the same way let your light shine before men, that they may see your good deeds and praise your Father in heaven."* We are the light-bearers. *"You are all sons of the light and sons of the day. We do not belong to the night or to the darkness,"* (I Thessalonians 5:5).

Light speaks of holiness, purity and truth.
- The first words spoken by God in the Bible are "Let there be light." And there was light! (Genesis 1:3) God spoke it and it came to be.

- God is light. He lives in unapproachable light (I Timothy 6:16).
- He wraps Himself in light as with a garment (Psalm 104:2).
- His Word is a light to my path (Psalm 119:105).
- The unfolding of His Word gives light (Psalm 119:130).
- His light is shed upon the righteous (Psalm 97:4).
- God keeps my lamp burning & turns my darkness to light (Psalm 18:28).
- By His light I walk through the darkness (Job 29:3).
- Let us walk in the light of the Lord (Isaiah 2:5).
- The Lord will be the everlasting light (Isaiah 60:19).
- Light dwells with him (Daniel 2:22).
- The people living in darkness have seen a great light (Matthew 4:16).
- A light for revelation to the gentiles (Luke 2:32).
- I (Jesus) am the light of the world (John 8:12).
- The Word is the light of men (John 1:4).
- The Lord is my light (Psalm 27:1).
- Put your trust in the Light (Jesus) so you may become sons of light (John 12:36).
- Light has come into the world (John 3:19).
- Jesus is the light of the world (John 9:5).
- Father of heavenly lights (James 1:17).
- God called you out of darkness into His wonderful light (I Peter 2:9).
- The description of the heavenly city where we will dwell tells us there is no need for the sun, for the glory of God gives it light and the Lamb is its lamp (Rev. 21:23). We will walk by its light (Rev. 3:24).

The Lampstand in the Tabernacle was both the LIGHT and the Light-bearer. We, as His lampstands reflect His marvelous light! The light does not originate with us. We reflect His light into the areas of influence where He has placed us. Light exposes the darkness and provides the way out of darkness! Light reveals things as they really are. Light promotes life. Light awakens us.

The lamps on the golden lampstand were lit by divine fire that consumed the sacrifice on the bronze altar (Leviticus 9:23-24). Coals of fire were taken from the bronze altar to be placed onthe golden altar of incense(so incense could be burned) and to light the oil in the Golden Lampstand. The Lampstand burns continually which speaks of an eternal light and revelation. No dimensions were given for the size of the Golden Lampstand constructed for the tabernacle. This speaks to the immeasurable work of the Triune God. God is light. Jesus is the light sent to all men, and the Holy Spirit is the oil that lights our lamps, so we can shine brightly among the earth.

As we tarry in the Holy Place, in the light of the Holy Spirit, we will become more aware of the darkness of our soul. Bob Sorge says it this way in the book <u>Dealing with the Praise and Rejection of Men</u>, "I'm living in greater light, and the brighter the light the uglier the stain appears to be," (page 70). The good news is that Jesus loves us so very much, that He shines His light upon the areas of darkness, so they can be exposed, brought into the light, trimmed off and our hearts are set ablaze with increasing holiness, truth and purity.

STUDY GUIDE
Chapter 5: The Lampstand
(Exodus 38:17-24)

Scripture to memorize: Matthew 5:16 *"In the same way, let your light shine before men, that they may see your good deeds and praise your Father in heaven."* *(NIV)*

Key Questions:

1) Share your diagram of the Outer Court (what it looks like for you)~ with the Gate, Bronze Altar & Bronze Basin~ and write out what the Outer Court means to you:

2) What are your thoughts about the numbers seen in the Lampstand?

3) How do we "let our light shine before men"?

This week we are moving into the "Inner Court". The Tabernacle is broken into several sections; the Outer Court, the Holy Place and the Holy of Holies. The Holy Place and the Holy of Holies are in the "Inner Court". For the time that we spend on the Holy Place and the Holy of Holies, we will refer to this place as the "Inner Court." Before you begin each day's study, ask the Lord to illuminate your mind to understand all that He has for you. "Let there be light!"

Day 1: Outer Court

We have spent the last several weeks examining the Outer Court of the Tabernacle. The size of the Outer Court measured 150 feet long (North & South sides) and 75 feet wide (West & East sides). The 12 tribes of Israel encamped around the Tabernacle ~ which was significant to the centrality of the Tabernacle to their lives. Fine linen curtains made the walls surrounding the Outer Court. They were hung hook to hook on 20 pillars on the north & south sides and on 10 pillars on the west side. The gate (entrance) to the Tabernacle is 30 feet wide and 7 ½ feet high. The curtain was blue, purple and scarlet~ a stark contrast to the white finely twisted linen curtains around the perimeter of the Tabernacle. Four pillars set in bronze sockets supported the curtain. When entering through the east gate (the only way into the Tabernacle), the first piece of "furniture" we see is the Bronze Altar (upon which all sacrifices were offered for the atonement for the sins of the Israelites). The next article in the Outer Court is the bronze basin. Only the Priest, to cleanse them before ministering before the Lord, used this. The Priests cleansed continually at the Bronze Basin. The Outer Court deals with salvation and sanctification. These two need to be in order before we can move beyond the second curtain into the Holy Place.

1) Use this space to draw a diagram of the Outer Court (what it looks like for you)~ with the Gate, Bronze Altar & Bronze Basin~ and write out what the Outer Court means to you:

Day 2: Inner Court

Today we are moving from the Outer Court into the Holy Place. We can only enter the Holy Place because of the ministry of the Outer Court. We have been justified (Rom. 4:25; Acts 13:39) by the blood of the Lamb and we have been cleansed from the defilement of the world (Eph. 5:26-27; Psalm 51:7). Now we have permission to enter through the curtain to the Holy Place.

The curtain at the entrance to the Holy Place was made of the same beautiful colorful fabrics of blue, purple and scarlet with cherubim woven into the fabric. The word veil (Hebrew = paroketh) means to separate. The veil acted as a barrier between God & man, shutting God in and keeping man out. The priests could have access to the Holy Place after they had met the requirements written out in the Mosaic Law. This veil (separating the Outer Court from the Inner Court) was supported by five pillars made of acacia wood & overlaid with gold. Gold hooks were used to attach the veil to the bronze sockets. (Exodus 26:36-37). (We will look more closely at each of the three veils in the coming weeks.)

As we peer into the Holy Place, we see the lampstand that is illuminating the Holy Place, serving as the only source of light. It stands on the south side of the Tabernacle (Exodus 40:24-25). The Table of Showbread stood on the north side and the altar of incense stood in front of the third curtain, which separated the Holy Place from the Holy of Holies, where the Ark of the Covenant was held.

Read Exodus 25:31—40. This gives us the instructions for the construction of the lampstand.

1) What metal was it made from? (verse 31)

2) What kind of flowers would be "hammered" in the design? (verse 33)

3) What other accessories were to be made out of pure gold? (verse 38)

The weight of the gold is averaged between 75—90 pounds. This was one very heavy and expensive lampstand! It was part of the Priests ministry to keep the lamps burning continually (see Exodus 27:20-21) by filling them with olive oil. The Priests trimmed each lamp (the wicks) each morning & evening with the pure gold wick trimmers (Exodus 30:7-8). This lampstand was different that a candlestick. With a candlestick we think of burning candles (where the source is themselves & eventually burn themselves out), but that is not the case with the lampstand~ these lamps burned by the continual supply of oil being poured into them.

Gold needs to go through a refining process in order to look like gold (in the sense that we know it). The purifying fires cause the impurities to be removed, for it is in the fire where the gold is brought forth. The gold then needs to be shaped in the hands of a goldsmith. Then the gold needs to go through the hammering and beating work of the goldsmith. This is a long, painful process, but when the work is completed, it is a rare & beautiful metal.

4) Have you been through the refiner's fire? Explain. What does I Peter 1:7 mean in light of what we are studying?

5) Have you felt the hammering and beating work of the goldsmith? How?

Gold also symbolizes the Deity of Christ, God's son. Jesus stepped out of heaven into the stream of humanity, living a perfect, spotless life (I Peter 1:19).

We read in Exodus 25:33 that almond flowers with buds & blossoms are to be on the branches of the lampstand.

6) Read Numbers 17:8. What happened to Aaron's staff? Aaron's staff budded, flowered, and brought forth almonds. The almond tree is the first of all trees to bud in Palestine, so we see the message of life from death.

Day 3: Numbers in the Lampstand

It is time to take a look at some numbers and their significance in the Lampstand.

1) How many pieces of gold were to be used in the making of the Lampstand? (Exodus 25:31, 39)

1~ The **number one** is significant of unity, oneness, one accord or one Church. We serve the LIVING GOD. John 17 was the prayer that Jesus prayed for believers that we would be ONE (the church) in unity just as He and the Father are one. Oneness is the mark of the Lampstand.

2) How many branches are there to be on the Lampstand? (Exodus 25:32)

The Lampstand will have one center shaft with six branches (three on one side and three on the other). Each branch is to have three cups shaped like almond flowers extending from the Lampstand.

3~ The **number three** is significant as the Godhead~ Father, Son, Holy Spirit. The Godhead is our foundation and He sustains the church.

3) How many cups shaped like almond flower with buds and blossoms are on the shaft? (Exodus 25:34)

4~ *Four* is the number of earth. There are four seasons, four winds, and four corners of the earth. This light is to shine to the four corners of the earth. We, the church are to carry God's light to the nations!

    4) How many branches extend from the lampstand?

6 ~ *Six* is the number for man – the number of branches; the center shaft is Jesus –as branches, our connection with Christ brings life & light.

    5) How does John 15:1-5 speak to our connection to Christ?

7~ The ***seven*** lamps signify fullness, completeness, perfection. The seven lamps sit at the end of the seven branches. There are seven lamps and yet one light (Lampstand). The seven lamps represent the Spirit of the Living God.

There are a couple references we will look up today:

    6) Read Isaiah 11:1-4. The Spirit of the Living God pours out (**list the seven gifts of the Holy Spirit~** these are the seven spirits of God spoken of in Revelation 1:4 & Revelation 4:5):

    7) Read Ephesians 4:4-6. What do these verses say to the church?

9~ Here are a couple more interesting number facts in the Lampstand~ the ***number nine***. In each of the six branches, there were three almond flowers, three buds, and three blossoms. Each branch had nine designs hammered into it. The number nine is the number that signifies the Holy Spirit.

8) Read Galations 5:22-24. How many fruit of the Spirit are there? Name them.

9) Read I Corinthians 12:7-11. How many gifts of the Holy Spirit are there? Name them.

12~ On the center shaft of the Lampstand, there were four sets of the almond flower cups, buds and blossoms, which gives us a total of twelve. The **number twelve** is the number of Divine Government, Apostolic Fullness. We see this number over & over in the scriptures. Examples: 12 tribes, 12 disciples, 12 loaves of showbread, 12 stones in the breastplate of the Priest, 12 gates in the Holy City, 12 foundations in the Holy City...

66~ The last number we are going to see today in the Lampstand is the **number 66** which is the number of books in the Bible. Add together the flowers, buds, blossoms on the three branches on one side, and the flowers, buds, blossoms on the shaft and you get thirty-nine (3 x9=27 + 12=39). Thirty-nine is the number of the books in the Old Testament. Then, add the remaining branches to get twenty-seven (3 x 9 = 27). Twenty-seven is the number of the books in the New Testament. The grand total=66! The Bible is sixty-six books unified in ONE book.

Day 4: Light!

The Lampstand was used to illuminate the Inner Court. The Lampstand was the only source of light in the Holy Place. The Inner Court (which included the Holy Place & the Holy of Holies) measured 10x10x30 cubits. Four large canopies covered it as the ceiling. They hung down over the North, South and West sides in divine order. The first curtain (canopy) was the curtain made of blue, purple and scarlet with Cherubim woven into the fabric (Exodus 26:1).

The second curtain (canopy) was that of goat hair (Exodus 26:7). The third curtain (canopy) was made of rams' skins dyed red (Exodus 26:14). And the last curtain (canopy) to be the covering over the Inner Court is to be made of sea cows (Exodus 26:14). We will look at these covering curtains in more detail in several weeks. For now, we just need to have the understanding of the darkness of the Inner Court by all these coverings. Without the light from the Lampstand, it would be dark as night inside.

1) Draw the Inner Court on your diagram. (The outer court of the Tabernacle is outlined on the diagram). The Inner Court should be near the back half of the Tabernacle outline with space around the entire place. This is a rectangular space (10x10x30). The Holy Place of the Inner Court is the largest area (it makes up two-thirds of the Inner Court space). The Holy of Holies is a square (10x10).

2) Draw the Lampstand in the space inside the Holy Place on the south side (Exodus 40:24).

The light speaks of holiness, purity and truth.

3) What does I John 1:5 say?

4) Read John 1:4, 7-9. Who is the light that this scripture is referring to?

5) Read John 8:12. What does this say?

6) Read Luke 1:78-79. Who is the light?

7) Psalm 27:1. David says that the Lord is His:

8) .Read James 1:17. What does it say concerning our Father?

9) Read John 9:5. Who is the light?

10) Read Genesis 1:1-3. What are God's first recorded words in the Scriptures?

11) What do these verses say concerning the light:
- Psalm 119:105, 130?
- John 3:19?
- Revelation 21:23?
- Revelation 21:24?

We know that God is light & Jesus is the light of the world. We will dwell in the Holy City where there will be no sun, because the light will come from the glory of God! God's Word also calls us the light. We are found in the Lampstand in the Holy Place. The church, His body, His bride are called to be the light of the world. *"You are the light of the world. A city on a hill cannot be hidden. Neither do people light a lamp and put it under a bowl. Instead they put it on its stand, and it gives light to everyone in the house. In the same way **let your light shine before men**, that they may see your good deeds and praise your Father in heaven." (Matthew 5:14—16)*

12) How are we a light; a city on a hill? How are we to let our light shine before all men?

The Lampstand was both the LIGHT & the light-bearer! We, the believers are to walk in the light so we have fellowship with the Lord. (I John 1:7) Revelation 2 & 3 refers to the seven churches as Golden Lampstands (this is in direct reference to the Lampstand in the Tabernacle). The church today needs to heed the warning given to the seven churches written about in these chapters; that we may let our light shine before men!

Day 5: Lampstand tools

There are no dimensions given for this Lampstand. This speaks to the immeasurable work of Triune God. We see that God is Light, Jesus is the light sent to all men, and the Holy Spirit is represented in the oil that lights the lamps.

The tools to be used (made also of pure gold) in regards to the Lampstand:

Wick trimmers~ Daily the Priests removed any dead material from the wick that might prevent the light from shining brightly. If our "wick" is defective, the oil of the Holy Spirit will not be able to flow through us causing the light to be dim & eventually die out is not tended to.

1) What does Hebrews 12:5-11 say regarding the "trimming of the wick"?
2) Read John 15:1-2. What does the Gardener do?

Snuff Dish~ The used portions of the wick were placed in the snuff dish & carried out of the Tabernacle to be disposed of properly. Just as our sins are disposed of *"as far as the east is from the west, so far has he removed our transgressions from us." (Psalm 103:12).*

The Lampstand was divinely lit but was kept lit by the supply of the oil (daily) by the Priests. Divine Fire came out from the Glory of God & burned up the sacrifice on the Bronze Altar (Leviticus 9:23-24); consequently lighting the fire which was to burn continually and never go out (Leviticus 6:12-13). From this fire were taken the coals of fire for the Golden Altar of Incense, and the fire to light the

Lampstand. The Lampstand burns continually speaking of an eternal light & illumination (revelation).

We, the believers have been "lit" by the fire of God and it is the responsibility of every believer to receive a continual supply of DIVINE oil (the Holy Spirit) to keep our lamps burning before the Lord.

3) What does Ephesians 5:18 say?

4) In the space provided, draw what this lampstand looks like in your life today.

Let's be BRIGHT LIGHTS shining in the darkness of this world! Shine on! Lord, "let there be light!" Keep the fire burning brightly. Holy Spirit, burn in us!

CHAPTER 6:
The Holy Place: The Table of Showbread

Opposite of the Golden Lampstand, inside the Holy Place, sits the Table of Showbread.   This is the first time in scripture from the creation of the world to the wilderness that God uses this word "table". It is from the Hebrew word *shulchan* which means "a meal or spread or a place of communion and fellowship". What an inviting picture we have of the Table of Showbread. How often in our home is fellowship done around a meal or even sitting around a table, munching on snacks. It speaks to relationship. From the beginning, God has been about relationship. He desires a relationship with us. Relationships were his idea. In the Garden of Eden, after creating man from the dust of the earth, God knew that man needed a companion. Adam didn't say to God, "You know, this would be a whole lot more fun if I had someone to talk with." God designed Eve to be a companion to Adam. Relationships. Fellowship. Communion. This all happens around a table. In the beauty & stillness of the Holy Place, God is calling the priests to relationship, fellowship and communion with Him.

Psalm 23 speaks of a table, which is the same Hebrew word used in the account of the Tabernacle's Table of Showbread. *"You prepare a table before me in the presence of my enemies,"* Psalm 23:5. In the midst of enemy territory, God is inviting David (and us) to fellowship & communion with Him. Several years ago, I experienced the West Nile virus, the disease that affects someone who has been bitten by a mosquito. I suffered for a couple weeks with a high fever, vomiting, lethargy, dehydration, body aches, and intense headaches (like a migraine).   I had been to the doctor a couple times during those two weeks and the problem wasn't diagnosed, so an IV of fluids would be given to me and then I would be sent home. After two visits to the Urgent Care in the third week of my illness, the emergency doctor asked if I had been tested for the West Nile virus. At this point, I was so sick that I couldn't really remember anything about the doctors' visits. I seemed to be getting worse instead of better. He decided to check for that virus. This was a simple blood test; however, with the dehydration my body was experiencing, my veins kept popping when a needle was inserted. (Sidenote: I do NOT handle needles well. I have fainted anytime I have given blood or had a shot, so this was not a highlight in my adult life. ☺)   Eventually the blood was drawn and within an hour the diagnoses was given and I was put in an ambulance and sent to the hospital. I was the only case of West Nile in this facility, so I had doctors in and out of my room day and night. There wasn't much to do; but to wait. I would either get better or worse. I spent time in the quiet and pain, believing God had the best for me, no matter the outcome. Those days and nights in the hospital I felt the presence of the Lord, even in my delirious state; trusting Him in the midst of this "enemy territory". I was released after day five in the hospital and made my way to our bedroom (which is on the second floor of our home). I remained in our bed for more than a month~ the stairs were too exhausting to go down. My energy level was gone. I knew that if I walked down the stairs, I would not be able to get back up them. My mom came and stayed with us for several weeks to help with the kid stuff, because my husband was working six hours away from our home and I homeschooled. My oldest daughter became a nurse and a part-time teacher! I did recover with no side effects, which is a miracle.

I recently saw an article about a young woman, who contracted the West Nile virus roughly around the same time I did. She was eighteen at the time. She is just now recovering and learning to walk. Her nervous system is gaining strength. I realize that my life and recovery are a total miracle of healing from God, Jehovah ~Rapha.

When I read about the table being prepared in the midst of enemies, I immediately thought of my enemy, West Nile. God prepared a table of fellowship and communion in the midst of my enemy. He had to carry me to the table, because I wasn't strong enough to get there on my own. But isn't that just like our loving Heavenly Father. The God of the Universe, The Creator God, Yahweh, The Everlasting God, The Beginning and the End, The First and the Last, The One who was, who is and who is to come~ This God desires to commune with you and me. Let's take a look into the Table of Showbread.

Exodus 25:23-30 gives us the description of this table. It was constructed of acacia wood; three feet long and one and a half feet wide and two and a quarter feet high. The wood being a product of the earth speaks to Jesus' humanity. Isaiah 11:1 says this about Jesus, *"A shoot will come up from the stump of Jesse; from his roots a Branch will bear fruit."* Jesus is this shoot, this branch. He was perfect and lived a life that was much like the wood of the acacia tree, incorruptible and indestructible; nothing could harm him. Hebrews 7:16 tells us of Jesus, *"one who has become a priest not on the basis of a regulation as to his ancestry but on the basis of the power of an indestructible life."* The metal used to overlay the acacia wood is gold. Gold signifies the Deity of Christ. In the table we see the two elements in union in the life of Christ; the acacia wood (Jesus' perfect humanity) and the gold (Jesus' deity). Jesus had both natures. Both natures were united in One man.

He is unique among all other humans. He alone is the God-Man. Philippians 2:6-7 says of Jesus, *"Who, being in very nature God, did not consider equality with God something to be grasped, but made himself nothing, taking the very nature of a servant, being made in human likeness."* Jesus willingly gave up His God-ness to come and dwell among man as a man. In God's infinite design of the Tabernacle, we see the very essence of Jesus in everything.

Around the edge of the Table of Showbread was a gold molding rim three inches wide all the way along the perimeter. This rim was to protect anything from falling off the Table of Showbread. We see the hand of Jesus in this rim of gold. He keeps us from falling. He is our protection. In John 10:28, Jesus is talking about how His sheep hear His voice and then he says, *"I give them eternal life, and they shall never perish; no one can snatch them out of my hand."* Thank you, Jesus. What security! What love! During my two month illness, I felt His hand holding me on the table of fellowship and communion. He met me right where I was. He didn't expect anything from me, but fellowship. I couldn't open my Bible, because I couldn't open my eyes from the intensity of the headaches and fever. So, I had to sit (lay) before the Lord~ with no agenda, no way to "do" anything for Him. I had His love and He had mine. Many conversations and tears were poured out before Jesus during that time. And I heard His sweet voice, the voice of my Shepherd, tenderly loving me and comforting me in my time of sickness and pain. When you are hurting, He is enough. He will keep you from falling. You just need to reach out your hand and His hand will grab yours and firmly hold onto you. Peter experienced the mighty hand of Jesus reaching down to grab him, firmly. Matthew 14:22-33 records this account. Jesus was walking on the water to the disciples and Peter got out of the boat and began to walk on water toward

Jesus. *"But when he saw the wind, he was afraid and beginning to sink, cried out 'Lord, save me'! Immediately Jesus reached out his hand and caught him..."* (verses 30-31) Jesus has a mighty right hand, mighty in power and authority, security and protection. He is able to keep us from falling!

Four gold rings were placed each of the corners of the Table of Showbread , which stood on the four legs of the table. Four symbolizes the number for the earth: four seasons, four winds, four corners of the earth, four quarters of the moon.

- The four corners of the Table tell us that we are to take the bread of life (Jesus) to the ends of the earth, the four corners of the world. Matthew 28:18-20 records the Great Commission which is our assignment from Jesus!
- The four legs of the Table represent the four gospels (Matthew, Mark, Luke and John) which are the foundation of the Table standing. The ministry of Jesus is set in the gospels. And those men used their legs to do a lot of walking to the corners of their world! ☺
- The four gold rings~ a ring has no beginning and no end; it is a common symbol representing eternity and these rings were gold which symbolizes Deity.

Who brought the Gospel of Christ to you? Who faithfully carried His message? Where are you carrying the message of Christ? To whom are you going?

Poles were constructed for carrying the Table of Showbread when the Israelites were to pack up and journey to another destination. Just like the Israelites, we are reminded that we too, are on a journey or pilgrimage.

We are strangers and aliens on this earth. We are not to be too comfortable here. Hebrews 11 recounts the lives of the men and women who had lives surrendered to God so He could use them for extraordinary purposes. Each of them did not consider this world to be their home. They were looking forward to their heavenly home. *"By faith he (Abraham) made his home in the promised land like a stranger in a foreign country; he lived in tents, as did Isaac and Jacob, who were heirs with him of the same promise. For he was looking forward to the city with foundations, whose architect and builder is God....all these people were still living by faith when they died. They did not receive the things promised; they only saw them and welcomed them from a distance. And they admitted that they were aliens and strangers on earth." (Hebrews 11:9,10,13).* The Israelites had the poles as a reminder of the journey. What do you need to remind you? Maybe we all need to construct a couple poles made of wood & covered in gold (or gold spray paint) as a visual to point us to our city with foundations whose architect and builder is GOD!

With every table, come accessories. This is my favorite part about the table. My husband would say it is a weakness of mine. When I go shopping with my mom & sister, Greg sends me with a stern warning: "Do not come home with anymore dishes for the table. We don't have room for the dishes we have." I have to say that this is my favorite vessel that is found in the Tabernacle, because of my love for relationships, fellowship and communion with God and others. So often, our home is open to many~ gathering around the table. With every holiday comes a set of dishes for that holiday, along with placements or charger plates to match. Candles and candy dishes or serving trays are also a must have for the various seasons! When I call my family and friends to "Come to the table" it means so much more than just eating. It is the life-line of relationship. That is seen in this Table of Showbread. It was the life-line of the priests' relationship with God and with one another.

The accessories on this table included: dishes and plates, incense cups and bowls and pitchers. Exodus 37:16 says (NKJ), *"He made of pure gold the utensils which were on the table: its dishes, its cups, its bowls and its pitchers for pouring."* Let's examine each accessory.

- Dishes and plates~ used for carrying the bread into the Holy Place and for holding the bread on the table. *"The changing of the showbread was an elaborate service. The Mishna (the first section in the Talmud) explains the procedure the priests had in changing the bread. Four priests entered the Holy Place, two of them carrying the piles of bread and two of them the cups of incense. Four priests had gone in before them, two to take off the two old piles of showbread, and two to take off the cups of incense. Those who brought in the new bread stood at the north side facing southward, those who took away the old bread, at the south side, facing northward. One part lifted off and the other put on, the hands of one being over and against the hands of the other, as it is written, 'Thou shalt set upon the table bread of the Passover always before me' (Men. XI,7). The loaves that were removed were delivered to the priests for their consumption within the Tabernacle, the whole quantity to seventy-five pounds of bread per week."* *~The Tabernacle: Shadows of the Messiah (p.52-53)*

- Incense cups~ were filled with frankincense (a sweet smelling gum resin), which was set out as a memorial portion to the Lord and burned on the Altar of Incense (Leviticus 24:7) when the priests ate the bread at the Table of Showbread in the light of the Golden Lampstand. Imagine that scene. The priests ate at the table (representing relationship, fellowship and communion) in the illumination of the lampstand (which represents for us the Holy Spirit's anointing), while the frankincense was burned at the Altar of Incense. Frankincense was the purest incense. When it was burned, it produced a white smoke symbolizing prayers, worship and praise ascending before the presence of God, Almighty.

- Bowls and pitchers~ contained wine, which was poured out in connection with the eating of the bread on the table before the Lord (Numbers 28:7). This "drink offering" was used in relationship to the Table of Showbread. The bread and wine foreshadow the New Testament table of communion. Jesus' life (in the bread) was broken for us and His blood (in the wine) was poured out for us (Matthew 26:26-28, I Corinthians 11:23-25). Paul speaks of his life being poured out as a drink offering in Philippians 2:17, *"But even if I am being poured out like a drink offering on the sacrifice and service coming from your faith, I am glad and rejoice with all of you."*

Leviticus 24:5-9 gave the instructions to the priests for the bread. There were twelve baked breads containing about six pounds of flour that were arranged in two rows of six each. The scripture doesn't tell us that it was unleavened bread, but because it was a meal offering to be used in the Tabernacle, it had to be unleavened. The divine recipe from God was to use fine flour in the baking of the bread.

162

Fine flour begins as a whole kernel of wheat. In order to make this wheat useable, it had to be ground into a powder. Ground and crushed, words that would seem to describe the beating that Jesus allowed his body to suffer, on our behalf. Jesus, the kernel of wheat was crushed and ground, beaten and broken in his body to become the bread of life for us, so we could partake of Him. John 12:24 speaks of this process, *"I tell you the truth, unless a kernel of wheat falls to the ground and dies, it remains a single seed. But if it dies, it produces many seeds."* This fine flour was then made into cakes and then baked, symbolizing the suffering that Jesus would endure on our behalf, for the cakes were baked in the fire. Twelve cakes (breads) were then placed before the Lord on His table, one for each tribe. All the tribes were represented before the Lord. These twelve loaves were collected from each tribe on the Sabbath. They were twelve separate tribes, yet part of one nation. I Corinthians 10:17 says of us, *"For we being many are one bread, and one body; for we are all partakers of that one bread."* Jesus is that Bread that unites us in Him. The twelve breads sat in two rows on the Table of Showbread. It was to always be before the Lord. *"Put the bread of the Presence on this table to be before me at all times," Exodus 25:30.* Showbread, which is Hebrew for "bread of presence or bread of faces", was before the presence of YHWH who dwelt in the Holy of Holies above the cherubim. This Showbread was a foreshadowing of Jesus Christ, who is the true bread of life, giving sustenance to all who partake of Him. Showbread means "to show; to declare; to tell forth" which was speaking of the Bread of Life, Jesus, who was to come. Jesus Christ was born in the city called Bethlehem, which means "house of bread". God doesn't miss a detail!

The twelve cakes which sat in the two rows on the table represents the double portion to the priests. As priests, they received His presence and His provision. We are His priests and receive from God the double portion in the spiritual and physical provisions found in Jesus. The bread was eaten by the priests, on the Sabbath in the Holy Place (Leviticus 24:5-9). We, too, are to "feed" on the Bread of Life, Jesus, to receive spiritual and physical sustenance. He is our source of life! The bread and wine that sat on the Table of Showbread represents the fellowship, relationship and communion that the priests had with the Lord.

Jesus is the Bread of Heaven. He, the sustainer of our physical and spiritual life came down from heaven to dwell among us. Matthew 4:4 says that *"Man does not live on bread alone but on every word that comes from the mouth of God."* There are two definitions of the word "word". *Logos* is the term which describes the written Word of God, that which is written on the pages of Scripture, and *rhema* which is a word (verse or part of a verse) that comes alive to you. You may have read the same verse one hundred times and then one time as you are reading, the word or passage seems to jump off the page and speak right to your heart. That is a *rhema* word. We need the Holy Spirit to illuminate the Word of God to us in such a way that it is *rhema* to us. Rhema words breathe the breath of God onto the pages of Scripture. That is the type of relationship we are to have with the Word of God.

Partaking of the Word at the table is a different experience than being washed with the Word (at the Bronze Basin). In the outer court, at the bronze basin, we are washed with God's Word (Ephesians 5:26-27), being transformed more and more into the image of Christ (2 Corinthians 3:18). The Word is used as a cleansing instrument~ to show us defilement from the world. Moving through the veil into

164

the Holy Place is representative of a pressing in to the deeper things of God. One must tarry at the table to receive revelation or a fresh word or a rhema word from God. That takes time. It requires time in God's presence and time being still before Him. It will demand time to listen, moving away from all distractions.

How do we get to know someone better? We give them our time. We listen to their story. We ask questions about who they are. We sit around a table, sharing a meal and conversation. If you want to get to know someone better, invite them over for dinner or dessert or snacks! Food speaks a language of relationship. Most of my dearest friendships have been forged over meeting together for a meal, then sharing dreams and passions and heart-aches. God designed relationship, so this is not a foreign concept to our Creator. In the light of the lampstand, the priests would share bread, spending time with one another and with their God. For us, illuminated by the Holy Spirit, eating the Bread of Heaven, communion with Him draws us to a deeper knowledge of who Jesus is. The logos Word of God becomes rhema (life to us that feeds us). As we spend time with Jesus, we will hunger for more of the Bread of Heaven.

How hungry are you?

Matthew 6:11 tells us *"Give us this day our daily bread."* This is a continual, daily need. As the Israelites were given manna from heaven daily, so we too are to partake of the manna from heaven (Jesus) daily. Remember our key principle as we study the Tabernacle: Everything God did with the Israelites in the realm of the seen, He deals with us in the realm of the unseen. The Israelites could not keep any manna for the following day (except for the Sabbath). They needed fresh manna daily. So too for us, we cannot rely on the manna from a month ago or a week ago or even yesterday. We need a fresh supply of manna daily.

In the book of John, chapter 6, we see Jesus as:
- True bread of heaven (6:32)
- Bread of God who gives life to the world (6:33)
- Bread of life (6:35)
- Bread of life (6:48)
- Bread that comes down from heaven (6:50)
- Living bread (6:51)
- Bread is my flesh (6:51)
- Bread that came down from heaven (6:58)
- Feed on this bread (6:58)

Jesus is the bread of heaven. As we feed on this bread, we are strengthened in our inner man spiritually and physically. Here is another principle to remember: We crave what we feed on. If I am feeding on the Word and being in the presence of the Lord, I will crave that more and more. If I am feeding on television and media, I will continue to crave that more and more. Sometimes we need to starve ourselves in order to develop a new craving! When I was in bed with West Nile virus and could not read the Word of God because the headaches were too severe to open my eyes, I would lay in bed and dream of the time when I would be able to open the pages of Scripture again. I craved the Living Word of God. The first time I was able to go back to church (after two months), when the Pastor said, "Open your Bibles to _____", I closed my eyes and just listened to people turning the pages of Scripture to the text. I was so weepy to hear the beautiful sounds of God's Living Word being opened to so many. I still listen to others opening their Bibles when a Pastor or speaker says to turn to such and such. It is a sweet sound in my ears.

What do you crave? Do you crave time with the Bread of Heaven? Do you crave to meet at the Table of the Lord? Spend some time asking God to show you what you crave. If you are not hungry of things of God, ask the Holy Spirit to give you a hunger for righteousness. God's desire is for you. He craves you. He wants you. He loves you. He longs for relationship with you.

"Blessed are those who hunger and thirst for righteousness, for they will be filled," Matthew 5:6.

STUDY GUIDE
Chapter 6: The Table of Showbread
(Exodus 25:23—30)

Scripture to memorize: John 6:35 *"Then Jesus declared, 'I am the bread of life. He who comes to me will never go hungry, and he who believes in me will never be thirsty."* (NIV)

Key Questions:
  1) Remember a time when you tarried before the Lord (partaking of the bread of life) & the Spirit illuminated or revealed something to you & your response was prayer, worship and/or adoration.
  2) Describe a time when you have experienced God's supernatural provision physically and/or spiritually?
  3) Can you think of a time when the logos word became rhema for you?

This week we will be studying the second piece of furniture in the Holy Place, the Table of Showbread. Before you begin this week, consider "fasting" as you study this week; to allow the Lord to show you that He is the **Bread of Life**! When we fast from feeding our physical self, Christ can use those "hunger pangs" to fill our spiritual self.

Day 1: Materials used in the Table of Showbread

This is the first time from the time of creation to the wilderness that God uses this word, table (Hebrew = *shulchan*) that means "a meal or spread or a place of communion & fellowship".

In the construction of the Table of Showbread, every detail is given, as with all the vessels used in the Tabernacle.

After it was completed, it was set on the North side of the Holy Place, opposite the Golden Lampstand. The Lampstand lit the Holy Place to illuminate the Bread on the Table.

1) Read Exodus 25:23. What is the table made of? What are the dimensions?

The acacia wood speaks to Christ's humanity (as we saw in the Bronze Altar). Acacia was found in the Sinai Desert. It was a hard, indestructible, incorruptible wood. It could survive the harsh environment because its roots grew very deep. The tree was not affected by disease nor animal infestations because of the strong odor in the fiber of its wood. Insects would not borough into it. The wood was a product of the earth, which speaks to the humanity of Jesus. He was without sin, without blemish or any other defect. His human living withstood all the evil and nothing could attack him (Hebrews 7:16).

The Table of Showbread was three feet long, one and a half feet wide and two and a quarter feet high.

2) Read Exodus 25:24-25. What metal is used to overlay the acacia wood? What else is constructed around the perimeter of the Table?

Gold signifies the Deity of Christ. In the Table we see the two elements in union in the life of Christ: the acacia wood (Jesus' humanity) and the gold (His deity). Jesus had both natures. Both natures were united in one man. He is unique among all other humans~ He alone in the "God-man").

3) Read Philippians 2:6-7. What do we see in these two verses about Christ?

There is a gold molding around the Table of Showbread. A rim 3" wide was around the perimeter of the Table with a gold molding on the rim also. This rim was to protect anything from falling off the Table of Showbread. We know that Jesus' hand is able to keep us from falling!

4) Read John 10:28. What does this say about Jesus' hand?

5) Read Exodus 25:26-27. What number is mentioned in these verses? List the references to that number.

There were four gold rings in the four corners of the Table of Showbread on the four legs of the Table. We have seen that the number four represents: earth; four seasons, four corners of the earth, four quarters of the moon.

- The four corners of the Table~ taking Jesus (the bread of life) to the ends of the earth (Matthew 28:18-20).
- The four legs of the Table ~ "These legs are made for walking" ☺ This is the gospels (Matthew, Mark, Luke, John) which those men walked the earth to bring the message of Christ to the earth! The legs of the Table are essential to the table standing. The Table (ministry of Jesus) is set upon the gospels.
- The four gold rings ~ a ring has no beginning and no end; it is a common symbol that represents eternity; gold meaning deity

6) Read Exodus 25:28. What are the poles made of?
What are they used for?

When we studied the Bronze Altar, we gleaned that the
poles that were used to carry the Bronze Altar were to
remind us that we are on a journey; pilgrimage; we are
strangers & aliens here on this earth. Just as the Israelites
wandered in the wilderness, we are also on a journey.

7) Read Hebrews 11:9-16. What are we looking
forward to? (We are in good company~ Abraham,
Isaac, Jacob) ☺

8) On the Tabernacle diagram, draw a rectangle to
represent the Table of Showbread on the north side of
the Holy Place, across from the Golden Lampstand.

Day 2: Accessories of the Table of Showbread

Today we will be studying the plates and dishes and
pitchers and bowls~ the accessories that sit upon the Table
of the Showbread.

1) Exodus 37:16 says, *"He made of pure gold the
utensils which were on the table: its dishes, its cups,
its bowls, and its pitchers for pouring." (NKJ).*
Highlight the serving utensils, in the scripture
above, that were used in the Holy Place in regard to
the Table of Showbread.

- **Dishes & plates:** Used for carrying the
bread into the Holy Place; for holding the
bread on the Table
- **Cups (incense cups):** Filled with
frankincense, which was set out as a
memorial portion to the Lord and burned on

the Altar of Incense (Lev. 24:7) when the Priests ate at the Table of Showbread in the light of the Golden Lampstand. We see the three connected: As we eat at the bread of life at the **Table of the Lord** in the illumination of His Spirit (**Lampstand**), we offer up prayer, worship, adoration (**Altar of Incense).**

- **Bowls & pitchers:** These bowls & pitchers contained wine, which was poured out in connection with the Table of Showbread before the Lord (Numbers 28:7). This "drink offering" was only used in association with the Table of Showbread. Bread & wine are brought together here foreshadowing the New Testament "Table" of communion; the bread of life being broken for us and His life being poured out (I Corinthians 11:23-25; Matthew 26:26-28).

2) Remember a time when you tarried before the Lord (partaking of the bread of life) & the Spirit illuminated/revealed something to you & your response was prayer, worship and/or adoration. Can you share it here?

3) What does it mean for you to commune at the Table?

4) Draw the Table of Showbread with the serving utensils here.

Day 3: The Bread on the Table

"Put the bread of the Presence on this table to be before me at all times," Exodus 25:30. "Showbread" (which is

Hebrew for "bread of presence" or "bread of faces") was before the presence of YHWH (who dwelt in the Holy of Holies above the cherubim).

The showbread was a foreshadowing of Jesus Christ, who is the true bread of life, giving sustenance to all who partake of Him. Jesus was born in the city called Bethlehem, which means "house of bread".

Leviticus 24:5-9 gives the direction to the Priests for the bread. There were twelve baked breads containing about 6 pounds of flour that were arranged in two rows of six, each. The scripture doesn't tell us that it was unleavened, but because it was a meal offering to be used in the Tabernacle, it had to have been unleavened. The recipe given from God is to use "fine flour" in the baking of the bread. Fine flour begins as a whole kernel of wheat. In order to make this wheat useable, it had to be ground to powder. It was ground and crushed, which speaks to the beating that Jesus allowed for Himself. Jesus, the kernel of wheat was crushed, beaten and broken to become the perfect bread of life for us.

4) Read John 12:24. How does that verse relate to the bread of life?

The fine flour was made into cakes & then baked (which refers to the intense suffering that Jesus endured on our behalf).

5) Write a prayer of thanksgiving to the Lord for giving Himself unto crushing & suffering on your behalf.

Twelve baked cakes were set before the Lord on His table, one for each tribe. All the tribes were represented before the Lord. These twelve loaves were collected from each tribe on each Sabbath. They were twelve separate tribes; yet part of one whole nation. I Corinthians 10:17 says, *"For we being many are one bread, and one body; for we are all partakers of that one bread."*

The number 12 represents Divine Government, Apostolic Fullness/Authority/United. We see in the Table of Showbread, the 12 tribes (see above); the 12 disciples who were part of the miraculous feeding of the 5,000 (there were 12 baskets of bread left over of the 5 original loaves—5 is the number of grace).

The twelve cakes of bread sat in two rows on the Table of Showbread, which represents the double portion to the Priests (we are His Priests – I Peter 2:9). God gives physical provision & spiritual provision.

   6) How have you seen God's supernatural provision for you in a physical provision and a spiritual provision in your life?

The bread was eaten by the Priests on the Sabbath in the Holy Place (Lev. 24:5-9). We are to "feed" on the bread of life, Jesus to receive spiritual & physical sustenance. Jesus is our source of life! The bread and wine that sat on the Table of Showbread represents the fellowship (communion) that the Priests had with the Lord.

   7) Explain the fellowship (communion) you experience with the Lord.

   8) Are you "feeding" on the bread of heaven daily? Why/why not?

Day 4: Jesus is the Bread of Heaven

Bread is a food that sustains the body physically. As we have followed the Israelites in their exodus from Egypt, God provided manna, a type of bread, for their physical sustenance. Exodus 16:4 says, *"Then the Lord said to Moses, 'I will rain down bread from heaven for you. The people are to go out each day and gather enough for that day. In this way, I will test them and see whether they will follow my instructions'."* The Israelites questioned one another about the manna, asking one another *"what is it?".* Moses says to the Israelites *"It is the bread the Lord has given you to eat."* (Exodus 16:15).

The qualities of the manna: small, thin white flake; a daily provision; each one gathered according to their need (to be filled); God provided it in a miraculous way, but each one needed to "gather" it. The Israelites had a responsibility. The manna sustained the Israelites for the entire forty years in the wilderness. No one could "hoard" it, for it was a daily provision, except on the Sabbath, then there was enough extra for that day.

9) Read Deuteronomy 8:3. What does this verse tell us about the Israelites? What does this verse tell us about God?

10) Read Matthew 4:3-4. Who is Jesus talking to? What scripture is he referring to?

Jesus is the Bread of Heaven. He, the sustainer of our physical & spiritual life came down from heaven to dwell among us. Matthew 4:4 says that *'Man does not live on bread alone but on every word that comes from the mouth of God.'* In the scriptures, there are two descriptions of the "word"; logos & rhema. The logos word is the written

Word of God, what is written on the pages of Scripture. The rhema word is a Word (verse or part of verse) that comes alive to you. You may have read the same verse 100 times & then one time you read it and it jumps off the page and speaks right to your heart! That is a rhema word. We need to ask the Holy Spirit to illuminate the Word of God to us in such a way that it is RHEMA to us. Rhema words bring the breath of God onto the pages of Scripture.

11) Can you think of a time when the logos word became rhema for you?

"Give us today our daily bread." (Matthew 6:11). This scripture is part of the Lord's Prayer found in Matthew 6. Jesus is giving us a model of prayer. In this verse, He is teaching us to ask God to provide for our daily needs (physical & spiritual). Jesus, we know is the bread; He is our provision.

12) What are you in need of (daily provision)? Remember, Jesus is the provision for us. Write out a prayer asking God to "give you your daily bread".

13) Read John 6:1-15. Describe this miracle. What did Jesus do? How many baskets were filled with the pieces?

Jesus is always concerned about our spiritual condition. He speaks to a crowd (John 6) and the crowd is following Him based on the miracles He can do. They are asking Jesus for miraculous signs and Jesus responds, *"Do not work for food that spoils, but for food that endures to eternal life, which the Son of Man will give you. On him God the Father has placed His seal of approval." (John 6:27)* The crowd wanted to see miracles like the manna given in the desert.

14) Read John 6:32-33. What does Jesus say to the crowd?

15) Read John 6:34-59. How do the people respond? What is the condition of their hearts? What does Jesus say that causes them to "grumble"?

In this passage of John 6:25-59, we see Jesus as:
- True bread of heaven (6:32)
- Bread of God who gives life to the world (6:33)
- Bread of life (6:35)
- Bread of life (6:48)
- Bread that comes down from heaven (6:50)
- Living bread (6:51)
- Bread is my flesh (6:51)
- Bread that came down from heaven (6:58)
- Feed on this bread (6:58)

16) How do you feed on this bread from heaven?

Day 5: Table illuminated by the Lampstand

Jesus is the bread of heaven. As we feed on this bread, we are strengthened in our inner man (spiritually) and physically. The Golden Lampstand illuminates the bread of presence. The bread of presence symbolized God's presence waiting for fellowship with us. We see the symbolism of communion in the Table of showbread. When the Priests ate the bread of the Table, they drank the drink offering of wine:

"The Lord Jesus, on the night he was betrayed, took bread, and when He had given thanks, He broke it and said, 'This is my body, which is for you; do this in remembrance of me.' In the same way, after supper he took the cup, saying,

'This cup is the new covenant in my blood; do this,
whenever you drink it, in remembrance of me.' For
whenever you eat this bread and drink this cup, you
proclaim the Lord's death until He comes."
I Corinthians 11:23-26.

1) Today is a day to commune with the Lord. If you have bread & grape juice (wine) available to you, use that in your communion time with Him. If not, just get in His presence, remembering His gift of life to you. Get into His Word (a Psalm or where He might lead you) and ask the Holy Spirit (the Spirit of wisdom and of understanding, the Spirit of counsel and of power, the Spirit of knowledge and of the fear of the Lord) to illuminate the logos word to your spirit...to give you a rhema word! Oh, Bread of Heaven, come. We want to feed on You. (You may want to listen to a worship Cd, grab your journal & Bible and spend time with the bread of life).

2) Draw what the Table of Showbread looks like to you.

CHAPTER 7:
The Holy Place: The Golden Altar of Incense

Fragrant smoke ascended with the sweet smell of incense burning on the Altar of Incense in the Holy Place. This Golden Altar of Incense was located on the west end of the Holy Place, placed before the veil that separated the Holy Place from the Holy of Holies. This was as close as the priests could get to the presence of God, which settled between the cherubim on the Ark of the Covenant. As the priests stood at the Altar of Incense and offered up the sweet aroma before the Lord, they were near to God Himself. The priests were literally feet away from the Shekinah (real, tangible, manifest presence) glory of the Lord.

In my mind, I have a picture of the priest coming in to minister before the Lord at the Altar of Incense. He burns the incense on the Altar, watching the smoke rise and filling his nostrils with the fragrance of the incense. With a holy fear and reverence, he performs his duties, knowing that beyond the veil rests the Glory of God. What awe the priest had for His God.

How about us? Do we approach God with a holy fear and reverence, knowing who He is? Personally, I have rushed right into His presence, pushing the curtain aside and demanding, like a child, that He listen to me and answer my requests. Do you have a tendency to rush in?

The Tabernacle model teaches us to treasure the presence of God with honor and respect, remembering that the only way I even have access to a Most Holy God is based on the sacrifice of His perfect Son, Jesus, who willingly gave up

His life for me (and you). Then, using God's Word as a mirror and cleansing basin, I examine my heart. Am I conforming to the image of Christ, being transformed more and more into His likeness, from the inside-out? Can others see the change in my attitudes and behaviors? Next, my life should be marked by the continual filling of the Holy Spirit, and a waiting before the Lord, spending time "eating" of the Bread of Heaven. Being partakers of God's life to us, we then proceed to the Altar of Incense, which represents the ministry to the Lord in worship, prayer and intercession in the life of a believer. The placement of this Altar, in the Tabernacle shows us that this (worship, prayer, intercession) is at the heart of God. I want to take a few minutes to define the ministry of worship, prayer and intercession that takes place at the Altar of Incense.

- **Worship**~ Many people hear the word "worship" and immediately think of music. Now, music can be part of worship, but it is not the definition of the word. Worship is a life surrendered to God totally, in every area. In Bible references , when one would encounter the angel of the Lord or the manifest presence of God, the person would fall prostrate, on his face. The first mention of the word worship is in Genesis 22:5, "*Abraham said to his young men, 'Stay here with the donkey, and I and the lad will go over there; and we will worship and return to you.'*" There is no mention of singing praises to the Lord, in this case. In fact, as James Goll says, in his book, The Prophetic Intercessor, "We often connect worship with music and sometimes make them synonymous. But there is no mention of music here. The only instruments listed are wood, fire and a knife, and I don't think Abraham had in mind to whittle a flute and play a tune. All he offered was sacrifice, obedience and faith. This is

180

worship in its highest form~ a life prostrate before God. Worship is about bending the knee." (p.200)

- **Intercession~** There is a difference between prayer and intercession. James Goll describes intercession as "one who stands in the gap between God's righteous judgments and the people's need for mercy". (p. 27 in The Prophetic Intercessor). This was one of the ministries of the priest when he approached the Altar of incense. He stood in the gap between God and the people. That is our ministry of intercession as priests of the new covenant. And Jesus, the Great High Priest intercedes on behalf of His people, *"Therefore he is able to save completely those who come to God through him, because he always lives to intercede for them,"* Hebrews 7:25. What a privilege to participate in intercession. May we be faithful in this ministry. Ezekiel 22:30 gives us a warning: *"I looked for a man among them who would build up the wall and stand before me in the gap on behalf of the land so I would not have to destroy it, but I found none."* Oh Lord, let that not be said of us! Do you have a heart to intercede? Ask the Lord to give you a spirit of intercession; a desire to intercede; a heart that breaks over what breaks his heart. In intercession, we are asking God what is on His heart and then we intercede.

- **Prayer~** Richard J. Foster, in his book, The Celebration of Discipline speaks of prayer, "to pray is to change. Prayer is the central avenue God uses to transform us. If we are unwilling to change, we will abandon prayer as a noticeable characteristic of our lives. The closer we come to the heartbeat of God, the more we see our need and

181

the more we desire to be conformed to Christ" (p.33). Before we can move into intercession, we have to have our ears tuned to the voice of our Shepherd. Many people pray by handing their list of requests to Jesus and turning and walking away. The joy of prayer is listening to Him. What does He want to say to you? However, this is not a fast-food, drive-thru experience. It takes time to get to know the Father's whisper. He is wanting to tune our ears to hear Him. In order to do that, we need to turn off the television, the radio, the Ipods, the video games~ the noise and distraction of life. We are so accustomed to noise, that we don't know how to sit and be quiet. Begin by turning off the stuff of this world. Foster goes on to say of prayer, "Listening to the Lord is the first thing, the second thing and the third thing necessary for successful intercession." Do not wait to begin a life of prayer. Start today. Take five minutes to just listen to the voice of the Lord. Get a journal and pen. Be ready to write what you hear. It may take time and you may not hear anything for awhile, but the more you set your heart to listen, the more you will hear.

*Listen for five minutes

*Tell the Lord how much you love Him for five minutes. Pour your love on Him. Read through a Psalm & pray it back to Him. Or go through the alphabet saying one quality you love about Him for every letter (ex. A~ I Adore You Lord. B~ You are Beautiful Jesus. C~ You are the Creator.).

*Lay your requests before Him for the last five minutes. Keep a journal to see His faithfulness. And watch your heart grow and change.

Are you ready to take the 555 challenge?

5~Listen to Him, 5~Love Him, 5~Lay your requests before Him

We see the word altar used for this piece of furniture in the Tabernacle. Altar means 1) "slaughter place", a place of sacrifice and 2) "lifted up" or "ascending". At this altar, there was no blood sacrifices made, just a heart sacrifice. It wasn't the scent of the shed blood rising up to the Lord; it was the rising of the fragrant incense before the Lord. What a beautiful picture. Psalm 51:17 says, *"The sacrifices of God are a broken spirit; a broken and contrite heart, O God, you will not despise."* A heart offered to Him, surrendered to God's will. *"Through Jesus, therefore, let us continually offer to God a sacrifice of praise~ the fruit of lips that confess His name, "* Hebrews 13:15. The sacrifice of praise ascends before the throne of God. It is sweet incense to Him. *"May my prayer be set before you like incense; may the lifting of my hands be like the evening sacrifice,"* Psalm 141:2.

Exodus 30: 1—10 gives us the description and construction of the Golden Altar of Incense. It was made of acacia wood, a hard, incorruptible wood that no animal or insect would burrow into. This wood, as we have seen in the Bronze Altar and Table of Showbread represents Jesus in perfect humanity, for He was sinless and incorruptible. This Altar was thirty six inches high (3 feet) and eighteen inches square (1 ½ feet); taller than the Table of Showbread in the Holy Place. There is a "squareness" seen in this altar, which is also present in the Bronze Altar (4 ½ feet high and 7 ½ feet square). The Holy of Holies was also a perfect square, which is representative of the Holy City. (Revelation 21:15-16 says of that city, *"The angel who talked with me had a measuring rod of gold to measure the city, its gates and walls. The city was laid out like a square, as long as it was wide. He measured the city with the rod and found it to be 12,000 stadia in length, and as wide and high as it is long.*" In our English measurement, the Holy City is 2,000,000 square miles; 600,000 stories high)! What a city in which we will dwell!)

The "squareness" of the Altar gives us four corners. The four corners in the Bronze Altar refer to Jesus' atoning sacrifice reaching to all mankind, all four corners of the world, throughout history for all who accept his sacrifice. The four corners in the Table of Showbread represent taking the gospel of Jesus to the four corners of the earth. Here, at the Altar of Incense, we see the ministry of intercession reaching into all four corners of the world. Prayers are to be lifted high from all four corners, from all believers, everywhere.

The horns in the four corners of the Golden Altar of Incense represent the powerful presence of God. The Hebrew word for horn is "qeren" meaning "a horn of an animal, a flask or cornet". It is a symbol of strength, power and victory. Because of Christ's victory at the cross (Bronze Altar), the horns at the Altar of Incense speak to us strength, power and victory as we worship, pray and intercede. It is not based on any good thing that we have done or could do, but based solely on the victory that Jesus had over death!

Exodus 30:3 tells us that this altar was overlaid with pure gold. Gold signifies Jesus' deity. Again, we see the two natures of Christ (his perfect humanity in the acacia wood and his deity in the gold). A gold rim or molding went around the perimeter, like a crown. Royalty wears a crown. We see this showing us the royal nature of Christ. John 18:37 begins with a question from Pilate to Jesus during his interrogation before Jesus' crucifixion. "'*You are a king, then,' said Pilate. Jesus answered, 'You are right in saying I am a king. In fact, for this reason I was born, and for this*

I came into the world, to testify to the truth. Everyone on the side of truth listens to me.'" On the Altar of Incense, this gold rim was to keep the coals from falling off the altar. We know that Christ is able to keep us from falling. *"For Christ did not enter a manmade sanctuary that was only a copy of the true one; he entered heaven itself, now to appear for us in God's presence," Hebrews 9:24.* He intercedes on our behalf. *"Therefore he is able to save completely those who come to God through him, because he always lives to intercede for them," Hebrews 7:25.*

This beautiful Altar made of acacia wood, overlaid with gold, three feet tall and 1 ½ feet square, horns at each corner, with a gold molding or rim around the perimeter had rings and poles used to carry it when the Israelites were led by the pillar of fire or cloud. Most scholars believe that there were only two rings (not like the four that we have seen in the Bronze Altar and the Table of Showbread). The poles would fit in the rings and as the priests carried the Altar. It would swing on the poles, becoming a large censor as they walked. Imagine the fragrance of the incense and the smoke ascending to the Lord, an offering that would be pleasing to the Lord, a continual fragrance.. This would be in the presence of all Israelites showing the reverence and awe due this Great God.

Having only two rings symbolizes for us the work of Jesus and the Holy Spirit in intercession. Hebrews 7:25 tells us how Jesus is always interceding on our behalf and Romans 8:26-27 tells of the Holy Spirit's work. *"In the same way, the Spirit helps us in our weakness. We do not know what we ought to pray for, but the Spirit himself intercedes for us with groans that words cannot express. And he who searches our hearts knows the mind of the Spirit, because the Spirit intercedes for the saints in accordance with God's will."* As we minister at the Altar of Incense, the

Holy Spirit and Jesus are offering intercession on our behalf. What incense!

We have the reminder again by the poles that we are on a journey. This place is not our home. We are strangers and aliens on earth. There will be a place for us when there will be no more wandering, no more need for prayer and intercession and our lives will be complete in worship as we live with Him in the Holy City. *"And I heard a loud voice from the throne saying, 'Now the dwelling of God is with men, and he will live with them. They will be his people and God himself will be with them and be their God. He will wipe away every tear from their eyes. There will be no more death or mourning or crying or pain, for the old order of things has passed away.'"* How I long for the heavenly city, to be whole and complete in Him. Until that time, we need to remember that this is not our home. The poles were a constant reminder to the Israelites that they were wanderers. May we keep before us the picture of the city of God, so that we do not get too comfortable here.

"Aaron must burn fragrant incense on the altar every morning when he tends the lamps. He must burn incense again when he lights the lamps at twilight so incense will burn regularly before the Lord for generations to come," Exodus 30:7-8. The Hebrew word for "regularly" means "continually, constantly, daily or always". The smell of the fragrant incense was constant in the Holy Place. Is there a continual fragrance of incense in your life, represented by prayer, worship and intercession?

Several years ago, our family experienced a time of pain, as we walked through a very difficult church split. For many months, we struggled in the desert, asking some hard questions: "Lord, where do you want us?" "What are we to do?" Dealing with the leadership failure, it caused our

186

hearts to press in closer to Jesus. He alone sustained us. It was a time of focusing our attention on our Savior, not on man. Have you experienced any loss? Or any hard time that has caused a refocus in your life? This happened at the beginning of the school year and I was missing corporate worship. The worship band, that my daughter was a part of, led worship at the chapel services weekly at her high school. My homeschooled son, Jon, and I decided to go to chapel weekly for our time of corporate worship. That worship time invited the Lord to come and heal the broken places in our hearts. For months, we trecked up to the high school on Thursdays for Chapel services. I cried through the entire half hour of worship, as these young people (ages 14-18) led me into the throne room of heaven. The tears that streamed from my eyes were healing to my soul. Those kids did not know what a healing balm their worship was to me. The Lord tenderly healed us, through worship, prayer and intercession. We met Jesus at the Altar of Incense and the fragrance of the tears of intercession rose before the Lord. I have shared with the worship team how their sweet, pure worship was the healing balm that moved us from woundedness to restoration. Praise the Lord, oh my soul and all that is within me; praise His holy name! What a fragrant offering! If you are in a place of brokenness or have experienced a wounded heart or have suffered loss, come to the Altar of Incense and let the incense ascend before Him. Do not be in a hurry. Come and tarry at the Altar.

A unique blend of spices were the ingredients used in the making of this fragrant incense. Exodus 30:34-38 gives us the ingredients: gum, resin, onycha, galbanum, pure frankincense, and salt. A gifted perfumer would combine the spices to create the incense. This was the only incense to be offered on the Altar of Incense. It was a sacred recipe. God would not accept any other incense. No substitutes could be offered on the Altar. Any other incense would have been an imitation. How do we bring an imitation to the Altar? Can you think of substitutes that we offer? God desires that we worship Him with REAL worship. John 4:23-24 tells us, "*Yet a time is coming and has now come when the true worshippers will worship the Father in spirit and in truth, for they are the kind of worshippers the Father seeks. God is Spirit and His worshippers must worship in Spirit and in truth.*"

- **Spirit** is the Greek word "pneuma", it is the inner person that can respond to God
- **Truth** is the Greek word "aletheia" meaning real, certainty.
- **Worship** is the Greed word "proskyneo" which is to pay homage, show reverence, kneel before or bow down. This is worship, to recognize WHO we are in relationship with; to give Him the respect due His Holy name.

It is our heart attitude that God sees. When we approach the Altar of Incense to offer our worship, prayer or intercession, He will only receive that which is real. Counterfeit or imitation doesn't count! It amounts to nothing. It is only smoke. True worship from man's inner spirit offered in reverence and humility is a fragrance that is lifted high. Because we are priests (I Peter 1:9), we have the privilege and responsibility to present our offering of incense at the Altar.

According to Exodus 30:10, once a year on the Day of Atonement (the 10th day of the seventh month), the High Priest took some of the blood of the sin offering (blood that was shed at the Bronze Altar) and placed it on the horns of the Altar of Incense, sprinkling them seven times (see Leviticus 16:18-19) to cleanse and consecrate the Altar from the uncleanness of the Israelites. This Altar of Incense had to be holy. So we see here in the Holy Place that this fragrant offering is only possible because of the blood sacrifice at the Bronze Altar. **Blood sacrifice makes fragrant offering possible**. We are able to come to the Altar of Incense and offer our fragrant worship, prayer and intercession because of the blood he shed to consecrate us.

Fragrant offering is only possible because of sacrifice.

Fragrance of the incense ascending to the King of Glory! John 12:1-3 shows us what fragrant offering looks like for us. *"Six days before the Passover, Jesus arrived at Bethany, where Lazarus lived, whom Jesus had raised from the dead. Here dinner was given in Jesus' honor. Martha served, while Lazarus was among those reclining at the table with him. Then Mary took about a pint of pure nard, an expensive perfume; she poured it on Jesus' feet and wiped his feet with her hair. And the house was filled with the fragrance of the perfume."*

1. **Fragrant worship is costly. It is a sacrifice.** Pure nard is one of the most expensive perfumes in that day. It was an uncommon perfume (we see that the incense used at the Altar was uncommon, it was set apart as holy). This perfume cost more than a year's wages. This was a true sacrifice. What was Mary saving that for? To sell it later in life? How do you sacrifice to bring a fragrant offering to the Lord? It will usually look foolish according to the world's standards. Certainly the people around Mary thought there was something wrong with her!

189

2. **Fragrant worship is real, not imitation**. Mary brought Jesus the real thing! Her actions revealed her feelings for Jesus. This perfume was used to anoint Kings and dignitaries. She showed that her love for Jesus had more of an impact on her life than anything this world could offer her. Is your love for Jesus more of an impact on your life than anything else this world might have for you?

3. **Fragrant worship is God-pleasing, not man-pleasing.** Mary was focused on the object of her affection, not with the people around her. They did not hinder her worship. Galations 1:10 tells us to be God-pleasers, not man-pleasers. Would we be people who are only concerned with Jesus, the one who we adore; that we would not be concerned with those around us? Keep us single-focused Jesus.

4. **Fragrant worship lingers on us for a while**! The perfume that was poured out on Jesus' feet would have brought fragrance to the whole room (even though the others weren't partaking in this worship experience). What a difference our worship makes on others! *"And the house was filled with the fragrance." John 12:3b* And Mary would have had the fragrance with her for a very long time, for she wiped Jesus' feet with her hair. Imagine, as the evening wore on, she would remember her time with him (the intimacy of the event). This happened less than a week before the crucifixion, so the fragrance of the pure nard would have probably remained on Jesus when he was

190

taken down from the cross. He had been anointed for his burial. Was the fragrance lingering while he hung on the cross? What about Mary? Could she still smell the fragrance on her hair?

5. **Fragrant worship is not released until the vessel is broken**. The perfume contained in the container was only fragrant when the container was broken. Then the fragrance began to fill the room. We are to be broken before Him. Then the worship that comes from us is real, costly, God-pleasing and it lingers. Each time the Lord has allowed me to be broken, the fragrant worship I bring Him is sweeter and more fragrant. Oh Lord, that we would be broken vessels before you.

The pouring out of this fragrant perfume filled the whole house with the scent of the fragrance. What fragrance is your home filled with? Is it the sweet fragrance of Jesus? Go through each point of the fragrant worship and ask the Holy Spirit to reveal to your heart: 1) how you sacrifice to bring an offering before Him, 2) if you are real or an imitation?, 3) are you single-focused or double-minded, 4) what is lingering on you?, 5) have you been broken before the Lord?

Intimacy is the reward of spending time at the Altar of Incense.

Tarrying at the Altar of Incense has several basic "ingredients" to get started:

1) Find a quiet place where you are not interrupted.

2) Begin by focusing on who God is. This gives focus to our minds (which often wanders). Read a Psalm

191

and highlight in your mind the character qualities
that are written about our God
God You are…
Jesus You are…
Holy Spirit You are…

3) I John 1:9. Spend a couple minutes in confession.
Ask God to reveal any sin. Agree with God about
your sin. Repent and accept God's cleansing.

4) Ephesians 5:20. Spend some time thanking the
Lord for His gifts of blessing upon your life. Thank
you Lord for:

5) Philippians 4:6. Bring prayers and petitions before
the Lord (for others & yourself).

In the Old Testament model, this altar stood before the Ark
of the Covenant, which held God's presence and we see
this mirrored in the heavenly city. *"Another angel, who
had a golden censor, came and stood at the altar. He was
given much incense to offer, with the prayers of all the
saints, on the Golden Altar before the throne. The smoke of
the incense, together with the prayers of the saints, went up
before God from the angel's hand."* (Revelation 8:3-4)
What a privilege to offer prayers, petitions, and intercession
to be gathered and placed in a golden censor before the
throne of God.

STUDY GUIDE
Chapter 7:
The Holy Place: The Altar of Incense
(Exodus 30:1-10,34-38)

Scripture to memorize: *"May my prayer be set before You like incense; may the lifting up of my hands be like the evening sacrifice." Psalm 141:2*

Key Questions:
1) Share something that you learned about the Altar of Incense.
2) In what ways do you want to increase your prayer life (your priestly ministry at the Altar of Incense)?
3) Any "breath prayers" (Day 4) that the Lord gave you?

The inner court held the Golden Lampstand, the Table of Showbread and the Altar of Incense. Imagine the sweet fragrance of incense rising up to the Lord from the Golden Altar. This week, we are going to get a deeper understanding of the Altar of Incense, which speaks to us of intercession. *"May my prayer be set before You like incense; may the lifting up of my hands be like the evening sacrifice." Psalm 141:2.*

Day 1: Materials used in the construction of the Altar (Part 1)

Altar has two meanings, which we discovered in the study of the Bronze Altar (in the outer court). An altar is a place of sacrifice. And it carries the meaning of being, "lifted high" or "ascending". What a beautiful description of the Altar of Incense! It is a place of sacrifice where the fragrant offering of the incense rises before the Lord~ it is "lifted high" or "ascending".

1) Read Exodus 30: 1. What is the purpose of this Altar? How is this different from the Bronze Altar?

2) What type of wood is the Altar made of? What does that symbolize?
   Refer to Week 3 (Bronze Altar) or Week 6 (Table of Showbread)

The Altar of Incense is 36 inches high and 18 inches square~ taller than the Table of Showbread in the Holy Place. We see the "squareness" in the Bronze Altar (it was 4 ½ feet high and 7 ½ feet square). The Holy of Holies is also square (15 feet x 15 feet square).

3) Read Revelation 21:15-16. What do we learn about the Holy City?

We also see the "4 corners" in a square. The ministry of Jesus is to be taken to the four corners of the earth. In the Bronze Altar, the four corners refer to Jesus' atoning sacrifice for all mankind ~ justification for all who would receive it. In the Table of Showbread, we saw the four corners of the ministry of Jesus ~ to take the gospel to the whole earth (all 4 corners; North, South, East & West)! Here, we see the Altar of Incense as the intercessory ministry reaching into the whole world (all 4 corners). Prayers are to ascend, be lifted high, from all around the world ~ all the believers.

4) Read Exodus 30:2. What is to be in the corners of the Altar?

We saw the horns in the Bronze Altar, in the Outer Court. Horns speak of salvation, strength, power, and authority. Horns on an animal are a weapon (shows power) and also their defense (to protect themselves). On the Bronze Altar the horns were used to tie down the animal sacrifice. We also saw a couple references where the horns on the Bronze Altar were a place of refuge (I Kings 1:49-53 and I Kings 2:28-34).

5) Read I Samuel 16:1 & 13. How is the horn going to be used?

6) Read Psalm 18:2. What does this "horn" represent?

The Hebrew word for horn is "qeren", meaning a horn of an animal; a flask or cornet; a symbol of strength, power and victory. This noun occurs more than 75 times. Horned animals, such as oxen, goats and rams are symbols of strength. The "Horns of the Altar" (Leb.4:7; 9:9; Psalm 118:27) are symbolic of the powerful presence of God.

Day 2: Materials used in the construction of the Altar (Part 2)

In Exodus 30:3 we see that the Altar was overlaid with pure gold. Gold signifies Jesus' deity. Again, we see the two natures of Christ (his perfect humanity~ acacia wood) and His deity (Gold).

1) A gold rim (molding) went around the Altar, like a crown on the head. Royalty wears crowns. Read John 18:37. Who does Jesus say that He is? Read John 19:1-5. Describe this scene.

The gold molding (rim) was to keep the coals from falling off the altar. Again, we see that Christ is able to keep us from falling. In the Golden Altar, we see that Christ is interceding on our behalf (Hebrews 7:25; Hebrews 9:24).

Read Exodus 30:4-5. What are used for the poles?

195

Most scholars believe that there were only 2 gold rings (not like we have seen in the Bronze Altar & the Table of Showbread). The poles would be fit in them and as the priests carried the Altar, it would swing on the poles~ thus being a huge censor as they walked. In this way, the incense would be burning before the Lord always.

2) What does Romans 8:26-27 say about the Holy Spirit's work in intercession?

3) What does Hebrews 7:25 say about Jesus' work in intercession?

The two rings represent the work of the Holy Spirit & the work of Jesus in intercession. And the gold of the rings speaks to the deity of the Holy Spirit & Jesus Christ.

4) What do the poles represent? (Do you remember from the Bronze Altar & Table of Showbread?)

The poles were acacia wood (speaking to Jesus' humanity) and overlaid with gold (Jesus' deity). The poles were a reminder that we are strangers and aliens on this planet~ we are on a journey. This world is not our home. We look forward to a heavenly home! (I Peter 2:11).

5) Read Exodus 30:6 to find out where the Altar of Incense was placed in the Holy Place. Describe its position.

6) Draw the Altar of Incense on your diagram of the Tabernacle.

The Altar of Incense was in the center of the Inner Court; placed before the curtain that separated the Holy Place from the Holy of Holies. This was as close as the priests got to the presence of God (the Shekinah glory, which rested between the cherubim on the Ark of the Covenant). As they stood at the Altar of Incense and offered up the sweet aroma before the Lord, they were near to God Himself. **We see that the ministry of intercession, prayer and worship are at the center (or the heart) of God**. His exact placement of the Altar shows us that this is nearest to His heart.

7) In Revelation 8:3-4 we see a picture of the Golden Altar. Where is it located? What is mixed with the smoke of the incense?

Day 3: The Incense at the Altar

"Aaron must burn fragrant incense on the Altar every morning when he tends the lamps. He must burn incense again when he lights the lamps at twilight so incense will burn regularly before the Lord for the generations to come." Exodus 30:7-8

1) From the above passage, when is Aaron to burn incense to the Lord?

2) Incense represents prayers rising up to heaven. According to this passage in Exodus 30, how should we start & end our day?

The word "regularly" in Hebrew means *"continually, constantly, daily, and always"*.

3) If our prayer is incense before the Lord, what should our lives be marked by? (Incense is to burn "regularly" before the Lord)

4) Read Exodus 30:34-38. What was unique about this blend of spices? Where was the only place this blend was used?

The spices were:
- gum resin (stacte)~ a sweet gum, or drops, that came from the storax tree or shrub which grew in Israel
- onycha~ a fragrant spice from a shell (taken from the Red Sea)
- galbanum~ aromatic gum resin that comes from the Syrian fennel (having a balsamic odor). This was used to drive away insects.
- Frankincense~ white gum that comes from a tree called the salai found in Arabia. (white speaks to purity and righteousness).
- Salt~ salt is used as a seasoning & a preserving ingredient. Colossians 4:6 says, "*Let your conversation be always full of grace, seasoned with salt, so that you may know how to answer anyone.*"

These spices were in equal measure and mixed by a perfumer. The mixture was then ground into powder and placed before the Lord on the Altar. Notice there were 5 ingredients in the incense that is holy & pleasing before the Lord. (5 meaning the number of grace.) His grace, which has redeemed us! His grace pours out daily upon us. His grace to commune with us! His grace, which reaches out to us!

This incense was to be:

- Holy~ Jesus is holy and He calls us to be holy (I Peter 1:15-16)
- Pure~ Jesus was pure. He calls us to be pure. (I John 3:3)
- Fragrant~ Sweet & fragrant was the ministry of Jesus (Ephesians 5:2). He calls us to be fragrant (2 Corinthians 2:16)
- Ground~ Jesus was crushed & ground (Isaiah 53:5). Jesus was crushed for us, on our behalf (2 Corinthians 4:8-10)
- Continual~ Jesus continually makes intercession for us (Hebrews 7:25) and calls us to intercede on others' behalf (I Timothy 2:1)

According to Exodus 30:10, once a year (on the Day of Atonement—the 10th day of the seventh month), the High Priest took some of the blood of the sin offering (blood that was shed at the Bronze Altar) and placed it on the horns of the Altar; sprinkling them seven times (Leviticus 16:18-19) to cleanse & consecrate the Altar from the uncleanness of the Israelites. The Altar had to be holy.

It is on the basis of the blood of Jesus that we can stand before a Holy God. By His blood sacrifice we are justified and cleansed to minister before our God (I John 1:7). Christ's blood gives value to our prayers.

5) Read Hebrews 9:24—26. What does this say to us about the blood of Christ?

Fragrant offering is possible only on the basis of sacrifice. (The coals from the Bronze Altar—the place of sacrifice were the only coals to light the fire on the Altar of Incense).

In Exodus 30:9 God says, *"Do not offer on this altar any other incense or any burnt offering or grain offering, and do not pour a drink offering on it."* God will not accept substitutes on the Altar. There can be no incense burned, except the Divine recipe. No imitation would suffice! For us, God desires a life of prayer, worship & intercession that is true worship~ in Spirit and in Truth (John 4:24).

God had divinely lit this Altar. When the fire came down from heaven & consumed the burnt offering on the Bronze Altar (Lev. 9:23-24), the Altar wood was lit. Coals were taken from the Bronze Altar and used to light the Golden Altar and the Golden Lampstand. Any other fire was forbidden and any other incense was forbidden.

> 6) Read Leviticus 10:1-3. What happened to the Nadab & Abihu (2 of Aaron's sons)?

Only the High Priest and the priests could minister at the Altar of Incense. Jesus is our High Priest (Hebrews 7:26-27) and we are priests (I Peter 1:9). We have the privilege of lifting our incense (prayers, intercession, and worship) before God.

> 7) Write out I Thessalonians 5:17.

Day : 4 Pray Without Ceasing

Exodus 30:10 ends with these words, *"It is most holy to the Lord."* The Altar of Incense is most holy to the Lord. Of all the articles in the Tabernacle, this is the first time we have seen this said. The closer we get to the Holy of Holies, the more holy the vessels become. This ministry of worship, prayer & intercession is most important to God. We cannot take it for granted.

1) How do you view prayer?

The priests entered the Holy Place (in the Inner Court) after being justified & cleansed. The ministry that was most important to them was the trimming of the wicks (in the Golden Lampstand) daily, partaking of the Bread of Presence each Sabbath (at the Table of Showbread) and burning incense on the Altar of Incense on behalf of God's people, the Israelites. This was a continual burning before the presence of the Lord.

2) We looked at I Thessalonians 5:17 yesterday which says, *"Pray continually."* As believers, how do we do that?

Today we are going to look at scriptures that refer to prayer and ask the Lord to transform us in such a way that this conversation with God Almighty is continual; and that we crave it!

"When the Spirit has come to reside in someone, that person cannot stop praying; for the Spirit prays without ceasing in him. No matter if he is asleep or awake; prayer is going on in his heart all the time. He may be eating or drinking, he may be resting or working ~ the incense of prayer will ascend spontaneously from his heart. The slightest stirring of his heart is like a voice which sings in silence and in secret to the Invisible." --Isaac the Syrian

Prayer is a gift that connects us with God's heart. Remember, the Altar of Incense (the place where prayers are lifted up) is most holy to the Lord.

3) What do these verses say about prayer:

- Romans 12:12
- Ephesians 6:18
- Colossians 4:2
- Philippians 4:6
- Luke 18:7
- Hebrews 13:15
- Luke 18:1
- Psalm 55:17
- James 5:13-16

Brother Lawrence who desired to *practice the presence of God (*and wrote a book with that title) urges us to "*make a private chapel of our heart where we can retire from time to time to commune with Him, peacefully, humbly, lovingly.* Brother Lawrence lived in such a way that he connected with the Lord in the morning and throughout the day and discovered "*those who have been breathed on by the Holy Spirit move forward even while sleeping*". To have a life of constant fellowship with the Lord does not come instantly. It is something that must be practiced. Brother Lawrence says that it took him ten years before he entered into the *practice of the presence of God* continually. But what a goal: to be with God; to enter into a life of constant prayer.

4) To begin, try some "breath prayers"; this is when you pray with every breath you take. Try it now. Write a couple of your "breath prayers" in this space.

- Here are several examples: 1) *Lord, show me if there is anything in me that is not pleasing to You.* 2) *Lord, I want to know You more,* 3) The *Holy Spirit, minister to my spirit—to refresh me and revive me,* 4) *Lord, give me deeper revelation of Your love for me,* 5) *Holy Spirit, will you light the fire in my heart.*

Rest in Jesus. John 15 is all about abiding in Christ. Let our hearts get fulfillment in Him. This will begin a lifelong passionate pursuit of continuous prayer. We saw in the Altar of Incense the work of both Jesus and the Holy Spirit:

Jesus interceded on our behalf before the Father continuously. Romans 8:34 tells us *"Who is he that condemns? Christ Jesus, who died ~ more than that, who was raised to life ~ is at the right hand of God and is also interceding for us."* We have looked at Hebrews 7:25 so many times that we should have that memorized! ☺ *"Therefore he is able to save completely those who come to God through him, because he always lives to intercede for them."*

The Holy Spirit is seen in Romans 8:26 as one who intercedes for us. *"In the same way, the Spirit helps us in our weakness. We do not know what we ought to pray for, but the Spirit himself intercedes for us with groans that words cannot express."* When we pray in the Spirit, it releases our spirit to touch the Holy Spirit. This brings encouragement, refreshment, revelation, a timely Word, an intimacy that exists between the two (spirit to Spirit). Jude 20 says, *"But you, dear friends, build yourselves up in your most holy faith and pray in the Holy Spirit."* Ephesians 6:18 tells us, *"And pray in the Spirit on all occasions with all kinds of prayers and requests."*

Jesus Himself and the Holy Spirit are interceding at the throne of God. The ministry of prayer & intercession is very important indeed. Take time in the Inner Court, at the Altar of Incense.

5) Draw a picture of what the Altar of Incense looks like to you~ as you bring your sacrifice of worship, prayer & intercession before the King

Day 5: Prayer & Intercession

Jesus said, *"My house will be called a house of prayer." (Matthew 21:13).* And we are His spiritual house. I Peter 2:5 says, *"You also, like living stones, are being built into a spiritual house to be a holy priesthood, offering spiritual sacrifices acceptable to God through Jesus Christ."*

What is prayer?

- Communication in a relationship that shows intimacy (James 4:8)
- Standing in the "gap" (Ezekiel 22:30)
- Claiming the promises He has given you (Joshua 23:14 & 2 Corinthians 1:20)
- Asking (Matthew 7:7-8)
- Abiding (John 15)
- Our ministry as priests to God (Deut. 10:8)
- Casting our burdens (I Peter 5:7 & Psalm 55:22)
- Moves God to act (Habakkuk 3:1-2)
- Beginning of revival (2 Chronicles 7:14)
- Watchmen posted on the wall (Is. 62:6)
- Praising God for who He is (Psalm 47)

We have seen who may come to the Altar of Incense. A priest; only after he has made atonement for his sin (at the Bronze Altar), having cleansed his hands & feet from defilement from the world (at the Bronze Basin). Then he may enter the Holy Place, in the light of the Lampstand, to minister at the Altar of Incense, which sat in front of the veil that separated the Holy Place from the Most Holy Place. At the Altar, holy hands were lifted up.

1) Read Psalm 66:18. What does this verse say to you?
2) Read Psalm 24:3-4. Who may stand in the holy place?

3) Isaiah 66:2. How should we approach God?

We know that worship, prayer and intercession is at the center of God's heart. James 5:16 says, *"the prayer of a righteous man is powerful and effective."* God turns His ear to His "priests" and answers them when they call. Spend some time today in intimate communication with the Lord. *"Deep calls to deep in the roar of your waterfalls; all your waves and breakers have swept over me," Psalm 42:7.*

Prayer has several basic "ingredients":
1) Begin by focusing on who God is. This gives focus to our minds (which often wanders). Read a Psalm and highlight in your mind the character qualities that are written about our God. Write out your Praise (worship) here.
God You are...
Jesus You are...
Holy Spirit You are...

2) I John 1:9. Spend a couple minutes in confession. Ask God to reveal any sin. Agree with God about your sin. Repent and accept God's cleansing.

3) Ephesians 5:20. Spend some time thanking the Lord for His gifts of blessing upon your life~ Thank you Lord for...

205

4) Philippians 4:6. Bring your prayers and petitions before the Lord (for others & yourself).

Chapter 8:
The Curtains and the Veils

In the Sinai Desert, the Tabernacle stood as a reminder that God is the God of the Israelites. He desired to make this nation His holy people. This chapter will delve into the curtains that surround the Tabernacle, the veil that separated the Holy Place from the Outer Court, and the veil that separated the Holy Place from the Most Holy Place. We will also take a look at the curtained roof that covered the Inner Court (which contained the Holy Place and the Most Holy Place).

Jesus said, *"I am the Way, the Truth and the Life. No one comes to the Father except through me."* John 14:6

Imagine the sight of the Tabernacle in the wilderness. Surrounding the Tabernacle were the Israelite s, placed by tribes. The center of their life was positioned in the center of their camp, the Tabernacle, which stood in stark contrast to the environment of the desert wilderness. The Tabernacle wall was covered with white finely twisted linen curtains on the North, South, West and part of the East wall. The curtains were supported by 60 pillars of bronze set in bronze bases around the perimeter of the Outer Court. These curtains were 7 ½ feet high all the way around the perimeter. (The Outer Court was 150 feet long x 75 feet wide), which formed a separation between God and man. Psalm 16:6 says, *"The boundary lines have fallen for me in pleasant places; surely I have a delightful inheritance."* These curtains were a boundary to keep man out and to keep God in. Each set of curtains or veils were created for our protection. We cannot accidentally come upon God's presence, thus being consumed by Him. Even in the placement of the tribes around the Tabernacle, we see the Levites and Priests set up first, for they too are a boundary line for the rest of the Israelites. God wants to protect His people from His holiness, so He has designed boundary lines. The only way into the Outer Court of the Tabernacle was through the gate. All Israelites were invited and could worship in the Outer Court.

The Way

This entrance or gate was placed on the East side of the Outer Court perimeter. It was the gate by which all men would enter. This curtained entrance was 30 feet wide, woven of blue, purple and scarlet fabric. We have seen the significance of the colors, but let me remind you of the beautiful representations: blue signifies heaven, communion, and revelation; purple signifies the royalty and authority of Jesus; and scarlet speaks to sacrifice and bloodshed. The white fine linen signifies righteousness and holiness. We have already studied that the white fine linen was the clothing of the Priests. We will call this entrance "the way" for there was no other entrance. One could not go under the white fine linen curtains around the rest of the structure, nor could one climb over. No, the only way in was through this beautiful curtained gate. Jesus tells us in John 14:6 that HE is the WAY. He is not just one way, but the **only** way. Just as the Israelites had one way into the Outer Court of the Tabernacle, to begin our journey as a believer or Christian, we must go through the gate.

One of my favorite books is the allegory, Pilgrim's Progress (in Today's English) by John Bunyan and it illustrates this truth well. Christian (the main character) comes to the cross of Jesus (the gate) and when he approaches the cross, his burden loosens, drops from his shoulders and he experiences a joy and lightness in his heart, because his burdened has been lifted. As he leaves the cross to walk along the path, he meets two other men who have climbed over a wall to enter the path.

"Christian: Why did you not come in at the gate at the beginning of the way? You know, it is written in the book by the Builder of the road: 'He that cometh not in by the door, but climbeth up some other way, the same is a thief and a robber (John 10:1)'. They told him that to go to the gate from where they lived was considered too far by all and that the usual way was to take a shortcut and climb over the wall, as they had done.

Christian: But will it not be counted a trespass and a violation of instructions by the Lord of the City where you are going? They said he need not trouble his head about that, for they had a long-standing custom where they lived to guide them in their practice, and they could produce plenty of testimony of its practicality over a period of more than a thousand years.

Christian: But will it stand the final test? They thought so. They said that a custom of such long-standing most certainly had been accepted and, without a doubt, would be admitted by the impartial Judge at the end of the way. 'And,' they reasoned, 'we are in the same way you are in. What does it matter how we got in? If we are in, we are in. In what way is your position better?'

Christian: I walk by the rule of the Lord of the way; you follow your own fancy: the crude invention of uninspired men. You are called thieves already by the Lord of the way. Therefore I doubt that you will be found true men at the end. You came in by yourselves without His direction, and you shall go out by yourselves without His mercy." (p. 42)

In John 10:9, Jesus says, *"I am the gate; whoever enters through me will be saved. He will come in and go out, and find safe pasture."* He is our gate; our entrance to Salvation. This is the beginning of our life in Christ, our eternal life. We enter through the gate, Jesus, for He is the Way.

This entrance can be compared for us to entering or gaining access into the entryway of a home. You must enter by the gate (front door) and fellowship can happen in the entry way. The Lord is drawing us, first into fellowship with Him in the entryway. Jesus, in the book of Revelation (which is the revelation of Jesus Christ) describes Himself to one of the Asia Minor churches as though He was standing outside a door, knocking. *"Here I am! I stand at the door and knock. If anyone hears my voice and opens the door, I will come in and eat with him and he with me."* *(Revelation 3:20)* Jesus is speaking to those **in the church.** How many in the church do not have a relationship with Jesus? How many have not entered through the gate? How many do not know Jesus as the WAY? Come through the gate. Pass through the curtain. Open the door to the One who is drawing you to Himself. For there is no other way. Church membership does not get you through the gate, being good does not allow you to pass through the gate, giving money won't do it, helping with the injustices of the world will not allow you entrance. The only way is through the gate.

Once inside the Outer Court, the ministry of the priests began. The Israelites' sins were atoned for at the bronze altar, so they could then worship the Lord God Almighty in the Outer Court. At the entrance gate to the Outer Court, the sacrifice was made. Bloodshed was the way into the Tabernacle courtyard. Bloodshed is the way of entrance into the life of a believer; not the blood of animals, but the blood of Jesus, who was shed once and for all. Jesus shed his blood, became the sin offering on behalf of all mankind. We need to make the decision to trust in that sacrifice, to walk through that entrance, to then enjoy the fellowship of the outer court. David loved to be in the courts of the Lord. Psalm 84:1-2 gives us a glimpse of David's desire to spend time in the Lord's presence, *"How lovely is your dwelling place, O Lord Almighty! My soul yearns, even faints, for the courts of the Lord; my heart and flesh cry out for the living God."* What a picture of David's love for His God. He entered through the gate, and that began a journey of desiring more and more intimacy with His Lord. How about you? Could the words of that psalm be your words? Do you yearn to spend time in God's presence? Does your heart and flesh cry out for the living God? Be honest. This study is to give us a chance to see the Tabernacle of the Old Testament in light of living in a new covenant. Have you entered through the gate? Do you watch others who have a love for the Lord, wondering how does that happen? Or maybe you are yearning to be in His presence. This leads us to the next curtain of the Tabernacle.

The Truth
The structure of the Inner Court (which held the Holy Place and the Most Holy Place) was made of 48 boards with five boards on each side as crossbars. The middle crossbar on each side was to extend from end to end. This reminds me of the center shaft of the Lampstand which connects the others together.

This veiled entrance into the Holy Place (from the Outer Court), was designed with blue, purple and scarlet with cherubim woven into them. At this curtain the cherubim are protecting the presence of the Lord. Again, we see a barrier, a boundary to keep man out so he does not stumble upon the presence of God Almighty. Remember, the

Priests were the only ones who could enter the Holy Place. This entrance leads us into a reality of Truth; a truth of who God is and who we are in Him. This is a deeper level of intimacy. For the Israelites, the Holy Place held the Golden Lampstand, which illuminated the Table of Showbread and the Golden Altar of Incense. The room would be dark, except for the light of the Lampstand. Light = Truth. John 8:32 says, *"Then you will know the truth and the truth will set you free."* The word truth is the Greek word "aletheia" meaning unveiled reality. The Lord opens His Truth to us, as we commune with Him.

This entrance for us, into the Holy Place can be compared to entering the kitchen; this is where relationship happens as we break bread with one another. Kitchen intimacy is deeper than entryway intimacy. Not everyone is invited to come on into the kitchen.

2 Corinthians 3:18 tells us, '*And we, who with unveiled faces all reflect the Lord's glory, are being transformed into his likeness, with ever-increasing glory, which comes from the Lord, who is the Spirit."* In the light of the Lampstand, which is the anointing of the Holy Spirit, and as we partake of His body and blood (representing communion at the Table of Showbread), and lift up our worship, prayer and intercession to the Lord, the TRUTH is unveiled. The Spirit of the Lord, which is the Spirit of Truth (John 14:17) and He reveals the truth to us! Isaiah 11:2, which we looked at as we studied the Golden Lampstand, reveals the seven Spirits of God (or seven ways the Spirit works in our lives). This verse says, *"The Spirit of the Lord will rest on him~ the Spirit of wisdom and of understanding, the Spirit of counsel and of power, the Spirit of knowledge and of the fear of the Lord"*. In the Holy Place, the place of intimacy, the Spirit of the Lord brings forth revelation of who He is and who we are in

Him. We are strengthened and equipped and loved by the Father. Let's take a look at the ways that the Holy Spirit reveals His truth to us by looking at Isaiah 11:2.

- ***The Spirit of the Lord will rest on him***~ The word for Lord is YAHWEH (YHWH) is our covenant God, the one who always exists. He who is involved in every detail of our lives, who wants a relationship with each person on earth. He is the one who wants to make a special revelation of Himself to us.
- ***Spirit of wisdom***~ Wisdom is the Hebrew word "chochmah" which indicates wise insight, skillfulness, whether in the artistic sense or the moral sense. YHWH desires to share His wisdom with us. His wisdom is from heaven, it is not from this earth. There is no limit to His wisdom. James 3:17 tells us about His wisdom, *"But the wisdom that comes from heaven is first of all pure; then peace-loving, considerate, submissive, full of mercy, and good fruit, impartial and sincere."* There is no agenda with God! He desires to make us wise by His Holy Spirit. That wisdom comes from heaven, so the only way to be equipped with heavenly wisdom is to sit quietly before the Lord, in fellowship with Him. This is what He wants to give His children~ wisdom that comes from heaven!
- ***Spirit of understanding***~ The word for understanding in Hebrew is "bina" which means insight, revelation, discernment, good sense. Imagine if we lived with insight, discernment, and good sense! This world needs the Spirit of Understanding to come! As believers commune with the Lord in the Holy Place, His Spirit will release insight, revelation, and discernment.

213

- *Spirit of counsel~* "Esa" is the Hebrew word which means a plan, purpose and strategy. What are you facing that you need the Spirit of counsel to give a plan or purpose of strategy to? We are told in John 16:7 that the Holy Spirit is the Counselor. And John 14:16 tells us that the Counselor will be with us forever! There have been many times in my life that I just didn't know what to do or which direction to go and the Counselor (Holy Spirit) was the one to give the plan, purpose or strategy. Sometimes it has been an obvious, hit me over the head explanation and other times it has been a feeling of peace that has washed over me or a feeling of "don't do that" that has stopped me in my tracks. The Holy Spirit will counsel. He is the Spirit of counsel. We spend much time and money on counselors of this world, seeking the answers to many of our questions or healing all the while the Holy Spirit is gently calling out "Come seek Me. I have the answers. Spend time with me in the Holy Place."

- *Spirit of power~* Might; strength, mighty works; source of strength are wrapped up in this Hebrew word, "gbura". I will ask: Anyone need a source of strength? Who needs might? Anything in your life that needs a mighty work of power? I can tell you that as a mother of three children, there have been plenty of times when my kids were babies when I have called out to the Holy Spirit for the strength to make it through the day! And as those kids walked through times of difficulty that I didn't know how to answer them or even pray for them, I would call out to God for His releasing of might to be my source of strength or to be their source of strength and might! Thank you for your Spirit of power which rests on me!

214

- *Spirit of knowledge~* Knowledge is the Hebrew word, "da'at" stands for learning; to have knowledge; to be well-informed; to have understanding. How I love to learn! I was made for school! In fact, my college degree is in Education, so I went from elementary, middle, high school, on to college, then back to Elementary School! I had Christmas vacation and Easter break and summers off until I was 29 years old. Studying the Word of God is my favorite book to study. And God is faithful to release His Spirit of Knowledge as I study His Word. John 14:17 calls the Holy Spirit "the Spirit of Truth". As you are studying God's Word, His truth will be revealed in your life, an unveiling into the deeper realities of God's Kingdom.

- *Spirit of the fear of the Lord~* This Hebrew word for fear of the Lord is "yira" which indicates a reverence, worship, awe, to revere or lift high. How do you reverence God's name? What are the ways you worship Him or lift high His name? This is part of the Holy Place. The closer you get to Him, the more reverence for Him you will display in your life.

This is the seven-fold Spirit who changes us and transforms us as He invades us. That happens as the TRUTH is illuminated in the Holy Place.

LIFE
The veil into the Most Holy Place, separated even the Priests from the Shekinah Glory of God (the place where His presence dwelt). LIFE is represented in this veil. God Himself dwelt between the Cherubim on the mercy seat in the Most Holy Place (resting on the Ark of the Covenant). Only the High Priest could enter into the Most Holy Place

215

through the woven veil and that happened only once a year, on the Day of Atonement. Moses was the only one who could approach God at any time. He would meet with God to hear what He had to say to the people and he would talk with God like a man speaks with a friend. Moses was the only one who had access to the Holy of Holies, which held God's presence.

Cherubim were woven into this veil of blue, purple and scarlet. The Cherubim were the powerful creatures and guards of the MOST HOLY ONE! Their presence announced God's presence (just beyond the veil) and they protected His presence. To see the Cherubim on this veil would signify the magnificent presence of God Almighty. This was the One who, in the wilderness, led the Israelites by day in a pillar of cloud and by night in a pillar of fire. They have witnessed His power in the wilderness by a cloud covering the Mountain of God when Moses visited with God to receive the instructions for the people and the pattern for the Tabernacle (Exodus 24). *"To the Israelites the glory of the Lord looked like a consuming fire on the top of the mountain," (Exodus 24:17).* The people had witnessed the miracles of God in the wilderness, beginning with the crossing of the Red Sea, where God parted the waters and provided dry land for them to pass through to nourishment given to sustain them in the desert (manna & quail), water had been miraculously turned from bitter to sweet. Oh, these Israelites knew the power in the presence of God. Each year when the High Priest would enter the Holy of Holies on the Day of Atonement, a rope would be tied around his ankle, so if God did not accept the offering of the Priest, the Priest would be consumed by the holiness of God. The Israelites would wait in quiet anticipation for the Priest to return from the Most Holy Place to the entrance of the Tent of Meeting (Outer Court) to have the

216

assurance that their sins had been atoned for ~ salvation had come for that year (Hebrews 9:28).

The Most Holy Place is a place of the deepest level of intimacy. This entrance can be correlated to the intimacy between a husband and wife. Many may be invited into the entryway, less will be invited into the kitchen to build relationship, but the intimacy between one man and one woman is the intimacy of the bedroom. No one *knows* my husband, Greg the way I *know* him. And no one *knows* me the way that Greg *knows* me. This is LIFE, intimacy. It is a relationship that can withstand any pressure from the outside or inside. This is the deepest place of intimacy. And God invites us to have that level of intimacy with Him. Hebrews 10:19-20 says, *"Therefore brothers, since we have confidence to enter the Most Holy Place by the blood of Jesus, by a new and living way opened for us through the curtain, that is, his body."* The curtain was torn from top to bottom at the moment Jesus died on the cross, giving everyone access to the Most Holy Place. *"And when Jesus had cried out again in a loud voice, he gave up his spirit. At that moment the curtain of the temple was torn in two from top to bottom. The earth shook and the rocks split open."* *(Matthew 27:50-51)* What an event that was! The thick curtain (4-8 inches wide) was torn from top to bottom. This curtain was 15 feet tall. Torn from top to bottom~ it is finished. God can now have a relationship with man that is full of intimacy. No more separation. No more blood sacrifice needed. Jesus paid the price and it is done! *"Let us then approach the throne of grace with confidence, so that we may receive mercy and find grace to help us in our time of need."* *(Hebrews 4:16)* The throne of grace is the mercy seat! We can approach the mercy seat of God with confidence. He desires us to sit with Him, seek His face, and approach Him when we are in need. He wants relationship with us. Thank you Jesus for paying the highest price, for being the atoning sacrifice for our sins, that we may have a relationship with the Most High God.

"Jesus answered, 'I am the WAY, the TRUTH and the LIFE. No one comes to the Father except through me." *John 14:6*

Spend some time thanking Jesus for being the WAY, the TRUTH and the LIFE in your life.

Jesus, you are THE WAY:
Jesus, you are THE TRUTH:
Jesus, you are THE LIFE:

STUDY GUIDE
Chapter 8: The Curtains & the Veils

Scripture to memorize: *"Jesus answered, 'I am the way, the truth and the life. No one comes to the Father except through me." John 14:6*

Key Questions:
1) Recall your experience of approaching God~ going through the gate. Can you share it?
2) Describe the Cherubim. What words & images come to your mind to express them.
3) How do you see the 3 curtains : The WAY (entrance into the Outer Court), the TRUTH (entrance into the Holy Place), and the LIFE (entrance into the Most Holy Place)?

In the Sinai Desert, the Tabernacle stood as a reminder that God is the God of the Israelites. He desired to make this nation His holy people. This week we are going to study further the curtains that surrounded the Tabernacle, the veil that separated the Holy Place from the Outer Court, and the veil that separated the Holy Place from the Most Holy Place. We will also take a look at the curtained roof that covered the Inner Court (which contained the Holy Place and the Most Holy Place).

Day 1: The Outer Court of the Tabernacle

 There was a stark contrast of the desert conditions and the fine white linen curtains that surrounded the Outer Court, on the North, South, West and part of the East side. These curtains were supported by 60 pillars of bronze with bronze bases around the perimeter of the Outer Court. The height of the wall created by these curtains was 7 ½ feet high. The Outer Court was the place where man began his approach to God.

The fine linen curtains (which acted as a wall surrounding the Outer Court) was a type of separation~ this spoke to the people; one could only enter by the gate (John 10:9). All Israelites were invited and could worship in the Outer Court.

1) Read Exodus 27:9-15. Recall your experience of approaching God. What was it that drew you through the gate?

2) Read Psalm 84:1-2 How does David feel about the outer court?

- Curtains of fine linen~ speaks of righteousness & holiness (this was the dress of the Priests – Exodus 28:39-41 & the saints in the Holy City—Rev. 19:8).
- Bronze pillars & bases~ speaks to the judgment of sin (the Israelites needed to recognize the reality of their condition—as a sinner. This was apparent in all aspects to the Outer Court; for bronze was the metal used in the Outer Court).
- Pillars~ speak to the standing, stability, uprightness (we see God appearing to the Israelites in the desert in a pillar of cloud or a pillar of fire).
- 60 pillars~ there are 60 men running through Joseph's side (Matt.1:1-16 & Luke 3:23-38) in the blood line from Adam to Christ. These 60 men were faithful, Covenant men. We also see the number 6 & 10 in sixty (6 speaks to man & 10 speaks to the law)

3) Read Exodus 27:17-19. What are the hooks and bands to be made of?

We, the pillars are set in bronze, but are connected with silver (the atonement money/ransom). These bands were used to keep the pillars in place, so they would not move around or sway with the weather. The hooks on the top of the pillars were to hold the curtains, so they wouldn't fall on the ground & be defiled by the dirt of the earth. We need to be like those hooks; holding a godly standard of righteousness in the earth.

4) What does Isaiah 54:1-3 say to the church (Christ's body)?

There was only one way into the Outer Court and that was through the gate. John 14:6 says, *"I am the Way, the Truth and the Life; no one comes to the Father except through me."* This Outer Court gate represents Jesus as the WAY.

5) Read Exodus 27:16-18. Describe what the gate (curtain) is made of?

6) Read Psalm 100:4. How should we enter through this gate?

We see the colors of Christ's beauty defined in this curtain. The blue signifies revelation, communion and heaven. Purple speaks to royalty & authority and scarlet as the sacrifice and bloodshed. And fine linen (Christ's righteousness) was woven in and through with the colored linens. Four (in the number of pillars supporting the curtain) speaks to the number of the earth~ Jesus wants the gate open to all who would come throughout the world (from the North, South, East & West). We also see the 4 gospels (Matthew, Mark, Luke & John), that point to the earthly ministry of Jesus.

Day 2: The entrance into the Holy Place
The next 2 veils we will study are the two entrances into the Inner Court. The first veil is into the Holy Place. We

saw in Day 1 that the curtains refer to the scripture John 14:6 *"I am the Way, the Truth, and the Life."* This second entrance represents Jesus being the TRUTH.

Let's take a look at the structure of the Inner Court (the Holy Place & the Most Holy Place).

1) Read Exodus 26:15. What wood is used for the frames? How are they to be placed?

2) Read Exodus 26:16—24. How many frames (boards) are to be standing to support the Inner Court coverings?

We see again the acacia wood (shittim) that the boards/frames are constructed with. The acacia represents the sinless, incorruptible life that Jesus lived. And each is covered with Gold (representing His Deity), see Exodus 26:25. Each board was standing up to be upright before the presence of the Lord.

3) Read Ephesians 6:10-18. How many times do you see the word "stand"?
We need to be upright & standing, just like these boards.

The 48 boards were standing on their own, and yet they were to stand together to create the dwelling place for God Almighty. We see in the church today, there are many believers and we need to be able to stand on our own, however we, collectively make up the body of Christ. We are to be unified as His body.

4) Read Ephesians 2:21-22. What does this say to us, His body?

48 boards standing upright~ the number 48 has the number 4 (representing earth & the number 12 meaning Divine Government/Authority/United). We also see in Joshua 21, there are 48 cities given to the Levites. WOW! God is in every detail! We see that over & over!

The silver bases speak to the ransom. Jesus was sold for 30 pieces of silver. I Corinthians 6;20 says, *'you were bought at a price."*

5) Read Exodus 26:26-29. How many crossbars are used?

We see the number 5 repeated. Five is the number of grace. We see God's grace in each side of the Tabernacle! As they were inserted into the gold rings, it would make a very firm structure. The center crossbar was to extend from end to end. We see the center shaft of the Golden Lampstand in this crossbar—Jesus is what joins us together. The frames were overlaid with Gold (showing the humanity of Christ, in the acacia wood and the Deity of Christ, in the gold). This is the recurring theme in the Tabernacle.

A veil is used to hide something. When a bride walks down the aisle at her wedding, her face is veiled (it hides her face from her beloved), until at the altar, the veil is removed and her face is seen in all its radiance! The veil at the Holy Place entrance was there to keep the presence of God inside.

Read Exodus 26:36. What is this curtain (veil) made of?By this entrance, only the Priests could enter. The Outer Court gate was open to all who would come. All the Israelite community could worship in the Outer Court. But only the Priests could pass through this curtain. The ministry of the

Priest took place behind the veil. We see the colors of blue, scarlet & purple intertwined with the white fine linen.

6) Write out what the colors represent (refer to Day 1):

Exodus 26:37 says, *"Make gold hooks for this curtain and five posts of acacia wood over laid with gold. And cast five bronze bases for them."*

Again we see the perfect humanity of Christ in the acacia wood and His deity in the wood overlaid with gold. The 5 gold hooks speak to the grace of God. Five also represents the first five books of the Bible (the Torah for the Hebrews). The bronze bases show again the judgment of sin that was laid upon Jesus. This is the basis that we have access into the Holy Place.

7) Draw in the Inner Court on your Tabernacle diagram. Draw dots for the posts (you may have already drawn the small rectangular shape on your diagram). Just add some detail. The posts and the curtain entrance (of blue, scarlet & purple).

Day 3: The Veil into the Most Holy Place

John 14:6 says, *"I am the WAY, the TRUTH and the LIFE"*. The veil into the Most Holy Place reveals Jesus as the LIFE!

1) What do the following verses say about the Cherubim?
   - Psalm 18:9-10:
   - I Samuel 4:4
   - I Kings 8:6-7
   - Numbers 7:89
   - Psalm 80:1

224

- Psalm 99:1
- Ezekiel 9:3

Cherubim were powerful guards to the Divine Throne. We see them as "living creatures" in Ezekiel. "Living creatures" means "burning ones". What a description!

2) Describe the living creatures (Cherubim) in Ezekiel 1:5-11.

3) Describe the living creatures (Cherubim) in Revelation 4:6-9.

These Cherubim are what was woven into the veil leading into the Most Holy Place. They were guards of the Most Holy ONE! Their presence in the veil (& we will see later that they are woven into the 1st layered curtain of the roof of the Inner Court) served two purposes. They announced God's presence~ beyond the veil and they protected His presence. They watched over the mercy seat (where the presence of the Lord rested). The Cherubim guarded the shekinah glory of God from the eyes of the Priests.

Exodus 26:32 tells us that the veil was hung upon four posts of acacia wood overlaid with gold and standing on four silver bases. Again, we see the two natures of Christ represented in the wood & the gold (his perfect humanity and the gold, his Deity). He was the God-man. The four posts speak to us of the 4 gospels of the New Testament that are to go to all the earth (4 being the number of earth). The posts stood on the base (foundation) of redemption (we see that in the silver—which speaks to ransom/redemption).

4) Read Hebrews 9:7. How often did the High Priest enter the Most Holy Place?

5) Paul tells us how we enter through this veil into the Most Holy Place. Read Hebrews 10:19-20. On what basis do we have access?

6) What happened when Jesus gave up his spirit while he was hanging on the cross? See Matthew 27:51.

The veil was torn in two from the top to bottom symbolizing the fulfillment of the Old Covenant, the Mosaic Law with all its sacrifices and rituals.

Hebrews 9:10 speaks to the Old Covenant:
"They are a matter of food and drink and
various ceremonial washings~ external
regulations applying until the time of the new order".
The new order came with the death & resurrection
of Jesus Christ~ The God-Man! He paid the highest
price. He became our once and for all atoning
sacrifice, so that we might have entrance into the
Most Holy Place. It is now available to all. *"For this*
reason Christ is the mediator of a new covenant, that those
who are called may receive the promised eternal
inheritance~ now that he has died as a ransom to set them
free from the sins committed under the first covenant."
Hebrews: 9:15

Day 4: The curtains that make up the covering over the Inner Court (Part 1)

There were four layers of curtains that formed the covering over the Inner Court (which consisted of the Holy Place and the Most Holy Place). They were hung over the framework of the Inner Court (we studied the framework on Day 2). God gave the Divine design of the order of the curtains. Today we will study those four layers of curtains.

226

1) Read Exodus 26:1-6. The first layer: These curtains were placed directly over the structure of the Inner Court. It was the roof that the Priests would see if they looked above them.
    - How many curtains of finely twisted linen (blue, purple and scarlet)?
    - What is to be woven into the linen?
    - How long & wide are the curtains to be?
    - How many curtains are joined together?
    - What are the loops to be made of?
    - How many loops on each curtain?
    - How many gold clasps are used to fasten them together?

2) Read Exodus 26:7-13. The second layer: These curtains were placed over the finely twisted linen curtains.
    - What were they made of?
    - How many altogether?
    - How long & wide are the curtains to be?
    - How many curtains into one set?
    - How many in the other set?
    - How many loops in each set?
    - How many bronze clasps to fasten the tent together?
    - How is the curtain to be hung over the rear of the Inner Court?

3) Read Exodus 26:14. The third & fourth layer: These coverings were to be placed over the second layer (Goat hair).
    - What is the third layer to be made of?
    - What color is this skin to be dyed?
    - What is the outer layer to be made of?

- Was the outer covering over the Inner Court attractive?

Let's take a look more closely at these curtains & coverings.

The first layer of finely twisted linen had the Cherubim woven into the fabric. Imagine that scene for when the Priests lifted their eyes up to the roof of the Inner Court, they would see the deep beautiful colors of linen fabric with the powerful Cherubim embroidered into the fabric. We studied the Cherubim in Day 3 in a little detail.

4) Imagine you are a Priest standing in the Holy Place at the Altar of Incense; ministering before the Lord there. You watch the smoke from the incense rise up and you glance up to watch it rise. What you see are the Cherubim woven in the linen curtains. Describe what you feel?

5) How would the following verses be significant (in the Inner Court):
- Psalm 63:7 ~
- Psalm 91:4~
- Psalm 17:8~
- Psalm 61:4~

There were ten curtains of the same size (42 feet long and 6 feet wide). They were joined in two groups of five. Ten speaks to the law. There were 10 commandments. The number 10 also means a "journey", and we know that the Israelites spent their lives wandering on a journey in the wilderness. The curtains were arranged in two groups of five: 5 being the number for grace and the number 2 speaks to multiplication. The grace was multiplied in this Inner Court to the Priests. For us, as we take refuge under his wings. His grace is sufficient for us and it is multiplied unto

228

us. The loops were made of blue fabric (blue meaning heaven, revelation & communion). And the gold clasps were used to fasten the curtains together. Gold represents the Deity of Christ. There were 50 loops & 50 clasps~ the number 50 signifies freedom! The Year of Jubilee was the 50th year. We also see Pentecost celebrated on the 50th day. Pentecost means "fifty". This curtain was foreshadowing the freedom to come!

> 6) Can you summarize this curtain's meaning? What does it mean for you?

Day 5: The curtains that make up the covering over the Inner Court (Part 2)

The second layer was a curtain of goats' hair. This was placed over the curtains of fine linen. This was the second covering over the structure of the Inner Court. The goat hair used here was most likely black. That was common in that part of the world. In Song of Songs 1:5, the Beloved is comparing herself to the tent curtains: *"dark like the tents of Kedar, like the tent curtains of Solomon."*

The number of curtains of goats' hair is to be eleven. This is a number that means disorder and lawlessness. (We see this in the behavior of the Israelites, almost from the beginning of their deliverance.) It is one more than ten (the number for order & law).

We see the goat being used in the sacrifices on the Day of Atonement. Two goats were used. One was sacrificed and the other was a "scapegoat" carrying the sins of the people into the wilderness (Lev. 16:5, 15-22).

We see the goat used in the Covenant that God made with Abraham.

1) Read Genesis 15:9-21. Describe the scene.

The goat was used in the burnt offering, fellowship (peace) offering and the sin offering ~ all that were offered on the Bronze Altar for the people.

There were two sets of curtains of goats' hair. One set was of five (number 5 is the number for grace) curtains and another set was made up of six (number six is the number for man) curtains. God's grace is upon all mankind, even in the midst of disorder and lawlessness (represented by the number 11). It is his grace that draws us to himself.

2) Read Ephesians 2:1-5. How do you see these verses in the curtain made of goats' hair?

The 50 loops again (speaking to freedom & liberty) and 50 bronze clasps were used to fasten them together as a unit. The bronze was seen in the offerings made at the Altar (the Bronze Altar—symbolizing judgment of sin). Isn't it fitting that this covering would be black? Our sin results in death (the color black). Thank you, Jesus that you paid the sin offering on our behalf! Jesus took our sin to the cross~ the Altar.

3) Respond to these curtains. What do they mean to you?

The next layer is the covering of rams' skins dyed red. This covering was laid over the goats' hair. So, the progression: The linen curtain woven with the Cherubim, the goats' hair (black), and next is the rams' skins dyed red.

4) Read Genesis 15:9. What animal is used here in the Covenant that God makes with Abraham?

5) Read Genesis 22:1-13. What animal was used in the sacrifice?

The ram was used in the sacrifices at the Bronze Altar, in the burnt offering, the fellowship offering (peace), guilt offering, and in the ordination of the Priests. The Ram was symbolic of strength and power. A ram is a male sheep.

The rams' skins were dyed red. Red is the color of sacrificial blood. Jesus is seen in this covering. The blood sacrifices at the Bronze Altar were a foreshadowing of the blood that Jesus would shed on the cross. The spotless lamb of God to take away the sins of the world! And we will see the blood-stained robe again. In Revelation 19:13 we see the picture of the Victorious One on a white horse. *"He is dressed in a robe dipped in blood, and His name is the Word of God."* I can't wait for that Glorious Day!

6) What does this covering speak to you?

The final covering of the Inner Court is the hides of sea cows (or badger skins or dolphin hides or seal skins). These were animals of plenty in the Red Sea. They were a blue-ish gray color. This would be a heavy protective covering from the elements of the earth in the desert regions. These hides or skins were also used to cover all the furniture of the Tabernacle while the Israelites traveled.

From the outside, there was nothing to attract one to the Tabernacle. We have seen this comparison with Jesus, that there was nothing to attract one to him—no physical beauty. Isaiah 53:2. *"He had no beauty or majesty to attract us to Him, nothing in his appearance that we should desire him."*

7) Thank the Lord for His protection for you from the "elements" in the world..

8) To conclude the study this week, draw the curtains & coverings. This is a good way to solidify what you have learned. Write a key verse or thought to remind you of its significance to you.
   - Finely twisted linen curtain (blue, purple and scarlet) with Cherubim woven in the fabric
   - Goats' hair curtains
   - Rams' skins dyed red
   - Hides of sea cows (dolphins/badgers/seals)

Chapter 9:
The Priests

We see God's plan unfold in part in Exodus 19:5-6. This gave the people a glimpse of what God was doing and the call that He brought forth. God was initiating the institution of the priesthood. *"Now if you obey me fully and keep my covenant, then out of all nations you will be mine, you will be for me a kingdom of priests and a holy nation." (Exodus 19:5-6).* Three months after the Israelites left Egypt in the miraculous Red Sea crossing, God speaks these words of covenant to the Israelite community. How He loves His chosen people. He calls them out from all other nations to be separate; to be a kingdom of priests and a holy nation. Without the Priesthood, the Tabernacle would have been useless. The Israelites were unable to minister before the Lord, they needed a mediator, someone to go between them and God. This was the reason of the establishment of the Priesthood.

The office of Priest is mentioned 700 times in the Old Testament, and approximately 80 times in the New Testament. Since it is mentioned so often, we need to pay attention; dig deep to uncover the importance of the priesthood and how it relates to us today. In our study of the Tabernacle, we have studied the "what" of the Priests (their work & ministry to the Lord), now we are going to see the "who" of the Priesthood. Throughout the week, as you go day by day, you will study who the priests were, the consecration of the priests, the specific clothing of the priest and High Priest: looking at the specifics of the Aaronic priesthood, the Old Testament priesthood.

In the fulfillment of the Old Testament Tabernacle model, Jesus is our Great High Priest. Hebrews 8:1-2 says this, *"The point of what we are saying is this: We do have such a high priest, who sat down at the right hand of the throne of the Majesty in heaven, and who serves in the sanctuary, the true Tabernacle set up by the Lord, not by man."* The priest acted as the mediator between the people and God. Hebrews goes on to say in chapter 8:6, *"But the ministry Jesus has received is as superior to theirs as the covenant of which he is mediator is superior to the old one, and it is founded on better promises."* Jesus is our great high priest. And He has established a new order of priesthood. We have studied that the Old Testament Tabernacle was just a shadow of what is to come. Even the priesthood was foreshadowing the Great High Priest, Jesus, who even now, continues to appear before God on our behalf. *"For Christ did not enter a man-made sanctuary that was only a copy of the true one; he entered heaven itself, now to appear for us in God's presence. Nor did he enter heaven to offer himself again and again, the way the high priest enters the Most Holy Place every year with blood that is not his own. Then Christ would have had to suffer many times since the creation of the world. But now he has appeared once for all at the end of the ages to do away with sin by the sacrifice of himself."* (Hebrews 9:24-26)

Jesus has a new order, a new priesthood, under the new covenant. We are that priesthood of believers. We have been called into the priesthood, just as Aaron was called into the Old Testament priesthood. Our calling is one to minister to the Lord and declare His praises to the earth! And His calling upon is secure. Romans 11:29 tells us, *"for God's gifts and his call are irrevocable".*

The calling ~ For the Israelites, that calling to the priesthood was to Aaron and his descendants only. Exodus

28:1 says, *"Have Aaron your brother brought to you from among the Israelites, along with his sons Nadab and Abihu, Eleazar and Ithamar, so they may serve me as priests."* This was the beginning of the priesthood, called the Aaronic Priesthood (named after the first High Priest, Aaron). They had the privilege to enter the holy place as priests and to minister before the people and before God Almighty. And this privilege was only given to Aaron and his descendants. No other tribe would be called. And this was God's establishment. No resumes going out, no job interviews~ it was the Lord's decision. For us, every believer is called to be a priest. We have been called & chosen. No others have been called, but the believers. For it is said of us, *"But you are a chosen people, a **royal priesthood,** a holy nation, a people belonging to God, that you may declare the praises of him who called you out of darkness into his wonderful light."* (I Peter 2:9) Do you hear the echo of God's early plan from Exodus 19:5-6? God is establishing this new kingdom of priests in you and me. What a privilege to be called!

The service ~ Read the two verses above (Exodus 28:1 and I Peter 2:9). What is the number one service reflected in both of these priesthoods? Serving God is how it is written in the Old Testament and in the New it is written "to declare the praises of him". To serve the living God in the Tabernacle is our first responsibility. We have read this in previous chapters, worship before work! Keep the main thing the main thing! Sit at Jesus' feet, like Mary did. She chose the better thing, scripture tells us. This service or ministry to Jesus is all about relationship: spending time with Jesus in the inner sanctuary of your heart to know Him, to know what He loves and what He hates, to know who He is, to know how much He loves you & all the people of earth, to keep your focus on those things that last for eternity. This knowing is discovered in relationship, like a bride discovering more and more of her groom. For that is who we are—His bride. And He wants to tell us the secrets in His heart. He desires to pour His love upon us more and more; to increase our understanding and wisdom; to seek Him, as David did. Oh that we would desire to gaze upon Him in the beauty of His Temple. Psalm 27:4, *"One thing I ask of the Lord, this is what I seek; that I may dwell in the house of the Lord all the days of my life, to gaze upon the beauty of the Lord and to seek Him in his temple."* In what ways do you serve Jesus? How do you minister to Him in the Tabernacle of your heart? Is worship the highest goal of your heart?

The priest was the mediator between God and man, so not only did the priest minister to the Lord, he also had the duties of mediating between God and man. We have witnessed this as we studied the various vessels in the Tabernacle. At the bronze altar, the priests made atonement for the sins of the people and at the golden altar of incense the priests ascended the fragrance of incense to the Lord, as they interceded on behalf of the Israelites. When the priests would exit the Tabernacle, a blessing would be spoken over the community. Numbers 6:22-27 reads, *"The Lord said to Moses, 'Tell Aaron and his sons, 'This is how you are to bless the Israelites. Say to them: "The Lord bless you and keep you; the Lord make His face shine upon you and be gracious to you; the Lord turn his face toward you and give you peace." So I will put my name on the Israelites, and I will bless them.'"* This was a pronouncement over the people's lives. God is marking His people with His name. Since we are a priesthood, we need to make this pronouncement over others. Do you know people who need His NAME marked upon them? Begin to speak this out over them, that the presence of heaven would be upon their lives. The peace spoken of in the verse, is the shalom of God, which is a wholeness of body, soul and spirit. Oh that believers would walk in the shalom of God; that the Lord would restore His people with His protection, His mercy and compassion upon, His approval, and with His NAME.

The inheritance ~ We have the priesthood as our inheritance, just as Aaron and his descendents experienced this inheritance. They were "born into" the priesthood and so are we! We see this today in our culture when a father has a son who will take over the family business and the business stays in the family for generations. For Aaron's sons, they did not think "Oh I wonder what I will do with my life? Will I be a perfumer? Or maybe a metal-worker?" No, they were born into the priesthood. And it was secure. Exodus 28:43b says, *"This is to be a lasting ordinance for Aaron and his descendants."* What an inheritance we have. We are born into God's family so we are called children of God. We enter into His eternal dwelling place, to experience life with Jesus, the Son of God. John 1:12-13 says, *"Yet to all who received him, to those who believed in his name, he gave the right to become children of God—children born not of natural descent, nor of human decision or a husband's will, but born of God."* Romans 8:15-17 tells us, *"For you did not receive a spirit that makes you a slave again to fear, but you received the Spirit of Sonship. And by him we cry 'Abba, Father'. The Spirit himself testifies with our spirit that we are God's children. Now if we are children, then we are heirs—heirs of God and co-heirs with Christ, if indeed we share in his sufferings in order that we may also share in his glory."* What an inheritance! God calls us co-heirs with Christ. Do you have an understanding of what that means? He calls us his sons and daughters. Our inheritance is that of royalty. Our father is GOD Almighty. Our brother is Jesus. We will partake in the end of the age of the beautiful inheritance, sharing with the Son of God.

237

Oh Lord, that we would be Your people, walking in the knowledge of who we are; sons and daughters of the Great High King. We don't need to wonder about our future, it is secure in Christ Jesus. Read through Revelation 21-22 to see what we are inheriting!

The security ~ Aaron and his descendants had complete assurance that their position would not be taken away. We too have security in our position as sons of the promise. We are told in Hebrews 7:24 that because Jesus lives forever, His priesthood is permanent. It will not be taken from the believers. In Revelation 5:10 we are given the scene in heaven and the priesthood is identified. *"You have made them to be a kingdom and priests to serve our God and they will reign on the earth."* The establishment of the priesthood goes on forever; here on earth and at Jesus' return, we will reign with Him on earth as priests. Romans 8:38-39 gives us the security that there is nothing on earth or in the heavenlies that could separate us from Jesus, *"For I am convinced that neither death nor life, neither angels nor demons, neither the present nor the future, nor any powers, neither height nor depth, nor anything else in all creation, will be able to separate us from the love of God that is in Christ Jesus."*

We, the believers need to get an understanding of what we have been called to in Jesus. So many of us are deeply connected to the world, without the revelation that we are called to be in service (ministry) to Jesus first and foremost. Let's use David's cry in Psalm 27:4 to discover what it means to be a priest of the Lord:

Message translation, *"I'm asking God for one thing, only one thing: To live with Him in His house my whole life. I'll contemplate His beauty; I'll study at His feet."*

238

New King James (NKJ) translation, *"One thing I have desired of the Lord, that I will seek: That I may dwell in the house of the Lord all the days of my life, to behold the beauty of the Lord, and to inquire in His temple."*

New International Version (NIV), *"One thing I ask of the Lord, this is what I seek; that I may dwell in the house of the Lord all the days of my life, to gaze upon the beauty of the Lord and to seek Him in His temple."*

David's desire was to dwell with the Lord in His tabernacle. To dwell means "to live, inhabit, to be settled, stay, or remain". David restored the ark of God's presence in Jerusalem during his kingship. He established priests, worshippers and gatekeepers to minister to the presence of the Lord twenty four-seven. David sat before the Lord. He remained with Him. God is calling the believers to establish David's Tabernacle again on the earth, to have a place to hold His weighty presence; a place where His Glory can dwell. And God is moving on the hearts of His people around the world to be His priests, ministering to Him in the Tabernacle. God is looking for people to prepare a place for Him, that there would be a place where people may go and sit, like David before His presence.

David wanted to burn from the inside out! Moses, at the burning bush, left his flock to go after the flame! In John 12, Mary broke a jar of expensive perfume and poured it out upon Jesus' feet and wiped his feet with her hair. This was an act of extravagant worship. It was the fragrance of intimacy. David, Moses and Mary all experienced the beauty and friendship and intimacy of the Lord, for they remained with Him. Those who pursue Jesus in the Tabernacle gain intimacy with Him. Each of those laid aside their "reputation" to be close to Jesus. According to the natural man, sitting before the Lord, dwelling with Him in the Tabernacle is a waste of time. This is a spiritual desire. We are His priests, set to minister before Him. And as David says in 2 Samuel 6:22, "*I will become even more undignified than this, and I will be humiliated in my own eyes.*" Are you concerned about what you look like? Or do you desire to dwell with Jesus? What is your spiritual appetite for Him?

David's desire was to dwell in the house of the Lord all his days and to gaze upon his beauty. To gaze means "to seek; to look; to observe; to choose". I choose to look at his beauty. I observe his beauty. I look or seek His beauty. How do I accomplish this? If I am going to gaze at my husband, I look at him; almost like I am studying him. Or if I am gazing upon the night sky with the beautiful stars and the fullness of the moon, I set my face to the sky and observe the darkness and the lights that dot the background. I purpose to fix my gaze. That is what is meant in this verse, too. We purpose to look at the beauty of Christ. In order to seek Him; observe Him, I get alone with Him. I want to challenge you to delight in Jesus. At the end of this chapter, I have a page of scriptures that you can meditate on~ to fall in love with Jesus. My prayer for you is that you will hunger more and more after Jesus; that the ministry of worshipping Jesus and spending time in the Tabernacle before Him will burn in you.

To dig deeper to gain understanding of this royal priesthood, the pronouncement of who we are, I Peter 2:9 as our guiding verse gives some description of what it means to walk in this permanent priesthood of believers. "*But you are a **chosen people, a royal priesthood, a holy nation, a people belonging to God**, that you may declare the praises of him who called you out of darkness into his wonderful light.*"

We are a chosen people. We are chosen out of this world. We are a kingdom people. God has chosen us. Do you believe that? Is it easier to think of someone else as being a chosen one, but not you? Did you know that God chose you? He believes in you. He says to you "You have what it takes". To be chosen, gives a sense of belonging. When I was in high school, our choir was chosen along with only a handful of other choirs from around the country to go to a performance "camp" in Utah for a week. We were able to perform and receive instruction from a famous jazz singer at the time. It was such an honor to be chosen. Then, at the "camp" there were auditions for a couple solo parts. I tried out and was asked to perform a solo. I was chosen. It was so unbelievable to me that this man thought I was good enough, that at the night of the performance, I choked. I forgot the words and could not perform. I did not believe that I had what it takes. How could someone else believe in me? There are many believers walking around today that don't believe that they have what it takes…they wonder how God could really choose them for anything. Here is the truth we need to get a hold of: God says in His Word, His Word of Truth that we are a chosen people. He chose us. He chose you. He chose me. I was the apple of His eye before the world was even created. You were the apple of His eye before the creation of the world. Unbelievable! The Creator God had me in mind; had you in mind. We are not a random, by chance people. We are designed for His plan and purpose. *"For he chose us in him before the creation of the world to be holy and blameless in his sight." (Ephesians 1:4).*

We are a royal priesthood. We have surpassed the Aaronic priesthood. We are of the priesthood of Melchizedek (who was a king and a priest) which is a priesthood that will never end, *"..but because Jesus lives forever, he has a permanent priesthood" (Hebrews 7:24)*

241

Hebrews 7:1-2 gives us Melchizedek's title: King and Priest and that is what Jesus is. We follow in His lineage, so that is what we are. This is not a position of control or power, but one of a servant. David served as a king and a priest. Revelation 5:10 says, *"You have made them to be a kingdom and priests to serve our God, and they will reign on earth."* That's something to look forward to!

We are a holy nation. Holy means to be set apart; consecrated. When I have company over at Christmas or Easter, I get out the special dishes for those occasions. I use common dishes every other day, but on special occasions or holidays, we get out the special dinnerware. That is who we are. We are the special dinnerware. God made us for holy purposes, not for common use! *"If a man cleanses himself from the latter, he will be an instrument for noble purposes, made holy, useful to the Master and prepared to do any good work."* (2 Timothy 2:21). I want to be ready & prepared to do any good work. How about you? We are holy, set apart for His purposes. Hebrews 1:15-16 reminds us, *"But just as he who called you is holy, so be holy in all you do; for it is written, 'Be holy, because I am holy'."* Holiness is different than being religious. Religious people follow rules; the dos and don'ts. Holy people desire to be like Jesus! Paul tells us in Colossians 1:22-23, *"But now he has reconciled you by Christ's physical body through death to present you holy in his sight, without blemish and free from accusation—if you continue in your faith, established and firm, not moved from the hope held out in the gospel."* We have a part to play. Jesus makes us holy. We can't do that by ourselves. There is nothing we could do to make ourselves holy. However, we are to continue in our faith, being established and firm; without wavering; not allowing ourselves to be tossed to & fro by the winds of adversity or prosperity. Peter tells us to live as strangers here (he addresses the believers in I Peter 1:1 as *"God's elect, strangers in the world"*), not to be too comfortable or attached in this world. For our home is not here in this kingdom. We belong to a heavenly kingdom. This life is a journey, for the destination is our eternal dwelling. While we walk this earth, let's live a life of holiness, being set apart for His Glory.

We are a people belonging to God. We are a "peculiar" people; which means we are a unique possession of God. I love to be defined as a peculiar people. And I am sure that those who know me would agree that I am peculiar! What a term to describe His people, His royal priesthood. We are a peculiar people. Look at the lives of the early Christians. They were peculiar! They lived radical lives of obedience and so should we!

We are a people declaring His praise. This is our service to the Living God. We declare HIS praise in all the earth. Take a look at this amazing love that our Father has lavished on us!
*He has moved us from darkness to light (Eph. 5:8-9; I Thess. 5:5)
*He is the light of the world (John 8:12)
*He is the Good Shepherd (John 10:14)
*He has moved me from death to life (Eph. 2:4-5)
*He has set us free (Gal. 5:1)
*He has made me a new creation (I Cor. 5:17)
*He has made me righteous (Romans 3:22-24)
*He has made me his son (Romans 8:15-17)
*He has given me His Spirit (I Cor. 2:12)
*He is my comfort (2 Cor. 1:3-4)
*He has blessed me with every spiritual blessing (Eph. 1:3)
*He lived a perfect life of humility, so he could take my place on the cross (Phil. 2:6-8)
*He lives forevermore & His name is above every name! (Phil. 2:9-11)
*Jesus is the WAY, the TRUTH, the LIFE (John 14:6)
*He is going to prepare a place for us (John 14:2-3)
*He has the victory (2 Cor. 2:14; Col.2:15))
*He is the bread of life (John 6:35)

243

*He meets all my needs (Phil. 4:19)
*He is the Creator God (Col.1:16)
*He gives us His Spirit to guide us (John 14:16 & 26, 15:26 , 16:13)
*He has overcome the world (John 16:33)
*He has rescued me (Col.1:13)
*He is coming again (I Thess. 4:16-17)
*He is the God of Peace (1 Thess. 5:23, 2 Thess. 3:16, Is. 9:6)
*He is eternal, immortal, invisible, the only God (I Tim. 1:17)
*He is the Messiah (John 1:41)
*His throne will last FOREVER (Heb. 1:8; Heb. 12:28)
*God is the builder of everything (Heb. 3:4)
*Merciful, faithful High Priest (Heb. 3:17; 4:14; 6:20; Heb. 9:28—
when He appears again, he will bring salvation to those who are
waiting for Him—just as when the High Priest came out of the Holy of
Holies)
*Redeemer, Holy One (Is. 47:4)
*He is holy, blameless, pure, set apart (Heb. 7:26)
*The Son was sent as a sin offering (Rom. 8:3-4); Heb. 7:27; Heb.
9:26-27)
*He is the judge of all men (Heb. 12:23)
*He is the same yesterday, today & forever (Heb. 13:8)
*He is able to keep us from falling (Jude 24-25)
*He is the Alpha & Omega (Rev. 1:8,17b-18; Rev. 22:13)
*He is the Lamb of God (Rev. 5:12)
*He is the WORD OF GOD (Rev. 19:13)
*He is the King of kings & Lord of lords (Rev. 19:16)

That is worth declaring praise to our God and to make the
declaration of what God has done for us to the world!

Lastly, we want to imitate our Great High Priest, Jesus. He
lived a life of humility as he walked the earth. Philippians
2 tells us that he laid down his "God-ness" and took on the
form of a man. He lived a perfect, sinless life,
understanding completely our humanity. That is why it is
said of our great high priest, *"For we do not have a high
priest who is unable to sympathize with our weaknesses,
but we have one who has been tempted in every way, just as
we are~ yet was without sin." (Hebrews 4:15).* Jesus has
been tempted in every way. He knows what it feels like.
Whatever situation you find yourself in, He understands.

Jesus is full of compassion and love. Let's follow His example: To be the priesthood of believers is to live a life of: humility, gentleness, meekness, peace, not defending ourselves, regarding others better than ourselves, being kind, long-suffering, bearing with one another.

Meditate on Matthew 11:25-30 (this is the only passage where Jesus speaks of Himself). Study who He is so we can imitate our high priest.

Meditation Practice

"One thing I ask of the Lord, this is what I seek: that I may dwell in the house of the Lord all the days of my life, to gaze upon the beauty of the Lord and to seek Him in His temple." Psalm 27:4

Goals for this time:
*To get alone with the Lord & listen to Him
*To restore our hunger and desperation for Him
*To empty ourselves of ourselves!
*To grow in knowing Him intimately
*To learn to LOVE Him
*To be restored & refreshed by His presence

To "enter into His presence":
*Invite the Holy Spirit to come and do what He desires (John 14:17; 16:13; 4:14; 7:38; I Corinthians 3:16, Colossians 1:27). You may want to play a quiet worship cd to move your mind and heart to focus.
*Go to a spot where you can be alone

Practical Guidelines:
1) Give all your worries & concerns over to the Lord. Talk to Him about them. Pray a prayer that says something like this: *"I invite you to come and*

search my heart. Come close and let me know Your love. I want to taste and see that the Lord is good."

2) Write out a scripture to help your mind focus on Him. You may want to use one of the scriptures from the section on "Declaring His Praises" on who God is. This can help you begin to clear your mind from the distractions of the world—focus on God. (This is NOT to be confused with a mantra, which is part of the meditation in false religions. In that, your mind is to go blank, we want you to focus on Jesus).

3) It takes most people 10-20 minutes before they stop thinking about the day's events or future plans, etc. and come to a place of rest. Don't be discouraged if your mind wanders. Keep refocusing on God.

4) If you don't "feel" anything, that is OK. God communes directly with our spirit. By faith we know something is happening even though we don't feel it. Your thoughts may tell you this is a waste of time. Do not give in to those thoughts…keep pressing in to Jesus. Trust that the Lord is doing something whether you feel it or not (2 Corinthians 3:16-18). We are to spend time loving Jesus.

5) Have your journal out, so when you hear from the Lord, you can write down what He is saying to you. This is a sweet time between you and your love, Jesus. He desires to commune with you. He wants to abide. He desires to make His home in your heart. Make this a habit and you will be overwhelmed by the love that comes from Him unto you.

246

6) Here are some scriptures to meditate on. Studying and meditating on the Word of God are essential, so we fall more in love with Jesus.
Psalm 4:4, Psalm 62:1, Matthew 11:28, Hebrews 4:9-11, Is. 55:1-3, Psalm 91:1, Luke 9:35, I Samuel 3:9, Lamentations 3:25-26, Psalm 27: 4, 14, Psalm 130:5-6, Luke 10:39, Song of Songs 2:3-4, Hosea 2:14, Psalm 37:7, Psalm 131:2, John 15:9-11, Is. 30:15, Zechariah 2:12-13, Psalm 46:10, Proverbs 1:33, Ephesians 5:18, Is. 40:29-31

"Take time to be separate from all friends and all duties, all cares and all joys; time to be still and quiet before God. Take time not only to secure stillness from man and the world, but from self and its energy. Let the Word and prayer be very precious; but remember, even these may hinder the quiet waiting. The activity of the mind in studying the Word or giving expression to its thought in prayer, the activities of the heart with its desires and hopes and fears, may so engage us that we do not come to the still waiting on the All-Glorious One; our whole being is prostrate in silence before Him. Though at first it may appear difficult to know how thus quietly to wait, with the activities of the mind and heart for a time subdued, every effort after it will be rewarded. We shall find that it grows upon us, and the little season of silent worship will bring a peace and a rest that give a blessing not only in prayer, but all the day." From Andrew Murray, *Waiting on God;* Moody Press, pg. 124.

Study Guide
Week 9: The Priests
(Exodus 28)

Scripture to memorize: *"The Lord bless you and keep you; the Lord make his face shine upon you and be gracious to you; the Lord turn his face toward you and give you peace. "* Numbers 6:24-26 (NIV)

Key Questions:
1) Why did God set the Levites around the Tabernacle? What do we learn about God in the appointing of the Priest & Levites?
2) Draw a picture of the garments of the new priesthood~ the armor of God? (Ephesians 6:14-17)
3) Describe the Priesthood of Christ. It is far superior to the Aaronic priesthood.

The Israelites were unable to minister before the Lord. They needed a mediator, someone to go between them and God. This was the Priesthood. We see God's plan unfold in part by His words to the Israelite community in Exodus 19: 5-6. *"Now if you obey me fully and keep my covenant, then out of all nations you will be mine, you will be for me a kingdom of priests and a holy nation. "* God was initiating the institution of the Priesthood. Without the Priesthood, the Tabernacle itself would have been rendered useless.

The office of the priest is mentioned 700 times in the Old Testament, and approximately 80 times in the New Testament. We should study this concept of the Priest, because that is who we are! In our study of the Tabernacle, we have studied the "what" of the Priests; what they did, now we are going to see the "who" of the Priesthood.

As you study this week, remind yourself of the truth that you are a priest. If you have surrendered your heart to Jesus and have asked him to be your Lord & Savior, then You are a priest. *"But you are a chosen people, a royal priesthood, a holy nation, a people belonging to God, that you may declare the praise of Him who called you out of the darkness into his wonderful light." I Peter 2:9*

Day 1: The Priests & the Levites

The word Priest means "one who officiates". Chosen by God, the Priests were appointed by God, not man. There was no election process that determined who would serve as priests. God gave that divine order on the Mountain of God, when Moses met with Him.

1) Read Exodus 28:1. Who does God name as the Priests for the Israelite community?
2) Read Numbers 3:10. What would happen to anyone (who wasn't a priest) if they approached the Tabernacle's Inner Court?

The tribe of Levi was appointed by God to assist Aaron & his sons in the caring for the Tabernacle. The Levites were not priests but belonged to the priestly tribe. Levi means "joined". The Levites were joined to Aaron & his sons.

3) Read Numbers 3:5-9. What are the responsibilities of the Levites?
4) What were the names of the sons of Levi? (Read Numbers 3:17; see also Genesis 46:11)

In the arrangement of the tribes of Israel set around the Tabernacle, the Levites were closest to the Tabernacle. Numbers 2:53 says, *"The Levites, however, are to set up their tents around the Tabernacle of the Testimony so that*

249

wrath will not fall on the Israelite community." This was God's provision for his set-apart nation. Their presence around the perimeter of the Tabernacle protected the people! Numbers 3 gives us the placement of the Levites around the Tabernacle.

    5) Read Numbers 3:23. Where were the Gershonites to camp?

    6) Read Numbers 3:29. Where were the Kohathites to camp?

    7) Read Numbers 3:35. Where were the Merarites to camp?

    8) Take a look at these clans (in their prospective places) on the Tabernacle diagram.

The Priests & the Levites worked together in caring for the Tabernacle. Numbers 4 gives the specifics of the responsibilities of each of the clans of the Levites; and includes the Priest who is "in charge" for each clan.

    9) The Kohathites' responsibilities were: (Read Numbers 4:1-20)

    10) Who was the Priest in charge of the entire Tabernacle (over the Kohathites)?

    11) The Gersonites' responsibilities were: (Read Numbers 4:21-28)

    12) Who was the Priest in charge of the Gershonite clan?

    13) The Merarites responsibilities were: (Read Numbers 4:29-33

    14) The Merarites perform their duties under the direction of who?

    15) Read Numbers 4:46-49. What is the number of men (30-50 years) who did the work of serving & carrying the Tabernacle?

Day 2: Consecration of the Priests (part 1)

Today we will take a look at the ordination of the priests; what that ceremony looked like—to get them prepared for service in the Tabernacle. As we dive into the Old Testament example, ask the Holy Spirit to illuminate for you how you were "consecrated" as a priest.

Cleansing~ The ordination ceremony began with the cleansing of Aaron and his sons. Moses did the cleansing of the priests at this time. After this initial washing, the priests would cleanse themselves at the Bronze Basin. (See Exodus 29:4 & Lev. 8:6). Our ordination began with a cleansing by the blood of Jesus. We have been cleansed!

1) Read Hebrews 10:22. This is our cleansing done by the Lord. What does this say to you?
2) We need to be purifying our hearts & minds~ coming to the Bronze Basin. What does 2 Corinthians 7:1 say to you?

New garments~ After the initial cleansing, Aaron & his sons were given priestly garments to wear. Their old clothes were replaced with a new set! Moses dressed the priests with these divine garments. They included:

3) Read Leviticus 8:7-9. List the garments:
4) What are the old clothes that we (the priests) are to take off & what are we to put on. Read Ephesians 4:22-32. Make 2 columns and write the "put off" and "put on". As you are reading through the lists, ask the Lord to show you where there needs to be a putting off or a putting on.
5) The garments of the priests look a lot like the armor of God which we are to be clothed in. Read through Ephesians 6:14—17. Draw a picture of yourself

251

dressed in the clothing of a priest (this armor of God). Label the "clothing".

Anointing~ Moses anointed Aaron and his sons as priests (Ex. 29:7 & Ex. 30:30). Using this special blend of fine spices, the anointing oil became holy; to be used in an act of consecration. Leviticus 21:12 says of the anointing oil, *"he has been dedicated by the anointing oil of his God."* The anointing oil was a divine recipe (like the incense to be used on the Golden Altar). Exodus 30:22-33 gives God's directions in using this oil. It was sacred; only to be used on the priests and the vessels in the Tabernacle. *"You shall consecrate them so they will be most holy, whatever touches them will be holy." Exodus 30:29.* The anointing oil had a fragrance which would linger for a while. The anointing was done by anointing the head; it was not to touch the body (flesh).

6) The oil is the Holy Spirit. How interesting that the oil was to be poured over the head, not to touch the body (flesh). Our flesh counts for nothing! We are to put no confidence in the flesh. What does Paul say about the flesh in Philippians 3:3?
7) Read 2 Corinthians 2:14-17. The world will respond in two ways to the anointing fragrance of Christ in us. What do these verses say?

Day 3: Consecration of the Priests (part 2)

The sacrifice followed the anointing of the priests. In Exodus 29:10-34 we see the offerings made to consecrate the priests for service.

Offerings~ The first offering to be made was the sin offering (See Exodus 29:10-14). The sin offering was offered for unintentional and intentional sins committed for

252

which there was no restitution. The guilt for wrongdoing was transferred onto the animal that would be sacrificed at the Bronze Altar. Hebrews 9:22 tells us, *"In fact, the law requires that nearly everything be cleansed with blood, and without the shedding of blood there is no forgiveness of sin."* Aaron & his sons lay their hands on the head of a bull; this was done to transfer their sins onto the head of the animal. Moses killed the bull and put some of the bull's blood on the horns of the bronze altar and poured the rest at the base of the altar. The fat, the liver and the kidneys were to be burned on the altar. The bull's flesh, hide and waste parts were burned outside the camp. This was the first mention of the sin offering; all the preceding offerings were either burnt offerings or peace offerings. This was not an offering with a pleasing aroma rising to the Lord, instead it was one of transfer—to be an atoning for sin. The priests, covered by the sin offering, were now able to minister before the Lord. (To study the sin offering further, see Leviticus 4.)

1) Read 2 Corinthians 5:21. What does this say about Jesus being our sin offering?

The next offering was the burnt offering (see Exodus 29:15-18). A ram (male lamb without defect) was used in this offering. Aaron and his sons placed their hands on the head of a ram. It was slaughtered and the blood was sprinkled against the altar on all sides. The ram was cut into pieces, washed and the whole animal burned on the altar as a burnt offering for a pleasing aroma to the Lord. (To study the burnt offering further, see Leviticus 1.)

Read Romans 12:1. What are we to be?

2) What does I Peter 1:19 tell us about Jesus?

The next step in the consecration of Aaron and his sons was to offer a ram of consecration (see Exodus 29:19-21). Aaron & his sons lay their hands on the ram's head. The ram was slaughtered and the blood of the ram was put on the lobes of the right ear, on the thumb of the right hands, and on the big toe of the right feet.

The blood consecrated the **ears** (that the priest was to be listening to the voice of God, so they may instruct the Israelites). The blood consecrating the right thumb was to remind the priests that their **hands** are the Lords. And the sprinkling of blood to the big toe was to signify that the priest would **walk** in righteousness before the Lord.

We, the priests of the new covenant, are to be consecrated by the blood of the lamb.

3) How do these scriptures speak to our hands?
- I Timouthy 2:8
- James 4:8
- Psalm 63:4
- Psalm 18:20

4) How do these scriptures speak to our ears?
- Proverbs 2:2
- Luke 11:28
- Isaiah 50:4
- Mark 4:9

5) How do these scriptures speak to our walk (feet)?
- Luke 9:23
- Psalm 26:3
- Psalm 26:12
- John 8:12

Some of the blood of the ram sacrifice and some of the anointing oil were mixed together. The blood and oil was sprinkled on Aaron & his garments and also on Aaron's sons and their garments symbolizing the work of the cross in the blood (the death & resurrection of Jesus) and the anointing of the Holy Spirit (oil).

Exodus 29:22-34 tell us that Moses took the fat of the ram, the fat tail, the fat around the inner parts, the covering of the liver, both kidneys with the fat on them and the right thigh, an unleavened cake, a cake made with oil, and a wafer. These were a wave offering to the Lord. The wave offering was an offering before the Lord where the breast of the ram was waved (lifted up and down & back and forth) before the Lord. This was done in relation to the peace offering. Aaron and his sons cooked the meat of the ram (the wave offering) and ate it at the entrance to the Inner Court. They were to eat the bread & cake also.

These offerings were to be made before the Lord for seven days. (Read Exodus 29:35-41). Seven speaks to completeness. The seven days consecrated the priests for their service to the people of God.

6) Write out a prayer of consecration to God. Give him your ears, hands, feet and your whole self; to be a living sacrifice; to be wholly consecrated to HIM!

*For further study, Numbers 8 for the consecration of the Levites

Day 4: Clothing of The High Priest

In Exodus 28 we find the clothing of the High Priest. Verse 2 tells us, *"Make sacred garments for your brother Aaron, to give him dignity and honor."* The role of the

High Priest was a life-long commitment, and was assumed by the oldest qualified descendant of Aaron (after Aaron's death). This Priesthood was called the Aaronic priesthood. All male offspring of Aaron served as priests, except in the case of the physically impaired (see Lev. 21:17-23) or unless he became temporarily unclean (see Lev. 22:3). Only the High Priest was allowed to enter the Holy of Holies on the Day of Atonement each year (Lev. 16). Today we are going to look at the clothing of the High Priest (which set him apart from the other priests). We will see that there were sacred garments for the priests as well. The High Priest was divinely dressed.

The garments consisted of: a breast piece, an ephod, a robe, a woven tunic, a turban, and a sash. The fabric used was gold, blue, purple, scarlet and fine linen. We have seen these colors woven together in the curtains and the veils of the Tabernacle. Gold-- symbolizing Christ's Divinity, blue—speaks to heaven, revelation & communion, scarlet—speaks to the blood of Jesus shed for the atoning for sin, purple—the royalty of Christ, and the white fine linen—speaks to Christ's purity. Today we will take a look at each piece of clothing that the High Priest was to wear.

Ephod: This was two pieces (a front & back piece) that were held together at the shoulder by gold clasps, which held 2 onyx stones. On the onyx stones the sons of Israel (the tribes) were engraved on them; 6 on each stone). The garment was made of the finely twisted linen with the colors of blue, scarlet and purple along with the gold thread running through it. The stones were to be a type of memorial stone that Aaron would carry as a memorial before the Lord. Aaron was representing the 12 tribes of Israel every time He went before the Lord. Gold chains were attached to the shoulder straps to hold the breast piece (see below). The ephod was held to the body by a woven waistband (belt).

1) What does Isaiah 49:16 say in relation to the Ephod?
2) What belt are we, as priests, to wear (Ephesians 6;14)

Breast piece: This was made of the same fabric as the Ephod. It was called the "breast piece of decision" or the "breastplate of judgment". It was shaped in a square (9 inches high and long) and doubled-over. Four rows of three precious stones each were added; representing the twelve tribes. The names of Israel's' sons were engraved like a seal on each one. There was one name on each stone. In this way, the High Priest wore the children of Israel on his heart.

First row: Ruby, Topaz, Beryl
Second row: Turquoise, Sapphire, Emerald
Third row: Jacinth, Agate, and Amethist
Fourth row: Chrysolite, Onyx and Jasper

The breast piece also contained the Urim and Thummim, by which Aaron would know God's heart on decision making for the Israelites. These 2 stones were in the pocket of the breast piece, resting over Aaron's heart. Urim means "light" and Thummim means "perfection". God's perfect will for the people would be illuminated to the Priest (see Numbers 27:21). The breast piece was held in place by gold rings and gold chains. A blue chord held the breast piece close to the ephod, so the breast piece would not swing out from the ephod.

3) Look at I Peter 2:5. What does this say we are?
4) Ephesians 6:14 tells us to put on what?

Robe: The robe was made of blue fabric. It had an opening for the head & arms. The bottom of this robe was trimmed with pomegranates (made of blue, purple and scarlet yarn) and gold bells, alternating. The colors used to make the pomegranates speak to the ministry of Jesus and they speak to fruitfulness. The bells speak to testimony. The people would hear the sound of the bells and it was a type of call to prayer.

5) I Corinthians 15:20-23. What does this say about "fruit"?
6) What kind of robe are we clothed in? (Isaiah 61:10)

Tunic (Headdress): Tunic or miter means "to wrap around". It was made of the fine linen. A plate of pure gold engraved with "HOLY TO THE LORD" was fastened to the turban by a blue cord. It was on the front (on the forehead).

7) Ephesians 6:17 tells us the kind of headdress we are to wear.
8) Write out I Peter 1:15-16.

White Inner Tunic and undergarments: The white linen tunic (that was worn under the blue robe) was down to the feet and had long, tight fitted sleeves. The undergarments were also made of fine linen. They are dressed to be given dignity and honor.

9) What will we be wearing in the age to come? (Revelation 7:9-10).
10) Read Jude 17- 23. What are we to do about garments that are full of flesh?

Notice that Aaron's sons wore different garments than that of the High Priest. They were dressed in the white linen tunic, headbands of white linen and the sash (which was embroidered in blue, scarlet and purple), with undergarments of the white linen (see Exodus 28:40-43). These were the clothes of the priests. Only one was the High Priest.

We have a great High Priest. His name is Jesus. Aaron was a foreshadowing of the Great High Priest to come and Aaron's sons (the priests) were a foreshadowing of us, the believer-priests of this new order.

11) What do these verses tell us about our Great High Priest:
- Hebrews 7:26-27
- Hebrews 2:17-18
- Hebrews 4:14-16
- Hebrews 7:23-25
12) *"You are a priest forever in the order of Melchizedek,"* Hebrews 7:17. This is spoken about Jesus. Read Hebrews 7:1. What titles did Melchizedek have (there are 2)?
13) Describe the similarities between Jesus & Melchizedek: (See Hebrews 7:1-3)

Day 5: Priests of the New Covenant

"And when Jesus had cried out again in a loud voice, he gave up his spirit. At that moment the curtain of the temple was torn in two from top to bottom." Matthew 27:50-51. When the curtain was torn from top to bottom at the entrance to the Holy of Holies, God was establishing a new covenant with the people of God. The Old Covenant was fulfilled and abolished, and the New Covenant had come. We were given entrance into the Most Holy Place based on the death & resurrection of Jesus, the Great High Priest.

259

We, the believer-priests are consecrated by the blood of Christ, which cleanses us from all unrighteousness. We are made holy by the sacrifice of Jesus (Hebrews 10:10).

"You also, like living stones, are being built into a spiritual house to be a holy priesthood, offering spiritual sacrifices acceptable to God through Jesus Christ." Hebrews 2:5

We are to offer what kind of sacrifice to the Lord? What does our believer-priesthood look like for sacrifices?

"Therefore, I urge you, brothers, in view of God's mercy, to offer your bodies as living sacrifices, holy and pleasing to God—this is your spiritual act of worship. Do not conform any longer to the pattern of this world, but be transformed by the renewing of your mind. Then you will know what God's will it—his good, pleasing and perfect will." Romans 12:1-2

This is the sacrifice we are to offer before the Lord. We are to sacrifice our bodies as a living sacrifice to the Lord. It is a voluntary offering made to the Lord~ to give ourselves wholly to Him. This sacrifice is holy and pleasing to God. We crawl up on the Altar & offer ourselves to Him~ freely. Because of what God has done for us, we are to willingly give ourselves back to Him.

1) Have you offered yourself fully to the Lord? Why/why not?
2) What evidence in your life shows that you are offered wholly to the Lord?

"Don't let the world squeeze you into its mold". I heard that quote years ago (I was in high school) & I have never forgotten it. I desire to live in a way that is opposite of the world. How does that happen? We have to know the Word

260

of God. Hebrews 9:10 says, "*This is the covenant I will make with the house of Israel after that time, declares the Lord. I will put my laws in their mind and write them on their hearts. I will be their God and they will be my people.*" His Word is written on our hearts. In order for us not to live according to the pattern of this world, we need to be in His Word, spending time in the Inner Court, desiring intimacy with our God. We are to be holy, set apart people, to look different from the world.

3) I Peter 1:15 tells us what?

Our mind needs to be renewed. Transformed, changed, new mind-sets, new habits, new attitudes, new behaviors, new motives, new lives!

4) How do you see your life transformed into the likeness of Christ?

As we are transformed by the renewing of the mind (because the battle is in the mind) we will then know what God's will is~ His good, pleasing and perfect will! Oh Lord, how we desire to know your good, pleasing and perfect will!

5) Read Hebrews 13:15. What other sacrifice are we to offer to God?
6) What else should our lips declare? See Malachi 2:7.
7) Jehoshaphat set out to correct a Biblical illiteracy of His day. He sent the Levites and Priests to do what? (2 Chronicles 17:9). What are we, the priests of the New Covenant to do in this day of Biblical illiteracy?
8) Draw what the Priest looks like to you:

"May the Lord bless you and keep you; the Lord make His face shine upon you and be gracious to you; the Lord turn his face toward you and give you peace. So they will put my name on the Israelites, and I will bless them."
Numbers 6:24-27

This was the blessing or pronouncement that Aaron and his sons were to speak over the Israelites. God is marking His people with His name. Since we are the priesthood, we need to make this pronouncement over others. Do you know people who need HIS NAME marked upon them? List them here:

Begin to speak this blessing over them: That the presence of heaven would be upon their lives. The peace spoken of in this verse is the shalom of God, which is a wholeness of body, soul and spirit. May you be blessed as you serve the Lord in the priesthood of the believers.

Chapter 10:
The Ark of the Covenant

The first reference that I had personally to the Ark of the Covenant was from the Indiana Jones movie, "Raiders of the Lost Ark". The Ark of the Covenant is found in an archeological site, a battle ensues between the good guys and the bad guys, the bad guys win, tie up the good guys, the Ark is opened and its power is released. Eventually after the bad guys are destroyed by its power, the Ark is put in a wooden box and stored in an American government building. Harrison Ford's character, Indy, makes the comment about the Ark, "They don't know what they've got there."

Power, all consuming power was present in the original Ark of the Covenant. But it is the power of Almighty God who dwelt on the atonement cover (mercy seat) between the Cherubim. Power was not contained in the Ark itself. Constructed of acacia wood and covered inside and out with pure gold~, there was no super power in the materials. God Himself dwelt here and this was His desire; to live among His people. This was the sole purpose for the Tabernacle: to have a place where His Glory would dwell. *"Then have them make a sanctuary for me, and I will dwell among them." (Exodus 25:8)* And Moses, following the Divine pattern given to him by God had the Tabernacle and all its furnishings constructed.

After this long journey with the Israelites, we now come to the purpose and reason for the Tabernacle. God longed to dwell with His people and He pursued them and made a way for communication and intimacy. This was God's idea, not man's. The Ark of the Covenant was placed in the Holy of Holies. This was the only vessel in the Holy of

Holies. None of the priests could enter the Holy of Holies. The closest they came to the Shekinah Glory of God (His manifest presence) was ministering at the Golden Altar of Incense in the Holy Place. Imagine standing at the golden altar, burning incense and offering prayers on behalf of the Israelite community, knowing that on the other side of the veil was the presence of the Almighty One. If I had been one of the priests performing my duties, I would want to reach out and touch the veil. Would one touch cause my heart to stop? Could one touch draw me nearer to the Holy One? Would the power seep through the veil? Did I AM smell the incense at the altar?

The High Priest was allowed access to the Holy of Holies one day a year, on the Day of Atonement. Moses was the only one who had direct access to God. He would meet with God on a regular basis to gain wisdom on how to lead the Israelites. *"There, above the cover between the two cherubim that are over the ark of the Testimony, I will meet with you and give you all my commands for the Israelites."* *(Exodus 25:22)*.

God established the Tabernacle in the wilderness, where the Israelites spent 40 years. In this wilderness time, God met with His people, trained His people, revealed who He was to His people, consecrated His people, showed His Glory to His people. God did not establish the Tabernacle in Egypt, for Egypt was a land of idolatry. God did not wait to establish the Tabernacle in the Promised Land, the land of Canaan. He began this new, covenant relationship with the Israelites in the wilderness. Hosea 2:14 says, *"Therefore I am now going to allure her; I will lead her into the desert and speak tenderly to her."* God brought the Israelites into the wilderness to speak tenderly to her and to show His love to His people and also to break the bondage of idolatry. Hosea 2:17 continues, *"I will remove the names of the Baals from her lips; no longer will their names be invoked."* The wilderness was God's Divine choice for the Tabernacle. God was using the physical manifestation of the Tabernacle structure itself to show the Israelites and all other nations that this was a set-apart people. They were a chosen nation. And at the center of Israel's worship was the Ark of the Covenant, where the presence of the Living God dwelt. The omniscient God inhabited the Ark of the Covenant.

The Israelites had experienced the Shekinah Glory of God before the establishment of the Tabernacle. After their release from Egypt, the Egyptian army pursued the Israelites to destroy them and God, who had been leading the Israelites by a pillar of fire, moved behind them in a pillar of cloud, coming between the army of Egypt and the Israelites (Exodus 14:24-25). And the pillar of fire or cloud led them through the wilderness.

At Mount Sinai, the Glory of God settled on the mountain when Moses had gone up to meet with God. *"To the Israelites the glory of the Lord looked like a consuming fire on top of the mountain."* (Exodus 24:17) At that meeting, the Glory of the Lord enveloped Moses in a cloud. *"Moses was there with the Lord forty days and forty nights without eating bread or drinking water. And he wrote on the tablets the words of the covenant~ the Ten Commandments." (Exodus 34:27)* Being in the presence of Almighty God was fulfillment of all needs; physical, emotional, spiritual. Moses experienced communion with the Bread of Life and the Living Water. Moses was changed in the presence of God. When Moses came down from Mount Sinai, his face was radiant (the effects of being with God). Others noticed and were afraid to come near Moses. The light of God, which is part of His Shekinah Glory was radiating on Moses' face. The Israelite community was in awe and reverence and Moses had to invite them to draw near to him, so he could speak with them about the commands that God had given them. Moses placed a veil over his face when he was with the people, but would remove the veil when he went to commune with the Lord.

When Moses would meet with the Lord, in the Holy of Holies, a *"pillar of cloud would come down and stay at the entrance, while the Lord spoke with Moses. Whenever the people saw the pillar of cloud standing at the entrance to the tent, they all stood and worshiped, each at the entrance to his tent* (Exodus 33:9-10). At the completion of the Tabernacle, the glory of the Lord filled the temple (a cloud covered the Tabernacle). Moses could not enter the Tabernacle because the weight of the Lord had settled upon it (Exodus 40). What a sight! During the forty years wandering in the desert, the Israelites would settle in a place, and when the cloud lifted from the Tabernacle, they would set out again until the cloud stopped. The cloud settled over the Tabernacle by day and by night there was fire in the cloud that rested over the Tabernacle. The power and majesty of the Living God affected the whole community.

David was another who communed with God Almighty in intimacy. God says of David that he is a man after his own heart. Now most of us know the failures of David and may wonder how God could say that of David (David's life can be read about in I & II Samuel). David's life was marked with adultery, lying, murder, bigamy, lack of parenting, and the list goes on. However, as you read the Psalms (a large number of which were written by David), his heart cry is to please His King, to love Him with all that is in Him. David's desire was to provide a place for His Glory to dwell. But God did not appoint David for that assignment (Solomon, David's son would be the one to build a temple to hold His presence).   So, David set up a tent and placed the Ark of the Covenant in the simple tent and then he spent much time sitting before the presence of the Lord. Psalm 27:4 shows us David's heart, *"One thing I ask of the Lord, this is what I seek: that I may dwell in the house of the Lord all the days of my life, to gaze upon the beauty of the Lord and to seek Him in his temple."* This passion was stirred in David's heart to bring the Ark back to Jerusalem (the City of David).   You can read the account in I Chronicles 13-14-15. *"After David had constructed buildings for himself in the City of David, he prepared a place for the Ark of God and pitched a tent for it."* (I Chronicles 15:1). He gathered the Levites and priests for the task of bringing the Ark to Jerusalem. They all set out and the first time (you can read about it in I Chronicles 13) they tried to bring the Ark to Jerusalem, David had not known the proper instructions from the law of Moses, so the Ark was placed on a new cart. Uzzah (who was one of the men guiding the Ark) reached out and touched the Ark to steady it because the oxen had stumbled. The Lord struck down Uzzah because he had put his hand on the Ark. *"So he died there before God."* (I Chronicles 13:10b). David, afraid of God, spent some time studying how to bring the Ark to Jerusalem.

{A side-note: David had left the Ark at the home of Obed-Edom, a Gittite (Gentile)for three months, which was the time it took David to gain understanding of how to bring the Ark back to Jerusalem. While the Ark rested at the home of Obed-Edom, the Lord blessed his household and everything he had. And the next time we read about Obed-Edom, he is made a gatekeeper of the Lord's presence (I Chronicles 15:18). When someone encounters the presence of the Lord, he can never be the same. We see that Obed-Edom left his home to be around the Lord's presence. He couldn't get enough. He had experienced the

Shekinah Glory and would not be satisfied with anything less.}

So they start out again, a second time, with the priests and Levites, who had consecrated themselves, carrying the Ark of God on their shoulders. *"And the Levites carried the Ark of God with the poles on their shoulders, as Moses had commanded in accordance with the word of the Lord."* (I Chronicles 15:15). David and many others in his company set out from the house of Obed-Edom (about 10-15 miles from Jerusalem). Along the way, they stopped to make sacrifices (as prescribed in the law of Moses) of seven bulls and seven rams. David and all the priests, Levites, musicians, and singers were dressed in the clothing of a priest~ a robe of fine linen with a linen ephod. I love to picture that scene: A least a thousand men shouting and worshipping the Lord, dancing and sacrificing before their God; a messy, bloody and probably sweaty scene (with all that linen). As they approached Jerusalem, the harps & lyres, rams' horns & trumpets, shouting & singing was coming from those carrying the Ark of God. And *"as the Ark of the Covenant of the Lord was entering the City of David, Michal, daughter of Saul watched from a window. And when she saw King David dancing and celebrating, she despised him in her heart."* (I Chronicles 15:29). The longer that David and his company spent in the presence of the Lord, the more "undignified" they became. They carried the weight of His presence on their shoulders. Today, the Lord is looking for those who are consecrated and prepared to carry His weighty presence. Oh that there would be a place prepared for His Glory to dwell~ a place that people would say, as David did, "I will become more undignified than this." (2 Samuel 6:22). It is all about intimacy. David had experienced it. Obed-Edom had experienced it. Moses had experienced it.

I have experienced it. I will never be the same. If you have experienced intimacy with God, you cannot be the same. You will be changed. You will call out, "I will become even more undignified than this!" However, we do need to be aware of the Michals in our lives. There are many more who would point a finger and say, "Get your act together. Stop looking like a fool." These are the ones who have not had the touch of the presence; the Shekinah Glory of God. I find it interesting that the Bible tells us that Michal was barren from this point on. Barrenness is a result from lack of intimacy.

Under the Old Covenant, only a select few were able to meet with God, as one meets with a friend. That covenant was fulfilled in the cross. Jesus became our sin offering, gave Himself up willingly on the cross, so that a new covenant would be established. At His death, the curtain that separated the Holy Place from the Holy of Holies was torn from top to bottom. The way was made that we can enter the Holy of Holies. God's presence, in all His Glory is available to all of His children. We are His chosen ones, and His desire is to be in relationship with us. This is the most intimate relationship. God invites us to come into His presence. Seek Him out. James 4:8 says, *"Come near to God and he will come near to you."* This was the cry of David's heart. Psalm 27:4 we hear this cry, *"One thing I ask of the Lord, this is what I seek: that I may dwell in the house of the Lord all the days of my life, to gaze upon the beauty of the Lord and to seek him in his temple."* To be a "one thing" person~ that is my desire!

God set up the Tabernacle as a boundary or barrier to His Holy presence. He loved His chosen people so much that He did not want someone to stumble upon his presence. The cherubim were set as a protection of His presence. The Tabernacle was the immediate barrier, and then the Priests and Levite families were placed around the outer court of the Tabernacle.

We, too, do not want to stumble into the presence of the Most Holy God. To meet God in the Most Holy Place, to be in His presence requires that we have moved from the outer court to the inner court. This tabernacle model for us shows the journey we are on.

1) Have I entered the gate (accepted Jesus as the only Way, the Truth and the Life)?
2) Understanding that there is nothing that I can do on my own in order to be saved; that my salvation is based solely on the shed blood of Jesus (the sin offering on the bronze altar).
3) Do I cleanse myself daily at the basin (washing with the water of the Word~ Ephesians 5:26) to make sure that I have clean hands and a pure heart (Psalm 24:4)?
4) Am I pursuing a relationship of communion with the Lord by inviting the Holy Spirit to transform me by His counsel, guidance and truth? Am I fellowshipping with Jesus in the midst of all the circumstances of life? Is worship, prayer and intercession an integral part of your life?

When Moses went to meet with God, he had to climb the mountain. God is looking for mountain climbers! In this culture, it is a "climb" (maybe not in the physical sense) to get into God's presence. Our mountains are obligations, commitments, chores, busyness, distractions….are we willing to climb up to meet with Him? Will you be a mountain climber? The result was a transformation of who Moses was. He was different from the inside-out. God met Moses' needs (physically, emotionally & spiritually). As God was changing him from the inside, it was showing on the outside. His face was radiant from his time with the Lord. People withdrew from Moses. When we draw near to God and He to us, there will be those who back away. The presence of God on us will be life to some and death to others. But as Moses did, we just keep inviting others to come close, draw near, so they can hear what the Lord has spoken. And there are people who we will need to place a veil over our face, because they can't bear the radiance of the Lord. But when we return, up the mountain to meet again with the Living God, take off the veil that there is no barrier between Him and us.

This is the LIFE, the description of the last veil. We have entered the Way, the Truth and now the Life, experiencing an intimate relationship with the God of the universe, the Living One. When we tarry with the Lord and allow Him to transform us from the inside-out, all our needs are met (physical, emotional & spiritual). God shapes our priorities, removes the worry, gives us direction and counsel, moves us in the way we are to go. His light radiates any darkness in us!

The last reference we have to the Ark of the Covenant in the Old Testament is in Jeremiah 3:14-16. The last reference of the Ark in the New Testament is in Revelation 11:19, *"Then God's temple in heaven was opened and within his temple was seen the Ark of His Covenant. And there came flashes of lightning, peals of thunder, an earthquake and a great hailstorm."* When the Ark of the Covenant is exposed to the people of earth in the last days, power and authority will be released, as seen in the movie, "Raiders of the Lost Ark".

We can know, in an intimate way, this God who has All power, All authority, and All creation bows to Him.

"To Him who sits on the throne and to the Lamb be praise and honor and glory and power forever and ever!"
Revelation 5:13

Study Guide
Week 10: The Ark of the Covenant
(Exodus 25:10-22)

Scripture to memorize: *"Let us then approach the throne of grace with confidence, so that we may receive mercy and find grace to help us in our time of need."* Hebrews 4:16

Key Questions:
1) Why do you think that God's directions for building the Tabernacle were given from the "inside-out" (beginning with the Ark of the Covenant)?
2) In the Ark were 3 things: a jar of manna, Aaron's staff that budded, blossomed & gave fruit, and the stone tablets on which were written the moral law. Share what significance any of these have in your life? Did you gain any revelation on these contents?
3) What does the mercy seat mean to you?

We come to the reason for the Tabernacle~ The Ark of the Covenant. This is the place where the glory of God rested. This was the reason for the Tabernacle itself; to hold the presence of the Lord, so He would dwell among the people. On the mountaintop, when God gave Moses the directions for building the Tabernacle, the first vessel that was mentioned in Divine detail was the Ark.

Interesting, the ark has been seen in the history of the world two other times leading up to this wilderness experience of God's people. The first ark is in the book of Genesis, when God had Noah make an "ark" to preserve the people of God. Genesis 6:14 tells us *"so make for yourself an ark of cypress wood, make rooms in it and coat it with pitch inside and out."* Noah, his wife, sons & their wives (8 people in all) and 2 of every living creature, bird, animal, and every

273

kind of creature that moves along the ground were preserved in the ark. These of God's creation were saved from the destruction of the water that covered the earth. See Genesis 6-9 for more detail of that ark.

The second ark is the ark into which Moses was placed for his survival or to have his life preserved. Exodus 2:3 tells us about Moses' mother who made a *"papyrus basket for him and coated it with tar and pitch. Then she placed the child in it and put it among the reeds along the bank of the Nile."* This ark also was covered with pitch inside and out. It was used to preserve Moses' life from the destruction of the waters of the Nile. See Exodus 2:1-10 for more detail on this ark.

And here we are at the study of the third ark that God has designed to preserve His people. This ark is made of acacia wood and covered inside and out with gold (not pitch). Let's take a closer look at the "Ark of the Covenant" this week.

Day 1: Construction of the Ark

This ark has many different names. Read the following scriptures and write the name of the ark next to the scripture:

- Exodus 25:22
- Numbers 10:33
- Joshua 3:6
- Joshua 3:13
- I Samuel 3:3
- I Samuel 5:7
- Judges 20:27
- 2 Chronicles 35:3

Exodus 25:8 was one of our memory verses in the beginning of this study. God desired to dwell among His people. The sanctuary would be a way for His Glory to dwell with them. *"Then have them make a sanctuary for me, and I will dwell among them."* The first time this Ark of the Covenant is mentioned is here in Exodus 25. There are almost 200 references in the Old Testament to the Ark. Jeremiah 3:14-16 gives us the last account of the Ark in the Old Testament. In Revelation 11:19 we read, *"Then God's temple in heaven was opened and within his temple was seen the Ark of His covenant. And there came flashes of lightening, peals of thunder, and earthquake and a great hailstorm."* What POWER!

God's directions to Moses on building the Tabernacle are from the inside out. (Beginning with the Ark and making the way to the Outer Court).

1) Why do you think God gave the directions in that way?

Exodus 25:10 tells us the Ark's size and what it is made of. The Ark is constructed of acacia wood (again that is the reference to the life of Jesus lived in perfect humanity). The acacia trees, which were common in the Sinai desert, were indestructible; not even an insect would burrow into the bark. Just as Jesus being perfect in every way. Isaiah 53:2 says, *"he grew up before him like a tender shoot, and like a root out of dry ground."*

The measurement of the Ark is 3 ¾ feet long and 2 ¼ feet wide and high. It is in the shape of a box. The atonement cover will fit on the top of the box. That is where the Glory of God dwells (between the Cherubim).

2) Read Exodus 25:11. What is the Ark overlaid with (inside and out)?

Think of the significance of the gold inside and out. We see three "layers": gold, acacia wood, gold.

3) What do you think the three layers signify?

Gold represents Deity. So to see the acacia wood (Jesus) overlaid with gold, both inside and out. We see God the Father and God the Holy Spirit in the design. The Three in One.

This is the third piece of furniture that we have seen that has a "crown" or "molding" of Gold around it: 1) Table of Showbread, 2) Golden Altar, and 3) Ark of the Covenant. We saw in the other two pieces of furniture that the molding or crown was significant to show that Jesus was able to keep us from falling. He intercedes on our behalf (Hebrews 7:25) and His hand is holding them (John 10:28). In this piece of furniture we see the Crown of the King. This crown (molding) speaks of Jesus' kingship.

4) What do these verses say about our King?
- Mark 15:17-18
- Matthew 2:2
- Psalm 2:6
- Psalm 24:10
- Revelation 19:16

In Exodus 25:12 it tells us the four rings of gold were made (this was to hold the poles for carrying the Ark). There were two rings on one side and two on the other. They were to be fastened to the corners (or feet) of the Ark.

276

The feet, which are to carry the message of the cross to the ends of the earth!

The number four speaks to the earth (4 winds, 4 corners of the world). We also see four in the gospels (Matthew, Mark, Luke and John). And in the great commission that Jesus spoke before ascending into heaven, he told his disciples to go to the four corners of the world (Jerusalem, Judea, Samaria, to the rest of the world)! The gold speaks to the Deity of Jesus.

5) Read Exodus 25:13-15. What is unique about the poles?

We see the poles of acacia wood (representing Christ's perfect humanity) and being overlaid with gold (His Deity). The God-man; 2 natures in one. The poles were to be in place through the gold rings. In transit, the Ark would be carried upon the shoulders of the Priests, without having to touch the Ark itself. The poles were to remain in the rings, to remind the people that they are aliens and strangers here. They were wanderers. We look forward to *"the city with foundations, whose architect and builder is God."* *Hebrews 11:10.*

Day 2: The contents of the Ark

Hebrews 9: 4 tells us what was inside the Ark. *"This Ark contained the gold jar of manna, Aaron's staff that had budded, and the stone tablets of the covenant."* Let's take a look at each of these three items in the Ark:

Gold jar of manna: The miracle food~ Manna was the food that God fed the Israelites for the forty years that they wandered in the wilderness. Exodus 16:12 tells us what God will give the Israelites to eat. The word "bread" or "manna" in Hebrew means "whatness" or "what is it". There is no translation for the word. Manna was the "bread from heaven"; it was a small, thin, white, coriander-like seed, which tasted like wafers with honey (Exodus 16:31), a daily provision from the Lord. Each person gathered what he or she needed and were filled. Manna appeared every morning like frost on the ground (Exodus 16:14). On the sixth day, they collected twice as much for the Sabbath. Aaron was commanded to *"take a jar and put an omer of manna in it. Place it before the Lord to be kept for the generations to come." (Exodus 16:33)* God showed that He was the one who provided for the physical and spiritual needs of His people.

1) Jesus refers to Himself as:
   - John 6:32
   - John 6:33
   - John 6:48
   - John 6:51

Jesus is the true manna and is able to meet all of our physical and spiritual needs.

2) What does Philippians 4:19 say to you?

3) What does Matthew 6:11 say to you?

Aaron's staff that budded: Aaron's staff budded in the light of Numbers 16 & 17. There was a revolt against Moses and Aaron by Korah, Dathan and Abiram. They questioned the authority of Moses and Aaron. (Numbers 16:2) These men had gathered 250 Israelite men (well-know community leaders who had been appointed members of the council) and they came as a group to oppose Moses and Aaron. God dealt with their opposition by *"the ground under them split apart and the earth opened* *its mouth and swallowed them, with their households and all Korah's men and all their possessions...and fire came out from the Lord and consumed the 250 men who were offering the incense." (Numbers 16:32 & 35).*

The next day the Lord told Moses to have the Israelites bring 12 staffs (one from each tribe with the name of each man on his staff). On the staff of Levi, write Aaron's name, for there must be one staff for each of the tribes. Then Moses placed them in the Tabernacle, in front of the Ark. Whichever staff budded is the name that God chooses to be the high priest. *"The next day Moses entered the Tent of the Testimony and saw that Aaron's staff, which represented the house of Levi, had not only sprouted but had budded, blossomed and produced almonds...the Lord said to Moses, 'Put back Aaron's staff in front of the Testimony, to be kept as a sign to the rebellious."*
(Numbers 17:8 & 10). Aaron was the chosen one! This would be a sign for generations to come~ that the line of Aaron was to be the priesthood.

This staff is a picture of Jesus' resurrection. Jesus overcame death!

   4) John 11:25 says what?

Aaron's staff overcame death & then budded, blossomed and produced almonds (fruit). Fruit that will last.

   5) What does I Corinthians 15:23 say about Jesus?

   6) According to John 15:5 what must we do in order to produce fruit?

What does the fruit look like (our character)~ see Galatians 5:22-23.

279

7) What fruit do you see the Lord producing in you?

The stone tablets: Deuteronomy 10:2 tells us *"I will write on the tablets the words that were on the first tablets, which you broke. Then you are to put them in the chest."* This was the second set of tablets that God wrote upon. Moses threw the first set out of his hands and they broke to pieces (Deut. 9:17). The "book of the law" was to be set inside the Ark as a witness against the Israelites (Deut. 31:26). *"For I know how rebellious and stiff-necked you are. If you have been rebellious against the Lord while I am still alive and with you, how much more will you rebel after I die!"* *(Deut. 31:27).* Moses certainly knew the nation of Israel!

8) What does Matthew 5:17 say about Jesus & the Law?

9) John 1:17. What does this verse say about the fulfillment of the Law?

10) Galatians 3:13. How did Jesus fulfill the law?

11) What will happen when Jesus abolishes the Old Covenant? (Hebrews 10:16)

Jesus was the fulfillment of each of the articles in the Ark.

Day 3: The Atonement Cover (Mercy Seat): Part 1

Exodus 25:17-22 gives the description and meaning for the atonement cover.

1) According to Exodus 25:17 what is the mercy seat made of?

It's dimensions are the same as the Ark (to fit perfectly as a cover)~ 3 ¾ feet long and 2 ¼ feet wide.

2) What are to be carved into the lid with one piece of gold? (Ex. 25:18-19)

3) Describe the positioning of the Cherubim on the atonement cover (Ex. 25:20-21):

We looked at the Cherubim in the Week 8 study guide (the Veils and the Curtains). We saw that the Cherubim had two roles, 1) to announce God's presence and 2) to protect God's presence. To look at the scriptures on the Cherubim: Genesis 3:24, Psalm 18:9-10, I Samuel 4:4, I Kings 8:6-7, Numbers 7:89, Psalm 80:1, Psalm 99:1, Ezekiel 9:3.

Here, in the Most Holy Place, the powerful Cherubim point to the place where the Glory of God dwells (with their wings spread upward and facing each other with their faces looking down toward the cover).

The atonement cover (mercy seat) and the two cherubim were constructed out of one piece of gold to signify that there is only ONE God. He is the Father, Son and Holy Spirit~ the three in one.

Jesus is portrayed as the mercy seat. Romans 3:25 says, *"God presented him as a sacrifice of atonement (mercy seat), through faith in his blood. He did this to demonstrate his justice, because in his forbearance he had left the sins committed beforehand unpunished-* "Jesus is the mercy seat. He is the manifestation of God's glory. He is the location of reconciliation. He is the minister of reconciliation. He is the at-one-ment! Praise the Lord! There is redemption for sin once and for all!

4) Draw the Ark of the Covenant in the Tabernacle diagram. Your diagram should be complete; with all the furniture in place: The gate around the outer court, the Bronze Altar, the Bronze Basin, the veil leading into the Holy Place; in the Holy Place, the Golden Lampstand, the Table of Showbread and the Altar of Incense, then we see the veil leading into the Most Holy Place which holds the Ark of the Covenant (the dwelling place of God).

5) What does this Ark look like to you? Can you illustrate it? Or write it out?

Day 4: The Atonement Cover (Mercy Seat): Part 2

Moses had access to the Most Holy Place. He was permitted to meet with the Lord. Exodus 25:22 tells us, *"There, above the cover between the two cherubim that are over the ark of the Testimony, I will meet with you and give you all my commands for the Israelites."*

God would meet with Moses and share His heart for His people. The word *"meet"* in Hebrew means *"to meet by agreement; to come together"*. Can you imagine the reverence that Moses had as he went to meet with Yahweh? He had spent time on the mountain receiving instruction for the people. When Moses came down from the mountain, what had changed in his appearance? What were the effects of being in God's presence?

Read Exodus 34:29-35.
1) What happened to Moses' face?
2) Who was afraid to come near to Moses?
3) Who approached Moses first? Then who? Then who?

4) What did Moses put on after he spoke with the Israelites?
5) When he met with the Lord, what did he do with the veil?

What an amazing sight; Moses was glowing after being with God! We see these effects of being with God:

- A change took place~ change is inevitable when we are in God's presence
- True intimacy produces humility (Moses didn't even know that his face was radiant)
- True intimacy produces deeper intimacy (Moses entered the Lord's presence continually); as one communes with the Lord, he hungers and thirsts for more of Him.
- Others saw the radiance; intimacy with the Lord shows on our faces! Our countenance changes!
- The mark of radiance will eventually fade~ we need to continue meeting with the Lord; being in His presence

This Glory was dwelling in the Holy of Holies, above the cover between the two cherubim that are over the Ark, on the mercy seat. Moses was the only one who could meet with God at any time. The only other person allowed to enter the Lord's presence (remember that presence was guarded by the Cherubim woven in the veil leading into the Most Holy Place) was the High Priest. And he could only go behind the veil one day a year, on the Day of Atonement.

Leviticus 16 gives us the details about the Day of Atonement~ a very serious day.

The High Priest (Aaron is the first High Priest) first offered a bull for a sin offering and a ram for a burnt offering. He then bathed himself and then placed the sacred garments (refer to week 9 study guide). The High Priest then took a censor full of burning coals from the bronze altar and two handfuls of incense and took them behind the veil. He put the incense on the fire before the Lord and the smoke of incense would conceal the atonement cover above the Testimony. This cloud of smoke, representing the prayers of God's people was a protection for the High Priest.

The High Priest then goes back to the Brazen Altar and took blood of the bull, and again entered the Holy of Holies with the blood of the bull and sprinkled in on the front of the atonement cover (mercy seat) seven times. Sprinkling the blood seven times speaks to being complete (a complete atonement for sin). We see this fulfilled in John 20:17. Jesus said, *"Do not hold on to me, for I have not yet returned to the Father…"* Jesus needed to go to the Father to sprinkle blood on the mercy seat (atonement cover) to atone for the sins of the people once and for all!

The High Priest then chose 2 goats and presented them before the Lord. He casts lots for the two goats~ one lot for the Lord and one for the scapegoat. This goat was slaughtered and offered as a sin offering for the people and the High Priest took the goat's blood behind the veil and sprinkled the atonement cover (mercy seat) as he did with the bull's blood. Then the High Priest took the blood and sprinkled the horns of the Altar of Incense seven times to cleanse it from the uncleanness of the Israelites (see Exodus 30:10). Next, he went to the bronze altar and mixed the goat's blood with the bull's blood and dipped his finger in the blood and consecrated the bronze altar by sprinkling the horns, seven times. There could be no one in the Tent of Meeting (Tabernacle) on this day.

The High Priest would then place his blood-soaked hands on the head of the scapegoat, transferring the sins of Israel from that year onto the goat. He would then confess over the goat all the wickedness and rebellion of the Israelites. The scapegoat was then led away into the wilderness, signifying that the sins of Israel had been carried away for that year.

Next the High Priest went into the Holy Place and removed his sacred garments, washed his body and put on his regular garments. Then he shall come out and sacrifice the burnt offering for himself and for the people, to make atonement for himself and the people. He burned the fat of the sin offering on the bronze altar. The hides, flesh, and offal from the bull and goat for the sin offerings (whose blood was taken behind the veil) are to be burned outside of the camp.

The congregation waited patiently while the High Priest performed his duty. He would appear before the whole camp of Israel to tell the people that the blood covers them for his year.

We see this in Hebrews 9:28 *"so Christ was sacrificed once to take away the sins of many people; and he will appear a second time, not to bear sin, but to bring salvation to those who are waiting for him."* We see in this verse a picture of the Israelite community, who waited patiently for the High Priest to announce salvation for the people!

The final duty of the day was for the High Priest to offer the evening sacrifices and offerings to the Lord (see Numbers 29:7-11).

What a day! The patience, reverence, fear, blood, order, recognition of sin, cleansing from sin, holiness of God~ one day a year, the Israelites waited in hopes of redemption and salvation. The blood gives significance for that day. Leviticus 17:11 says, *"...it is the blood that makes atonement for one's life."* Jesus became the sin offering for us. *"First he said, 'Sacrifices and offerings, burnt offerings and sin offerings you did not desire, nor were you pleased with them'* (although the law required them to be made). *Then he said, 'Here I am, I have come to do your will.' He sets aside the first to establish the second. And by that will, we have been made holy through the sacrifice of the body of Jesus Christ, one for all."* Hebrews 10:8-10

6) Write a prayer out to God the Father thanking Him for the sacrifice of His son on your behalf.

Day 5: The Glory of God

The presence of God dwelt on the mercy seat. The "Shekinah" glory of God. Shekinah means "the one who dwells". It refers to God's dwelling visibly among His people. The Tabernacle was set up divinely; following the pattern of the Designer (Exodus 40). In Exodus 40:33 says, *"Moses finished the work."* Imagine that scene. The last piece is in place. They worked from the inside-out. Isn't that how God works in each one of us? He begins inside (our spirit) and then works His way out (soul and body) to line up everything in a Divine order. And what happens in Exodus 40?

"Then the cloud covered the Tent of Meeting, and the glory of the Lord filled the Tabernacle. Moses could not enter the Tent of Meeting because the cloud had settled upon it, and the glory of the Lord filled the Tabernacle."
Exodus 40:34-35.

286

The Shekinah glory of God was His "visible" presence. He dwelt on the mercy seat, between the two cherubim. The Tabernacle was constructed to provide a place for the Lord to dwell among His people. There was a reverence and a holy fear that came over the people. They knew the power in His presence. What about the church today? We are to be a place for His glory to dwell. Jesus **is** the mercy seat. Have we "constructed" a place for Him to dwell? Jesus came to dwell among a people. John 1:14 says, *"The Word became flesh and made his **dwelling** among us. We have seen His **glory**, the **glory** of the One and Only, who came from the Father, full of grace and truth."*

- The word "dwelling" means to "tabernacle". Just as the tabernacle in the wilderness carried the manifest presence of God (the Shekinah glory) above the cover, between the cherubim, so Jesus "tabernacled" among us. He put on flesh, identifying with humanity. And we have **seen His glory!**
- We have seen His **glory**, the **glory** of the One and Only~ this "glory" means "splendor, brilliance-the awesome light that radiates from God's presence and is associated with his acts of power, honor, praise, speaking of words of excellence and assigning highest status to God!

1) What does this verse (John 1:14) mean for you?

We see Jesus as the mercy seat in Hebrews 1:3. *"The Son is the radiance of God's glory and the exact representation of his being, sustaining all things by his powerful word. After he had provided purification for sins, he sat down at the right hand of the Majesty in heaven."*

Jesus dwelt among mankind and took on himself the punishment for all sin. What the High Priest could not do, Jesus did. He made the way of the "mercy seat" open to all at all times. No longer is the mercy seat a "throne of judgment" but to us it is a "throne of grace". Hebrews 4:16 tells us to "approach the throne of grace with confidence, so that we may find grace to help us in our time of need." We, the believers have access to the mercy seat!

2) We see the Ark for the last time in Revelation 11:19. Describe the ark.

3) Read Revelation 21:22-23. What do you see about the "Tabernacle" or "Temple"?

4) End this lesson praising the Lord for His grace & mercy upon you! Give Him all of your praise for HE IS WORTHY!!!!!! *"Worthy is the Lamb, who was slain, to receive power and wealth and wisdom and strength and honor and glory and praise." Revelation 5:12*

Chapter 11:
Looking Back & Looking Ahead

A survey was done recently, including 525 churches throughout the United States, surveying over 180,000 people. The questionnaire was completed online, so that each one would feel that they could give real answers, not "church approved" responses to the questions. Being anonymous lent itself to honest answers to spiritual questions. What came out of this survey is that four groups of people exist in every church. Based on this research, I immediately thought of the Tabernacle. Each of these four groups is seen in the Tabernacle that we have studied; for this is our "Journey of Faith".

In each of these groups, there is growth that is happening. No matter where you are in your journey with God, you can move from one area to the next at any time. God's desire is that each one of us would be found in the Holy of Holies. He loves us so much and longs to be in an intimate relationship with us.

The first group of people (labeled in this rectangle) is:

Outside the Tabernacle~

This is a time of exploring God and what He stands for; a knowing **of** God, but He is not a personal God. People in this group are examining the Bible, talking with Christians, asking questions, going to church to get some answers, maybe even involved in a Bible Study. This is the first step along the journey of faith.

Do you know anyone in this place? What characterizes these people? The first thing they need is the basics of what it means to trust God. It is important to answer questions from those who are searching. Think of this beginning place as a classroom setting. People here need to have a teacher to lead them and teach them. What moves someone from this place to the next step on the journey? **GRACE**. To move through the gate (the main entrance) into the outer court is grace, which is an understanding that there is nothing I can ever do to earn my salvation. It is by God's grace alone. It is a recognition of sin and realizing that payment needs to be made for my sin. This is a dramatic change from being in a place of self-sufficiency. When the Holy Spirit illuminates the truth and a heart is open to receive, all heaven celebrates! For those in this place, these scriptures are keys:

- Ephesians 2:8-9 *"For it is by grace you have been saved through faith ~ and this not from yourselves, it is the gift of God ~ not by works, so that no one can boast."*
- Romans 3:23 *"For all have sinned and fall short of the glory of God"*
- Romans 6:23 *"For the wages of sin is death, but the gift of God is eternal life in Christ Jesus our Lord."*
- Romans 10:9, 13 *"That if you confess with your mouth, 'Jesus is Lord', and believe in your heart that God raised him from the dead, you will be saved....for, 'Everyone who calls on the name of the Lord will be saved.'"*

The second group of people are those who have passed through the gate into:

Outer Court~
This group is beginning in God. They know God personally and are learning to love Him, getting to know Him better. They have met Jesus at the "altar" (cross) and are being cleansed/washed in the basin of God's Word, learning what to put off and what to put on. They are being transformed and becoming living sacrifices.

Do you know anyone in this place? What characterizes these people? This is like high school with some deeper teachings, and more freedom, but it is still a classroom setting with a teacher checking in to see how things are going. Many Christians never move from this outer court into the deeper things of God. They settle here, reminding themselves that they have been bought by the blood of Jesus and they are saved from eternal punishment. There is a lack of understanding of the love that God has for them and the intimacy that He desires. The Christian life looks more like rules and regulations (do's and don'ts). Is this you? In order to move into the next step along this journey of faith, the **BIBLE** has to become a love story that moves one's heart. The Word coming alive in a person's life moves them to the deeper things that are on God's heart to share with His children. Robert Morris, Senior Pastor at Gateway Church in Dallas says, the Bible is *"a spiritual book written by a spiritual being to spiritual beings. You cannot understand it with a natural mind."* From His Holy Spirit to our spirit-man, that is how the Word of God becomes alive and transforms us from the inside out. God meets with the human heart.

Here are some scriptures to meditate on, allowing the Holy Spirit to let these words go deep:

- Ephesians 4:22-23 *"You were taught with regard to your former way of life, to put off your old self, which is being corrupted by its deceitful desires; to be made new in the attitude of your minds"*
- Ephesians 4:29-32 *"Do not let any unwholesome talk come out of your mouths, but only what is helpful for building others up according to their needs, that it may benefit those who listen. And do not grieve the Holy Spirit of God, with whom you were sealed for the day of redemption. Get rid of all bitterness, rage and anger, brawling and slander, along with every form of malice. Be kind and compassionate to one another, forgiving each other, just as in Christ God forgave you."*
- Hebrews 4:12 *"For the Word of God is living and active. Sharper than any double-edged sword, it penetrates even to dividing soul and spirit, joints and marrow; it judges the thoughts and attitudes of the heart."*
- Romans 12:1-2 *"Therefore, I urge you, brothers, in view of God's mercy, to offer your bodies as living sacrifices, holy and pleasing to God~this is your spiritual act of worship. Do not be conformed any longer to the pattern of this world, but be transformed by the renewing of your mind. Then you will be able to test and approve what God's will is~ his good, pleasing and perfect will."*

The third group of people that were discovered in the survey were those who entered the:

Holy Place~

This group is close to God. God is becoming your best
friend~ talking to Him everyday, getting more intimate,
filled with the Holy Spirit, tarrying before the Lord
(meditating on the Word, worshipping and praying is a part
of your life). One in this place desires more and more of
God, being a "light-bearer" to those around you, enduring
God's discipline so that you will be more conformed to His
image. In this place, you are becoming more holy
(consecrated or set apart) in all you do and all you think.

Do you know anyone in this place? What characterizes
these people? This is like college! You are expected to
study much more than you go to class. You will go
backward if you are not studying, meditating and
communing with the Lord. In order to stay in the Holy
Place, one must tarry before the Lord. Time is invested in
this relationship. To move from the Holy Place (this step
in the journey) to the deepest level of intimacy, the Holy of
Holies or Most Holy Place, involves **GIVING.** Giving
your life! Totally surrendered in every area to the Lord~
finances, time, energy, schedule, relationships, career,
education, thought life, etc. It all belongs to the Lord! To
move to the deepest place of intimacy, let these words of
life wash over you:

- Ephesians 5:18 *"Be filled with the Holy Spirit"* (a
  continuous filling, meaning "be being filled")
- Matthew 4:14-16 *"You are the light of the world. A
  city on a hill cannot be hidden. Neither do people
  light a lamp and put it under a bowl. Instead they
  put it on a stand, and it gives light to everyone in
  the house. In the same way, let your light shine*

before men, that they may see your good deeds and praise your Father in heaven."

- Ephesians 1:17-19 *"I keep asking that the God of our Lord Jesus Christ, the glorious Father, may give you the Spirit of wisdom and revelation, so that you may know him better. I pray also that the eyes of your heart may be enlightened in order that you may know the hope to which he has called you, the riches of his glorious inheritance in the saints, and his incomparably great power for us who believe. That power is like the working of his mighty strength."*
- Psalm 119:11, 97, 127 *"I have hidden your word in my heart that I might not sin against you...Oh how I love your law! I meditate on it all day long...Because I love your commands more than gold, more than pure gold."*

In the Most Holy Place, there is a willingness to give everything; because all that He is - is so much more than what you could ever imagine. Intimacy is costly. Paul lived his life in the Most Holy Place, for we have his words, *"For to me, to live is Christ and to die is gain." (Philippians 1:21)* and in Galatians 2:20 Paul said, *"I have been crucified with Christ and I no longer live, but Christ lives in me. The life I live in the body, I live by faith in the Son of God, who loved me and gave himself for me."* Paul understood, as we have seen each week, that he was a stranger and an alien here on earth. Heaven was his home. So, he lived filled to the fullest of Jesus while he wandered here, giving his life to the King of Kings and Lord of Lords. Paul lived from this place.

Most Holy Place~

Life is centered on intimacy with God; committed to God no matter what; you would lay your life down for Him. You are under the power of God's Spirit who leads you and guides you; surrendering ALL to Him; mature in Christ. Your life is hidden in Christ; there is much fruit; you desire to minister to the Lord and hear His heart.

Do you know anyone in this place? What have you seen that characterizes these people? There are not many who live from this place. But this is where the Lord wants to take each one of us. He longs to have this intimate relationship with us. Life to the FULL happens here. Circumstances don't affect one who lives in this place! Take a look at these scriptures. Meditate on them. Invite the Holy Spirit to give you wisdom and fresh revelation. Psalm 25:14 says, *"The Lord confides in those who fear him; he makes his covenant known to them."* I want to be a friend of the Lord, one in whom He can share His secrets, one in whom He can share His heart. This is where I want to live.

- Matthew 10:28-29 *"And anyone who does not take his cross and follow me is not worthy of me. Whoever finds his life will lose it, and whoever loses his life for my sake will find it."*
- John 8:32 *"Then you shall know the truth, and the truth will set you free."*
- Philippians 3:7-11 *"But whatever was to my profit I now consider loss for the sake of Christ. What is more, I consider everything a loss compared to the surpassing greatness of knowing Christ Jesus my Lord, for whose sake I have lost all things. I consider them rubbish, that I may gain Christ and*

295

be found in him, not having a righteousness of my own that comes from the law, but that which is through faith in Christ~the righteousness that comes from God and is by faith. I want to know Christ and the power of his resurrection and the fellowship of sharing in his sufferings, becoming like him in his death, and so, somehow, to attain to the resurrection from the dead. '

- Exodus 34:18 *"Then Moses said, 'Now show me your glory."*

Before you move on to the study guide, ask yourself where you are? Are you outside the tabernacle, in the outer court, the holy place or the most holy place? Do you go from one to the next and back again. God knows our hearts. He knows that we are *"dark but lovely" (Song of Solomon 1:5)*, which means to say that He knows the darkness of our hearts and yet to him we are lovely. God sees us through the lenses of eternity~ He's got the "big picture"! Let the Holy Spirit set your heart free, so you can live in Him, with no condemnation, no legalism, just in love with your Jesus! Be real with yourself and with the Lord where you are at on this journey. Let Him lovingly lead you and guide you into each room of the Tabernacle, and enjoy the journey with Jesus.

What a study this has been! As you work through your study guide this week, you will look back (a review of the last ten weeks) and look ahead to the Heavenly City in which we will live with God!

Take some time to review. Don't rush through this chapter. Let the Holy Spirit lead and guide you, so He can reveal where you are in the Tabernacle. For this is "A Journey of Faith".

Study Guide
Week 11: Looking Back & Looking Ahead

Scripture to memorize: *"And I heard a loud voice from the throne saying, 'Now the dwelling of God is with men, and he will live with them. They will be His people, and God Himself will be with them and be their God."* Revelation 21:3

We come to the end of the study of Moses' Tabernacle. What an amazing 10 weeks it has been. As I have put this study together, the Lord has overwhelmed me week after week. I stand in awe of His Holiness, His Divine Design, His perfection, His compassion, His love, His grace, His favor, His desire to dwell among a people whom He calls His own. The Tabernacle study has been such a treasure to teach. It seems that each week we peel back the pages of history as we dig deeper and richer truths out of God's Word

"Now if you obey me fully and keep my covenant, then out of all nations you will be my treasured possession. Although the whole earth is mine, you will be for me a kingdom of priests and a holy nation." Exodus 19:5-6.

This was the establishment of a chosen people, a holy nation, a kingdom of priests. God chose a nation for Himself. God desired to dwell among them. *"Then have them make a sanctuary for me, and I will dwell among them."* (Exodus 25:8) Imagine that scene. Moses is meeting with God (the Creator who spoke the world into being) and He tells Moses that He wants to dwell among the people, His people. In order for that to happen, because of God's Holiness, God gives Moses the Divine Pattern for the Tabernacle (the place where His glory would dwell). Even writing those words, I am in awe. A Divine place for

HIS GLORY to dwell—on earth; in the desert; with this grumbling & complaining people; with an idolatrous nation; a double-minded people—are you kidding me? I think if I were Moses, I would've said, "Are you sure?" "Do you want to rethink this?" "Have you seen these chosen ones?" But God is GOD! He loves us! He wants us! He desires to live among us? It brings me to tears, even now. In order for His glory to dwell among us, God set in perfect order a plan for a Tabernacle; Sanctuary; Tent to hold His presence. God says to Moses, *"Make this Tabernacle and all its furnishings exactly like the pattern I will show you."* (Exodus 25:9) This is the pattern that we have studied over the last 10 weeks. Ten is a number of order & law. Interesting, that we studied the Tabernacle design for 10 weeks. My prayer has been that each one of you would "chew" on or meditate on the scriptures that describe the Tabernacle and you would have a deeper understanding of who God is, who Jesus is, and who the Holy Spirit is~ as you study and get revelation from His Spirit straight to your spirit!

Before we enter the "temple" in the heavenly city, let's take some time to review. Grab your study guide that you faithfully have completed and let's get started. What diligence and steadfastness to continue on in this study. Well done! Your spirit will be strengthened as you study God's word concerning all that is written. *2 Timothy 3:16-17 says, "All scripture is God-breathed and is useful for teaching, rebuking, correcting and training in righteousness, so that the man of God may be thoroughly equipped for every good work."* AMEN and AMEN! I have been taught, rebuked, corrected and trained as we have studied the Tabernacle. I hope that has been your experience as well!

Day 1: Outer Court

1) Describe the Tabernacle structure. What was the layout to look like? Diagram the entire Tabernacle here. (Be as specific or as simple as you would like.)

2) The Bronze Altar is described in Exodus 27:1-8. We studied this during week 3. Draw a picture of it here.

3) "Altar" has two meanings: 1) the slaughter place (sacrifice) and 2) lifted up; ascending. Describe how both of those meanings are seen in the Bronze Altar.

4) How is Jesus seen in the Bronze Altar?

The Bronze Basin was used only by the Priests. In this basin, cleansing bowl, the Priests washed their hands and feet for service before the Lord. Hands speak of what they did; their service. Feet speaks to where they went; their daily lives and ways; their walk had to be holy. No priest would minister without cleansing.

5) The Bronze Basin is described in Exodus 30:17-21, Exodus 31:9, and Exodus 38:8. We studied this vessel in week 4. Draw a picture of it here.

Day 2: Holy Place

The furniture in the Holy Place was only seen by the priests; it was an intimate place. For us, this is a place where the Holy Spirit illuminates God's truth to us. We partake in a deeper level of intimacy with Jesus. The Table of Showbread, the Golden Lampstand and the Altar of

Incense were placed in the Holy Place. Draw the Holy Place. Use as much or as little detail as you want.

1) The Golden Lampstand illuminates the Holy Place. Exodus 25:31-40 gives the description for the Lampstand. Draw it in the space provided. See week 5 for any additional reference.

2) What does Revelation 21:23 say concerning the light (in the heavenly temple)?

3) The Table of Showbread is described in Exodus 25:23-30. See week 6 for additional insight. Draw the Table.

4) What does it mean for you to commune at the table?

5) The Altar of Incense was a place where sacrifices were offered. The definitions for the word "altar" are: 1) a slaughter place (sacrifice) and 2) lifted up; ascending. How can we see both of the definitions in this Altar? **Fragrant offering is possible only on the basis of sacrifice, a broken vessel.**

6) Draw the Altar of Incense (see Exodus 30:1-10 and week 7 study guide).

7) How do you see the Holy Place come alive for you?

Day 3: Holy of Holies

The Holy of Holies or Most Holy Place contained one piece of furniture ~ the Ark of the Covenant, which was the reason for the Tabernacle. The Shekinah glory of God dwelt on the atonement cover (mercy seat) between the Cherubim.

300

1) Read Exodus 25:10-22 the description of the Ark. Draw a picture of it here (refer to week 10 for any additional insight)

Hebrews 9:4 tells us about the contents inside the Ark. *"This Ark contained the gold jar of manna, Aaron's staff that had budded, and the stone tablets of the covenant."*

2) Using week 10 study guide (if needed), draw each of these 3 contents and describe their significance revealed in Jesus.

3) Read Leviticus 26:11-13. Describe God's heart for His people.

The Holy of Holies was the most intimate place~ an encounter with the LIVING GOD in HIS GLORY! This "tangible" presence of God is experiencing heaven touching earth~ some call it a "thin space" (where the veil separating the two realms is very thin).

4) Have you had this type of encounter with the real presence of God? When?

Day 4: The Tabernacle of Man

The New Testament ushers in a new covenant. Jesus fulfills the law and sets up this new relationship with us.

1) Read Hebrews 9:11-15. Focus your praise and affection on Jesus, whose blood has redeemed you. Spend a few moments in adoration.

Here are some of the differences between the old covenant and the new covenant:

301

OLD COVENANT	NEW COVENANT
External	Internal
Based on a shadow	Based on a Savior
Continuous sacrifices	A one time sacrifice
Moses was the mediator between God and the people	Jesus is our mediator
Animal sacrifices	Living sacrifices
Freed from physical bondage	Freed from spiritual bondage
Tabernacle (God's presence) was in a building	Tabernacle (God's presence) is within a group of people
Priests were physically born into the priesthood	Priests are spiritually born into the priesthood
God led Israelites in a pillar of fire or a pillar of cloud	God leads His people (those who have put their trust in Jesus as their Savior and surrender to His Lordship) by the indwelling of the Holy Spirit

2) Can you think of any additional differences between the Old and New Covenant?

The New Testament opens with the announcement of the God of the Universe taking the form of a man and "tabernacling" among us~ the long awaited Messiah had come into the world!

Matthew 1:21-23 *"She will give birth to a son, and you are to give him the name Jesus, because he will save his people from their sins. All this took place to fulfill what the Lord had said through the prophet: The virgin will be with child and will give birth to a son and they will call him Immanuel~ which means 'God with us'."*

John 1:14 *"The Word became flesh and made his dwelling among us. We have seen His glory, the glory of the One and Only, who came from the Father, full of grace and truth."*

Jesus ushered in a new covenant with new covenant people

(2 Corinthians 3:7-18):

- No longer were the Israelites the only chosen ones. God desires that anyone who would call on the name of the Lord would be saved and be called His chosen people (Romans 1:16-17, John 3:16, Romans 3:22-26).
- No longer would the presence of God be constrained in a temple or tabernacle. His temple would be among a group of people who live in a personal, covenantal relationship with Him (Ephesians 2:19-22, I Corinthians 3:16)

Man is the dwelling place of God Immanuel, God with us. The Tabernacle of God is the people of God!

3) What does Acts 7:44-50 say to us?

4) What does 2 Corinthians 6:14-18 say to us concerning the "temple" of God?

God lives in the midst of His covenant bride. And each one of us is a "living stone" being built into an invisible building where the Spirit of the Living God dwells (I Peter 2:4-5).

Day 5: What's to Come?

We are at the last day of the last study! Take a deep breath before you dive in! Even as I write this, I am breathing deeply…getting ready to finish this wonderful study by looking at the Heavenly Tabernacle! For I am longing for my true home, my heavenly home, the city of God! How about you? Do you long for the "better country~ a heavenly one"? What good company we are in. Hebrews 11 gives us many heroes of the faith and we find in this chapter that these men and women longed for the city of God.

Hebrews 11:16 says, "*Instead, they were longing for a better country~ a heavenly one. Therefore God is not ashamed to be called their God, for he has prepared a city for them.*" And Philippians 3:20-21 reminds us that "*our citizenship is in heaven. And we eagerly await a Savior from there, the Lord Jesus Christ, who by the power that enables him to bring everything under his control; will transform our lowly bodies so that they will be like his glorious body.*"

Revelation 21 gives us a glimpse of our "new country" (the new heaven and the new earth) ~ the Holy City!

1) Read Revelation 21:1-4. How does this vision that John had, stir your heart?

2) Verse 3 speaks of the "dwelling of God" (God's tabernacle). Is this a physical building? What is the tabernacle of God?

3) Read 2 Peter 3:10-13. What does verse 13 call this new heaven and new earth?

What a vision! To dwell with God, the bride prepared for her groom. The old order of things will be passed away. God is a God of order; things will change. God is the God of the NEW! He takes us from old to new and eventually the old heaven and earth will pass away and behold, the new will come!

In the Old Testament model of the Tabernacle, the priests had no inheritance, for God Himself was their inheritance. They served God and ministered before Him and ministered to the people. We, the new kingdom of priests (I Peter 2:9) have God as our inheritance. We will be with Him in His Holy City. There will be unbroken fellowship with God.

4) Read Revelation 21:5-8. Who will dwell in the Holy City?

5) Read Revelation 21:9-21. This is our eternal city~ where we will have our inheritance. Describe this city.

What a sight! This is our reality: a city of pure gold, as pure as glass. The city is a perfect cube, a symbol of perfection (the Most Holy Place was a foreshadowing of the dwelling place of God). A city on whose 12 foundations are written the name of the 12 apostles of the Lamb. The message of Christ crucified, preached by the apostles (the beginning of the church) gives us the foundation to stand upon. Ephesians 2:20 tells us, *"...built on the foundation of the apostles and prophets, with Christ himself as the chief cornerstone."* The 12 gates of the Holy City (3 on the east, 3 on the north, 3 on the south and 3 on the west) represent the four corners of the earth, where the gospel had been preached, have the names of the 12 tribes of Israel written on them. There is no entrance into the city but through these gates. John 10:9 tells us that Jesus is the gate. *"I am the gate; whoever enters through me will be saved. He will come in and go out, and find pasture."* Each of these gates was made of a single pearl (which is representative of Jesus for these pearls are formed through the death of the animal in the shell). Jesus, is the pearl of great value (see Matthew 13:45-46).

6) Read Revelation 21:22-25.
- Is there a temple/tabernacle in the city? Explain.
- What gives the city its light?

The glory of God, the Shekinah glory, the manifest presence of God, who gives the city its light!

7) What do these verses say of God's light?
- Psalm 18:28
- Psalm 36:9
- Psalm 89:15
- Psalm 104:2
- Isaiah 2:5
- Isaiah 60:19-20
- Ezekiel 1:4, 27
- Daniel 2:22
- John 8:12
- I Timothy 6:16
- James 1:17
- I John 1:5
- Revelation 22:5

8) According to Revelation 21:26-27, who will dwell in this city?

Check out the following scriptures for more references on the Book of Life: Philippians 4:3, Luke 10:20, Isaiah 4:3

Praise the Lord that my name is written in the Lamb's book of life! I will dwell in the Holy City of God where the Lord God Almighty and the Lamb are its temple.

We started this study of the Tabernacle of Moses as a "journey of faith". We discovered with each curtain, base, post, piece of furniture, rings, pole, veil, metal used, material used ~ we saw the treasure of Jesus. The Tabernacle of Moses was only a shadow of what's to come. It serves as a model and symbol for us to find out where we are. We see Jesus in the fulfillment of the Tabernacle:

- Tabernacle itself~ John 1:14
- Gate~ John 10:9
- Bronze Altar~ Matthew 27:32-44
- Bronze Basin~ Ephesians 5:25-26
- Golden Lampstand~ John 8:12
- Table of Showbread~ John 6:35
- Altar of Incense~ Hebrews 7:25
- Veil~ Hebrews 10:20
- High Priest~ Hebrews 7:26-27, 8:1-2
- Ark of the covenant (mercy seat)~ Hebrews 4:16

Below are boxes that will help you determine where you are~ in the Tabernacle:

Outside The Tabernacle	Enter Throuh the Gate	Outer Court	Holy Place	Most Holy Place
*exploring God	*the gate into the outer court	*believe in Jesus' atonement *washing in the basin	*desiring to be close to God *filled with the Holy Spirit *enjoying the Word; spending time in worship & prayer	*life is centered on intimacy with Christ *Acts 17:28 is your lifestyle "For in Him we live and move and have our being."

Where are you? Have you entered the tabernacle or just curious about God? The cross is the way to enter. If you have not yet made a decision for Christ and are ready to now, spend some time asking God to cleanse you from your sin.

The first step is as easy as A, B, C:

A ~ Admit that you are a sinner. Confess your sins to God. You agree with God that there is nothing you could ever do to enter the "gate"; that it is based on His grace on your life.

B~ Believe that Christ died for your sins; that He took the penalty upon himself at the "altar". To believe is more than speaking it out, it is action from that belief. I believe that Jesus died on the cross for my sin (that He became my sin offering) and was resurrected and is alive and sitting at the right hand of God the Father Almighty. And because I believe that, my life has been transformed. I no longer live for myself, but I live for Christ who gave Himself for me and paid the highest price for me! I live in amazement that He loved me so much that He would lay His life down for me and now I lay my life down for Him.

C~ Confess to another (out loud) that you have accepted Christ's atonement for your sin; give yourself fully surrendered to Him! Share the good news with another. The enemy of your soul will try to convince you otherwise. Connect with others who love Christ, who are His disciples. They will help you grow in Him and walk along this journey of faith with you!

If you are in any other "box", continue to seek the Lord, get into His Word, and stay connected to others who will walk along this journey of faith with you. God's heart for each one of us is that we would tarry with Him and live our life in the Most Holy Place, where our life is centered on intimacy with Him, experiencing the joy and thrill of a personal, covenant relationship with God!

As you move deeper into the Tabernacle, discovering the glory of the Lord, may you say as David, *"One thing I ask of the Lord, this is what I seek: that I may dwell in the house of the Lord all the days of my life, to gaze upon the beauty of the Lord and to seek Him in His temple .*" Psalm 27:4